THE POEM
BEHIND
THE POEM

THE POEM
BEHIND
THE POEM

Translating Asian Poetry

EDITED BY FRANK STEWART

COPPER CANYON PRESS

A Kage-an Book

Printed in the United States of America

Cover art: Calligraphy by Quianshen Bai. The poem is "Drinking Wine," by T'ao Ch'ien.

Copper Canyon Press is in residence under the auspices of the Centrum Foundation at Fort Worden State Park in Port Townsend, Washington. Centrum sponsors artist residencies, education workshops for Washington State students and teachers, Blues, Jazz, and Fiddle Tunes festivals, classical music performances, and the Port Townsend Writers' Conference.

LIBRARY OF CONGRESS CATALOGING-IN-PUBLICATION DATA

The poem behind the poem : translating Asian poetry / Edited by Frank Stewart.
    p. cm.
Includes index.
  ISBN 1-55659-200-0 (alk. paper)
  1. Poetry—Translations into English. 2. Poetry—Asian authors. I. Title: Translating Asian poetry. II. Stewart, Frank, 1946–
PN6101
418'.02—dc22

2003021242

98765432
FIRST PRINTING

Kage-an Books (from the Japanese, meaning "Shadow Hermitage" and representing the "shadow work" of the translator) presents the world's great poetic traditions, ancient and modern, in vivid translations under the editorship of Sam Hamill.

COPPER CANYON PRESS
Post Office Box 271
Port Townsend, Washington 98368
www.coppercanyonpress.org

PERMISSIONS AND
ACKNOWLEDGMENTS

All essays are reprinted by permission. They first appeared in a two-part symposium on translation in *Mānoa: A Pacific Journal of International Writing* in Fall 1999 and Winter 2000, with the exception of the following: W.S. Merwin's "Preface to *East Window: The Asian Translations*," in *East Window: The Asian Translations* by W.S. Merwin, Copper Canyon Press 1998; Jane Hirshfield's "The World Is Large and Full of Noises: Thoughts on Translation," in *Nine Gates: Entering the Mind of Poetry* by Jane Hirshfield, HarperCollins, 1997; David R. McCann's "Translating Korean Poetry," previously unpublished. Some have subsequently been reprinted in new versions as noted, and the revised versions are printed here. Translations are reprinted by permission. We are grateful to the editors of the following publications where some of these translations previously appeared.

John Balaban: *Ca Dao Việt Nam: Vietnamese Folk Poetry,* Copper Canyon Press, 2003; *Spring Essence: The Poetry of Hồ Xuân Hương,* Copper Canyon Press, 2000.

Tony Barnstone: *Literatures of Asia, Africa, and Latin America: From Antiquity to the Present,* eds. Willis Barnstone and Tony Barnstone, Prentice Hall, 1999.

Willis Barnstone: *Literatures of Asia, Africa, and Latin America,* eds. Willis Barnstone and Tony Barnstone, Prentice Hall, 1999; *Laughing Lost in the Mountains,* University Press of New England, 1991.

Mark Bender: *Song Flowers of the Miao Ancient Songs* (*Banx Hxak: Maiozu gugu gehua*), Guizhou Nationalities Publishing House, 1999; *Selected Ququ Folk Songs* (*Ququ jingxuan*), Guizhou People's Press, 1996; *Passage from the Land of Sorcerers* (*Zou chu we jie*), Chengdu Press, 1995; *Selected Folklore of the Nationalities of Dayao County* (*Dayao xianminzu minjian wenxue jicheng*), Yunnan People's Press, 1992.

William I. Elliott: *Naked: Poems by Shuntarō Tanikawa,* Stone Bridge Press, 1966.

Ok-Koo Kang Grosjean: *Poems are previously unpublished.*

Sam Hamill: *Crossing the Yellow River: Three Hundred Poems from the Chinese,* BOA Editions, 2000; *Narrow Road to the Interior and Other Writings of Bashō,* Shambhala Publications, 1998.

Jane Hirshfield: *The Ink Dark Moon: Love Poems by Ono no Komachi and Izumi Shikibu, Women of the Ancient Court of Japan,* Vintage Classics, 1988.

Susie Jie Young Kim: *Korea Journal.*

Leza Lowitz: *Other Side River: Free Verse,* eds. and trans. Leza Lowitz and Miyuki Aoyama, Stone Bridge Press, 1995.

David R. McCann: *Early Korean Literature: Selections and Introductions,* ed. and trans. David R. McCann, Columbia University Press, 2000; *Modern Korean Literature: An Anthology,* ed. Peter H. Lee, University of Hawaii Press, 1990; *The Silence of Love,* ed. Peter H. Lee, University of Hawaii Press, 1980.

Ken McCullough: *Sacred Vows: Poetry by U Sam Oeur,* Coffee House Press, 1998.

W.S. Merwin: *East Window: The Asian Translations,* Copper Canyon Press, 1998.

Shogo Oketani: *Silence to Light: Japan and the Shadows of War,* eds. Frank Stewart and Leza Lowitz, University of Hawaii Press, 2001.

Hiroaki Sato: *The Girl Who Turned into Tea: Poems of Minako Nagashima,* P.S.: A Press, 2000; *Not a Metaphor: Poems of Kazue Shinkawa,* P.S.: A Press, 1999; *A Bunch of Keys: Selected Poems of Takahashi Mutsuo,* Crossing Press, 1984.

Andrew Schelling: *The Cane Groves of Narmada River: Erotic Poems from Old India,* City Lights, 1998. "Manuscript Fragments and Eco-Guardiens: The Estate of Sanskrit Poetry" has been revised since its publication in *Mānoa.* The revised essay, reprinted here, first appeared in *Wild Form, Savage Grammar: Poetry, Ecology, Asia,* La Alameda Press, 2003.

J.P. Seaton: *The Literary Review; Sulfur; I Don't Bow to Buddhas: Selected Poems of Yuan Mei,* Copper Canyon Press, 1997.

Eric Selland: *Rush Mats,* by Hiroya Takagai, trans. Eric Selland, Duration Press, 1999.

Gary Snyder: *Cold Mountain: 100 Poems by the T'ang Poet Han-shan,* Columbia University Press, 1970.

Arthur Sze: *The Silk Dragon: Translations from the Chinese,* Copper Canyon Press, 2001. "Introduction to *The Silk Dragon: Translations from the Chinese*" appeared in *Mānoa* as "Translating a Poem by Li Shang-yin." It appears here in its revised version, excerpted from *The Silk Dragon: Translations from the Chinese.*

Michelle Yeh: *Frontier Taiwan: An Anthology of Modern Chinese Poetry,* eds. Michelle Yeh and N.G.D. Malmqvist, Columbia University Press, 2001.

THE POEM
BEHIND
THE POEM

Translating Asian Poetry

A NOTE ON THE TRANSLITERATION
OF CHINESE

There are two systems currently in use for the transliteration of Chinese words into American English. The older system, and the one generally preferred by Copper Canyon Press and most literary translators, is "modified Wade-Giles." During the Cultural Revolution in China, the Chinese "official" system was changed to "Pinyin," a system most classical Chinese scholars dislike for various reasons. Since some of the essayists here have used modified Wade-Giles and others have used Pinyin, we have appended a list of names and places showing both.

(page)	Wade-Giles	Pinyin
3	Taoist	Daoist
3	Chuang Tzu	Zhuangzi
3	Szu-kong T'u	Sikong Tu
3	Liu Tsung-yüan	Liu Zongyuan
5	Su Tung-p'o	Su Dongpo
9	P'ei Ti	Pei di
12	T'ao Ch'ien	Tao Yuan-ming
13	Tu Fu	Du Fu
15	Li Ch'ing-chao	Li Qingzhao
29	Mao Tse-tung	Mao Zedong
29	Ko Ch'ing-po	Ge Jingbo
30	Yang Kai-hui	Yang Gaihui
30	Wu Kang	Wu Gang
30	Chang O	Jang E
30	Yeh Chun-chau	Ye Zhunzhan
31	Li Po	Li Bai *or* Li Bo
32	Shang P'ing	Shang Ping
35	Chang Yin	Zhang Yin
253	Chung-nan	Zhongnan
253	Meng Hao-jen	Meng Haoran
253	Chung Tzu-ch'i	Zhong Ziqi
254	Ch'ü Yuan	Qu Yuan
254	Ts'ang-lang	Canglang

CONTENTS

FRANK STEWART   Preface   XIII

TONY BARNSTONE   The Poem behind the Poem:
                     Literary Translation as American Poetry   I

JOHN BALABAN   Translating Vietnamese Poetry   17

WILLIS BARNSTONE   How I Strayed into Asian Poetry   28

MARK BENDER   Hunting Nets and Butterflies:
                     Ethnic Minority Songs from
                     Southwest China   39

WILLIAM I. ELLIOTT   A Poem Should Mean *and* Be:
                     Remarks on the Translation of
                     Japanese Poetry   55

OK-KOO KANG   The Way of Translation   62
GROSJEAN

SAM HAMILL   Sustenance: A Life in Translation   76

JANE HIRSHFIELD   *from* The World Is Large and
                     Full of Noises: Thoughts on Translation   90

SUSIE JIE YOUNG   Entering the Pale of Literary Translation   IOI
KIM

LEZA LOWITZ   Midwifing the Underpoem   II3

DAVID R. MCCANN   Translating Korean Poets   125

KEN MCCULLOUGH   Tuning In to the Poetry of U Sam Oeur   133

W.S. MERWIN   Preface to *East Window:*
The Asian Translations   152

SHOGO OKETANI   Some Thoughts on the Meaning
of Translation   163

HIROAKI SATO   Forms Transformed: Japanese Verse
in English Translation   175

ANDREW
SCHELLING   Manuscript Fragments and
Eco-Guardians: The Estate of
Sanskrit Poetry   189

J.P. SEATON   Once More, on the Empty Mountain   207

ERIC SELLAND   And Then the Whole Was Flooded
with Light: Hiroya Takagai Translated   221

GARY SNYDER   Reflections on My Translations of the
T'ang Poet Han-shan   233

ARTHUR SZE   Introduction to *The Silk Dragon:*
Translations from the Chinese   239

MICHELLE YEH   The Chinese Poem: The Visible and
the Invisible in Chinese Poetry   251

ABOUT THE CONTRIBUTING TRANSLATORS   265

ABOUT THE EDITOR   271

PREFACE

SEVERAL YEARS AGO, Tony Barnstone sent me a long essay called "The Poem behind the Poem," asking if I might want to use it in *Mānoa,* a journal of Asian and Pacific writing that I edit. For the past fifteen years, *Mānoa* has been publishing contemporary translations from Asian languages: Tibetan, Nepali, Chinese, Japanese, Indonesian, Korean, Vietnamese, and Khmer, to name only a handful. Occasionally we've published an essay that dealt in part with translation. But Tony's was the first that had crossed my desk addressing certain practical issues involved in translating Asian poetry into the contemporary American idiom. In addition to discussing word choices, lineation, and that sort of thing, the essay also imagines an ideal effort at translation that might accomplish two goals: deepen the conversation with English-language poetry that earlier Asian translations had begun, and help extend the boundaries of American poetic practices—which have already been significantly affected by Chinese and Japanese poetry since at least 1915, when Ezra Pound published *Cathay.*

Because of its passion and practical wisdom, Tony's essay appealed to me at once. It's in the tradition of commentaries on Chinese poetry by other American poets, such as Pound, William Carlos Williams, Gary Snyder, and Kenneth Rexroth, all of whom were influenced by Chinese translations. These poets in turn inspired generations of Americans to write in a clear, laconic, imagistic, and unadorned style about any subject—from atom bombs to turnips. Unfortunately, despite this profound influence, few collections of essays and worksheets from practicing literary translators have been published. Those that exist primarily discuss a single language and poetic tradition, such as Chinese or Japanese.

And so, with Tony's essay as a model—and perhaps a provocation— I invited translators working in an array of Asian languages to join in a symposium, by either responding directly to Tony's points or giving their own views, revealing their own approaches to translation's art, alchemy, luck, and sweaty labor.

The responses were all printed in *Mānoa,* and thanks to Copper Canyon Press they are reprinted here in book form to make them available to a wider readership. Some of the essays have been revised slightly by the translators, and each essay has been supplemented with several poems to serve as examples of the translator's work. The only essay that did not appear in *Mānoa* is David R. McCann's, which arrived too late to be included in the journal but, fortunately, could be added here. The result is an exaltation of superb translators, with a range of opinions and working methods, discussing poetry both ancient and contemporary.

If there is a thread that runs through the essays, it is the willingness of translators to allow themselves to be assimilated to the poems in the original language and to poetry. Their common approach is humility. Concerning the translation process, many assert it as a requisite to lose themselves—intellectually, emotionally, culturally—by a concentrated act of will that may take years of study and meditation, followed by a leap into a state of mind that can be described only indirectly and metaphorically. For example,

> A simple, surface act—that of linguistic transfer-
> ence—is in a sense an impossibility. The poem, the
> writer-translator, and language must give themselves
> over to the experience of death and transfiguration,
> in which new life appears.
>
> —Eric Selland

> The translator must love poetry so much that the
> poems become part of his breath.
>
> —Ok-Koo Kang Grosjean

> The poem becomes a part of my daily life: I dream
> about it, read supplemental texts, meditate on the
> process, learn all I can.
>
> —Leza Lowitz

> The translator who wishes to enter the creative terri-
> tory must make an intellectual and imaginative
> jump into the mind and world of the poet, and no
> dictionary will make this easier. In working with the
> poems of Han-shan, I have several times had a
> powerful sense of apprehending auras of nonverbal
> meaning and experiencing the poet's own mind-of-
> composition.
>
> —Gary Snyder

It's not surprising that translators of Asian poetry would describe their practice in terms associated more with Asian than Western sensibility and logic. The essays in *The Poem behind the Poem* frequently characterize translation as cooperation and even intimacy with the original poem. I'm reminded that in *Shōbōgenzō*, Dōgen advocates a similar attitude to things, which he calls nonopposition, "not opposing oneself and not opposing others." Dōgen expounds his meaning by saying:

> Because of assimilation to the human world, we
> know a Buddha must assimilate to other worlds.
> When one knows cooperation, self and others are
> one thusness. Their music, song, and wine accompa-
> ny people, accompany celestial beings, accompany
> spirits. People keep company with music, song, and
> wine; and music, song, and wine keep company
> with music, song, and wine. People keep company
> with people, celestials keep company with celestials,
> spirits keep company with spirits—there is such
> logic. It is the learning of cooperation.

> (trans. Thomas Cleary)

I wish to acknowledge Sam Hamill's sustained commitment to publishing this collection, as well as the staff at Copper Canyon, whose help was indispensable to the book's completion. I also thank the staff at *Mānoa* journal who helped at various times and in many ways, particularly Pat Matsueda, Kathleen Matsueda, and Michelle Tyau. Other individuals who assisted along the way include Daniel Cole of the Center for Chinese Studies at the University of Hawai'i and Ngô Thanh Nhàn. Special thanks to Leza Lowitz. The original publication of these essays in *Mānoa* was made possible by grants from the Witter Bynner Foundation for Poetry, the National Endowment for the Arts, and the Hawai'i State Foundation for Culture and the Arts. Their cooperation and support have made this book possible.

Frank Stewart
Near Kalopā, Island of Hawai'i, 2003

TONY BARNSTONE

The Poem behind the Poem: Literary Translation as American Poetry

I CAME TO CHINESE POETRY originally as an American poet learning how to make the image. Like many other American poets, I was led to China by my interest in Ezra Pound, William Carlos Williams, and other modernist poets who developed and modified their craft in conversation with the Chinese tradition. I came to China, in other words, to learn how to write poetry in English. This is also how I came to translation: as a way of extending the possibilities of poetry written in English. In fact, I would argue that historically the Chinese poem in English has allowed the American poetic innovator to invent a Chinese tradition filtered through the medium of translation in order to find new ways of writing American poems. A translation, after all, is the child of parent authors from different cultures, and however assiduously the translator attempts to remove his or her name from the family tree, the genetic traces will be found in the offspring. What the translator brings to the equation can never be reduced to zero. Translators bring their linguistic patterns, cultural predispositions, and aesthetic biases to the creative act, not merely holding up a mirror to something old, but also giving the original text new life in a strange environment. Even a perfectly translated poem—one in which every word magically is turned into its doppelgänger and in which form, sound, and rhetoric are retained—is still a product of misprision, and the translator does not so much create a text in the new language *equal* to the old one as a text that strives to be *equivalent* to selected aspects of the original.

This is particularly true of translators of Chinese poetry. From a set of monosyllabic, largely pictographic characters calligraphed on a Chinese painting, fan, or scroll, the poem proceeds through a hall of mirrors, reappearing on the other side of time, culture, and speech as a few bytes of memory laser-etched on a white page in the polysyllabic, phonetic language of the American translator. The effect is that of moving from the iconic, graphics-based Macintosh operating system to the text-based DOS system. It's very difficult to make the systems compatible because the conceptual paradigms that underlie them are so radically different. We can create a neutral language that will transfer information between the two systems, but small things will have changed: the formatting will have gone awry, certain special characters will disappear if their correspondents are not found, and attached files—such as graphics and footnotes, which modify our sense of the text—may become separated or lost. Raw information will be preserved, but the aesthetic unity, the gestalt of the poem, will be lost in the translation. Literary translation is more than anything else an attempt to translate that gestalt, which a machine isn't sensitive enough to detect, much less reconstruct.

Those who discount the creative element in translation believe that translations should consist of word-for-word cribs in which syntax, grammar, and form are all maintained, and in which the translator is merely a facilitator who allows the original poem to speak for itself in a new language. Poetry, however, can't be made to sing through a mathematics that doesn't factor in the creativity of the translator. The literary translator is like the musician who catalyzes the otherwise inert score that embodies Mozart's genius. In that act, musician and composer become a creative team. However, just because the musician can keep time and scratch out the correct notes in the correct order, it won't necessarily be good music. Musical skill inevitably enters into the equation. *Fidelity,* true fidelity, comes from a musician's deeper understanding of the music. As John Frederick Nims says, "The worst infidelity is to pass off a bad poem in one language as a good poem in another."

From the early metrical and end-rhymed translations of Herbert Giles to the so-called free-verse translations of Ezra Pound, Arthur Waley, and Kenneth Rexroth, Chinese poems have been reinvented as American poems. The Chinese poem in English is like a stolen car sent to a "chop shop" to be stripped, disassembled, fitted with other parts, and presented to the consumer public with a new coat of paint. But despite its glossy American exterior, it's a Chinese engine that makes this vehicle run, and fragments of the poem's old identity can be glimpsed in its lines, the purr of its engine, the serial number that we may still be able to read. The burden of my essay will be to discuss ways I've found of negotiating between Chinese and American poetic paradigms, and to engage in a limited discussion of what American parts have proved compatible with this Chinese vehicle, which has been a part of Western poetic traffic since the early years of modernism.

Daoist philosopher Zhuangzi says, "The fish trap exists because of the fish; once you've gotten the fish you can forget the trap... Words exist because of meaning; once you've gotten the meaning, you can forget the words. Where can I find a man who has forgotten words so I can have a word with him?" Words are the net we cast upon the waters in search of knowledge, meaning, enlightenment. Ultimately, though, the fish has to come to us of its own volition. (Native American hunters believe that when the hunter is in harmony with nature, the animal comes to him and sacrifices itself.) So Sikong Tu, a famous ninth-century poet whose *24 Styles of Poetry* is a Daoist treatise on how to write poems, speaks of the need to find poetic inspiration through *lack of effort* in his poem "The Placid Style": "You meet this style by not trying deeply; / it thins to nothing if you approach." There is always something ephemeral about the knowledge behind a poem, about the inspiration that creates it—or creates a translation. To find a poem in translation we need to discover what I call "the poem behind the poem." Sometimes we can't find this metapoem by looking; we also have to see. Sometimes we can't find it by trying; it comes to us while we're doing something else.

Before we discuss the next poem, "River Snow" by Liu Zongyuan— translated by Chou Ping and me—let's take a moment to read it aloud, slowly. Empty our minds. Visualize each word.

> A thousand mountains. Flying birds vanish.
> Ten thousand paths. Human traces erased.
> One boat, bamboo hat, bark cape—an old man.
> Alone with his hook. Cold river. Snow.

"River Snow" is considered a prime example of minimum words/maximum message and has been the subject of numerous landscape paintings. It is terrifically imagistic: the twenty Chinese characters of the poem create a whole landscape, sketch an intimate scene, and suggest a chill, ineffable solitude. To get this poem across in translation, I strove to reproduce the linear way the characters unfold in the reader's mind. The syntax is particularly important because it is perfectly constructed. We walk into this poem as if walking into a building, and the spaces that open up around us and the forms that revise themselves at each step unfold according to the architect's master plan.

The first two lines create a fine parallelism: birds passing through the sky leave no trace, just as human traces are effaced in the mountain paths. It makes me think of the Old English kenning for the sea: *whale path*.

Here the sky is *bird path*. In the second line, it's clear that the snow is the active agent in erasing humanity from the natural scene, yet snow is never mentioned. After the last trace of humanity disappears with the word "erased," a human presence is rebuilt in this landscape, character by character, trace by trace: "One boat, bamboo hat, bark cape" and—the sum of these clues—"an old man." These first two lines sketch a painterly scene: the vast emptiness of the sky above and the snowy solitude of the landscape below hit the reader like a glance at a Chinese landscape painting. And then the tiny strokes that create a man in the third line direct our imagination deeper into the poem, as if we had discovered a tiny fisherman's figure on the scroll. The next line tells us what the old man is doing. He is "alone with his hook." Silence. We take in the "cold river." The last character sums up the entire poem: "Snow."

Snow is the white page on which the old man is marked, through which an ink river flows. Snow is the mind of the reader, on which these pristine signs are registered, only to be covered with more snow and erased. The old man fishing is the reader meditating on this quiet scene like a saint searching himself for some sign of a soul. The birds that are absent, the human world that is erased, suggest the incredible solitude of a meditating mind, and the clean, cold, quiet landscape in which the man plies his hook is a mindscape as well. Thus, there is a Buddhist aspect to the poem, and Liu Zongyuan's old man is like Wallace Stevens's "The Snow Man," whose mind of winter is washed clean by the snowy expanse. He is

> …the listener, who listens in the snow,
> And, nothing himself, beholds
> Nothing that is not there and the nothing that is

"River Snow" is a perfectly balanced poem, a tour de force that quietly, cleanly, easily creates its complexly simple scene. To merely paraphrase it in translation is to ignore the poem behind the poem. The translator must discover the poem visually, conceptually, culturally, and emotionally, and create a poem in English with the same mood, simplicity, silence, and depth. Each word must be necessary, essential. Each line should drop into a meditative silence, should be a new line of vision, a new revelation. The poem must be empty, pure perception; the words of the poem should be like flowers, one by one opening, then silently falling. As William Carlos Williams was fond of stating, a poem is made up of words and the spaces between words.

A problem with this technique occurs if the translator takes it to extremes and makes a poem that sounds too choppy. Consider Wai-lim Yip's translation of "River Snow":

A thousand mountains—no bird's flight.
A million paths—no man's trace.
Single boat. Bamboo-leaved cape. An old man
Fishing by himself: ice-river. Snow.

Wai-lim is among the best-known contemporary Taiwanese poets, a well-respected translator and translation theorist. His translation is very, very close to mine, and I appreciate what he is trying to do, but I feel that all those dashes and that colon ultimately make the poem seem choppy. Still, the third and fourth lines are almost there.

For the sake of comparison with the translations by Wai-lim and me, take a look at this quite good but somewhat wordy translation from *Indiana Companion to Classical Chinese Literature:*

Over a thousand mountains, birds have ceased to fly,
On ten thousand paths man's tracks have been wiped out.
In a lone boat, in grass cape and hat, an old man
Fishes alone the cold river snow.

The translation is fine but, to my taste, prolix: filled with prepositions and articles that make the lines fluid, but dilute them in the process. This prosy version lacks the magical economy of "River Snow."

All three of these translations are very close to the original, and all attempt to reproduce the unfolding of visual clues. My point here is that the addition of a few parts of speech or an unfortunate choice of punctuation can pollute an otherwise excellent and accurate translation and weaken the poem's ability to catalyze a powerful reading experience.

The poetry of Wang Wei—the poet I've translated most extensively from Chinese—is often perfectly clean, like "River Snow." Each character resonates in emptiness like the brief birdcalls he records in one of his poems. The inventor of the monochrome technique, Wang Wei was the most famous painter of his day. In his work, both painting and poetry were combined through the art of calligraphy—poems written on paintings. As Su Dongpo said of him, "His pictures are poems and his poems pictures"; and as François Cheng has pointed out, painting and calligraphy are both arts of the *stroke,* and both are created with the same brush. I like to imagine each character in "River Snow" sketched on the page: a brush-stroke against the emptiness of a Chinese painting—like the figure of the old man himself surrounded by all that snow.

The most famous piece by Zen-influenced composer John Cage was titled "4' 32"." The audience came in and sat down, and for 4 minutes and 32 seconds nothing happened. The audience was the music. Their rustlings, coughs, chatter, the creaking of seats, perhaps the rain on the roof of the auditorium—all this was the music. In classical Chinese painting the white space defines what forms emerge, and in Buddhism emptiness is wholeness. The perfect man's mind, according to Zhuangzi, is empty as a mirror, and according to the Daoist aesthetics of Chinese painting, each stroke of the brush is *yin* (*dark, blackness, woman*) upon *yang* (*light, whiteness, man*). All the empty space reacts to one brushstroke upon the page. Each additional stroke makes the space adjust itself into a new composition, in much the way each great poem makes all of literary history readjust itself, as T.S. Eliot said. To make a Chinese poem in English we must allow silence to seep in around the edges, to define the words the way the sky's negative space in a painting defines the mountains.

As I stated earlier, I think the poem in translation must carry on a conversation with other poems in order to discover itself. For me, "River Snow" resonates with Japanese Zen poems and poems of the English Romantics, and it is this conversation that allows me to hear its silence. Consider these lines from a *haiku* by Japanese poet-painter Buson, translated by Robert Hass:

> Calligraphy of geese
> against the sky—
>   the moon seals it.

Here's the first clue: the birds are imagined as brushstrokes. Thus the empty sky is like a blank page. Consider now these lines from a poem by Japanese Zen poet Musō Soseki (1275–1351) translated by W.S. Merwin and Sōiku Shigematsu:

> Don't look back
>   to this world
>   your old hold in the cellar
> From the beginning
>   the flying birds have left
>   no footprints on the blue sky.

From Buson's image we come to Soseki's image of the flying birds passing through the sky without leaving a trace, as in "River Snow"; and as in "River Snow," there is a contrast of the human world with the natural. Here, the birds' trackless flight through the sky is a symbol of the enlightened mind's passage through the world without grasping or holding or desiring. Compare "On Nondependence of the Mind," a poem by Dōgen

(1200–1253)—founder of the Sōtō school of Japanese Zen Buddhism—translated by Brian Unger and Kazuaki Tanahashi:

> Water birds
> going and coming
> their traces disappear
> but they never
> forget their path.

The mind that doesn't depend on the world leaves no traces, just as the "water birds" don't forget their path—a path we can understand as a mystical Way. In these lines from Wordsworth's *Prelude,* he describes his hike through the Alps:

> Like a breeze
> Or sunbeam over your domain I passed
> In motion without pause; but ye have left
> Your beauty with me

Because he is in tune with the natural setting, Wordsworth's meditative mind passes through nature without leaving tracks. The inverse parallelism he sets up (his trackless passage through nature's landscape versus nature's beautiful inscription in his mindscape) is implicit in "River Snow" as well. "River Snow" is also a poem in which the mind is washed clean, like the sky empty of birds, the paths empty of humanity. Zhuangzi asks, "Where can I find a man who has forgotten words so I can have a word with him?" The fisherman in "River Snow" is that man.

Although I felt it necessary in "River Snow" to make an absolutely literal, word-for-word translation to get at the heart of the poem, in other cases I've translated lines in unusual ways to get at the poem behind the poem: the urgent image, the quiet mood, the sound that I felt resided in the Chinese poem and needed emphasis to be felt in English. Sometimes I've deviated slightly from a literal translation in order to get an effect that I believe is truer to the poet's vision. There are no fast rules; the translator has to feel it.

I want to close with a discussion of a translated line that is much more problematic than the ones above. First, though, I need to discuss what—somewhat idiosyncratically perhaps—I call deep-image lines in Chinese poetry. There are times when Chinese poets create a nature imagery that is almost surreal, incredibly evocative and strange. In order to learn how to recreate these lines in English, I think it's good to look at the school of deep-image poets in America. Most famous among them are Robert Bly and James Wright, though I would classify contemporary Native American poet Linda Hogan as deep-image as well (in her practice, as opposed to her literary history). Bly and Wright were deeply influenced by the combination of personal and impersonal perspectives and tones in Chinese and by Chinese rhetorical parallelism, clarity of image, and focus on implication. They blended these characteristics with a late strain of sur-realism derived from Trakl, Vallejo, Lorca, and Neruda. It is precisely this mélange of influences on Bly and Wright that opens up a space in American poetry for a blend of the Chinese tradition and the surreal—and that provides a model for translators.

Here are two examples of deep-image lines, the first from Linda Hogan:

> Crickets are pulsing in the wrist of night.

and the second from James Wright:

> A butterfly lights on the branch
> Of your green voice.

How do these lines work? They invert your expectation, blending the human and the natural or engaging in synesthesia (as in Su Dongpo's great line "With cold sound, half a moon falls from the painted eaves"). Similarly, in Wang Wei's poems "In the Mountains" and "Sketching Things," nature does strange things; the world is so lush that its green color becomes a liquid that wets his clothes:

> No rain on the mountain path
> yet greenness drips on my clothes.

and

> I sit looking at moss so green
> my clothes are soaked with color.

The strange beauty of James Wright's image taps into a profound psycho-logical mystery and opens up a space in the imagination that Wang Wei's lines also reach. Wright makes it possible for us to *see* Wang Wei's syn-esthesia, and to *see how* to translate him into English.

As with the Wang Wei lines above, the human and the natural are intertwined in Linda Hogan's line. It works because it imagines the world as a body through which the blood pulses, an intermittent action that is also a sound, the *ba-dump* of the heartbeat. The cricket sound is similarly an intermittent, two-beat sound, and it brings the night into our bedrooms, making it as intimate as our bodies—a small, internal event, like a pulse.

Of course I was thinking of Linda Hogan when translating one of my favorite lines of Wang Wei in which he sets himself the task of getting at the action-pulse of the cricket's song. Wang Wei's line comes from "Written on a Rainy Autumn Night after Pei Di's Visit": "The urgent whir of crickets quickens." I like the sound qualities here, the onomatopoeia, the internal off-rhymes, and the sense that the line is just beyond comprehension, yet intuitively right. However, this line as I translated it—in collaboration with Willis Barnstone and Xu Haixin—is extremely problematic: an example of the product of translation as reinvention. Literally, the line reads:

\	—	/	\	/
ts'u - chih	ming		ji	chi
urge + spin/weave (=cricket)	to sound/the sound of a bird or animal		intense	anxious/urgent/hurried

The urgent whir of crickets quickens.

The first two characters refer to the house cricket and mean "to urge into spinning" or "to urge into weaving"—an idiom derived from the similarity of a cricket's intermittent, two-beat chirp, produced by rubbing its wings together, to the *shhk-shhhk* of a shuttle on a hand loom, or the whir and whirl of a spinning wheel. In other words, the Chinese idiom for cricket has an onomatopoeic element. This element is also present in the English word "cricket," which derives from the insect's characteristic sound, *cricket, cricket*. Of course, we forget that, unless the word is heard freshly: the off-rhyme "crickets quickens" is therefore meant to focus our attention on the forgotten music of the word—to make us actively *hear* "cricket," perhaps for the first time.

Now what about "the urgent whir"? Isn't it mistranslating to add this image, using something that is simply an idiom? No, I don't think so. Idioms such as this add an idiosyncratic beauty to language, like the pillow words of Japanese poetics or the kennings of Old English. A translation that rendered Beowulf's "whale path" as "the sea" would be a very dull translation indeed. The Chinese idiom suggests an image that is inherent in the language, much as "foot of the mountain" bears a comparison, long forgotten, of the mountain to a human body.

This idiom allowed me entry to the poem behind the poem, to a sound that was also an action. I wanted to bring alive the complex image of the cricket wings shuttling like a cranky loom or lost in a whirring blur like a spinning wheel, so I had to analyze the phrase for what activated that metaphor: intermittency, quick action, noise. I imagined the blur of cricket wings rubbing themselves into song, and I imagined that song as both continuous and intermittent, both an act and a sound. The word "whir" suggested both the action of spinning—the insect's blur of wings—and the sound of that action: *whir*. I wanted a line that was musical throughout, wanted readers to sense the stuttering trochaic rhythm of a cricket's call (**crick**-et, **crick**-et) when they hear the line's rhyming, emphatic beat: "The **urgent whir** of **crick**ets **quick**ens." This goes beyond the question of whether to be true to the letter or the sense; it's a question of being true to the spirit of the line, which is both image and song. In this interpretive translation, I can't say that I truly got this line of Wang Wei's into English, but I do believe that I brought an analogous English poem to life—one closer to Wang Wei's imagination and to the imagination inherent in the Chinese language than one merely translated as "the cricket's loud sounds speed up."

I have argued elsewhere that Chinese poetry in English has deviated deeply from the form, aesthetics, and concerns of the Chinese originals and that this is the result of willful mistranslation by modernist and postmodern poet-translators. In the first decades of the twentieth century, Chinese poetry was a powerful weapon in the battle against Victorian form, and thus it was brought over into English in forms resembling the free verse that it helped to invent. Rhyme and accentual meter were quietly dropped from the equation because—unlike Chinese use of parallelism, caesura, minimalism, implication, and clarity of image—they weren't useful in the battle for new poetic form. However, we are now in a different century and need no longer be constrained by past literary conflicts. While the elimination of rhyme and meter from translations of Chinese poetry has created a distinguished English-language tradition of "Chinese" free verse—one that has influenced successive generations of American poets—it has also denied the poem its right to sing. I don't recommend a return to the practice of translating Chinese poems into rhyming iambics (generally, this overwhelms the Chinese poem with our pastoral tradition). But I do think that as much attention should be given to the way the Chinese poem triggers sound as to how it triggers sight, and that translators should use the whole poetic arsenal—syllabics, sprung rhythm, off-rhyme, half-rhyme, internal rhyme, assonance, consonance, and so forth—to try to give the English version of the poem a deeply resonant life. Too often translators have given Chinese poets the resolution powers of an electron microscope, but have cut off their ears. By being cognizant of the poem's song, we are less likely to be deaf to the poem behind the poem, and less likely to be satisfied with clumsy rhythms and a lack of aural pleasure.

If my examples are notable less for their similarity than for the apparent divergence of the translation principles by which they were created, this is the essence of my argument. There are many roads to China. So that the original's voice and silence can be heard, the poem behind the poem may require word-by-word fidelity—that is, for translators to restrain their inventiveness. Or the poem may require a radical departure from convention to arrive where it began. In either case, the translator must keep faith with the deeper need that poetry fulfills in our lives. Like a cricket's song, a poem is an arrangement of sound and image that is also an action affecting the reader. If we are very quiet, can we feel its tiny pulse fluttering in our wrists? If we listen like Stevens's snow man, if we become nothing long enough, we may discover not what the poem *says* but what it *does*. A poem is a machine made out of words, as William Carlos Williams once wrote, and like a wheelbarrow or a can opener or a telephone, it is a machine reduced to an economic efficiency of parts and designed for a specific function. It doesn't matter whether we take the original poem apart with an Allen wrench or a Phillips screwdriver, or whether we build the translation out of wood or plastic or burnished copper. What matters is that the gears engage and the wheels turn and that the poem's *work* is done in the translation as well. All translation is mistranslation, but a translator's work and joy are to rig, out of the materials at hand, something that opens cans, or carries hay, or sends voices through the lines. We will never create a truly Chinese poem in English, but in this way we can extend the possibilities of the translation, which may in turn reveal to the imaginations of American poets unforeseen continents.

From the series "Drinking Wine"

I built my hut near people
yet never hear carriage or horse.
"How can that be?" you ask.
Since my heart is a wilderness the world fades.
Gathering chrysanthemum by the east hedge,
my lazy eyes meet South Mountain.
Mountain air is clean at twilight
as birds soar homeward wing to wing.
Beneath these things a revelation hides
but it dies on the tongue when I try to speak.

Tao Yuan-ming (aka Tao Qian) (365–427)

Translated by Tony Barnstone and Chou Ping

Thoughts While Night Traveling

Slender wind shifts the shore's fine grass.
Lonely at night below my boat's tall mast.
Stars hang low as the vast plain broadens,
the swaying moon makes the great river race.
How can poems make me known?
I'm old and sick, my career over.
Drifting, just drifting. What kind of man am I?
A lone gull floating between earth and sky.

Du Fu (712–770)

Translated by Tony Barnstone and Chou Ping

A Hundred Worries

I remember I had a child heart at fifteen,
healthy as a brown calf running wild.
In August, when pears and dates ripened in the courtyard
I'd climb the trees a thousand times a day.
All at once I am fifty,
and I sit and lie around more than I walk or stand.
I force smiles and small talk to please my patrons,
but a hundred worries tangle my emotions.
Coming home to the same four empty walls,
I see this grief mirrored in my old wife's glance.
My sons don't treat their father with respect.
They greet me by the door with angry screams for rice.

Du Fu (712–770)

Translated by Tony Barnstone and Chou Ping

To the Tune of "Dream Song"

I'll never forget sunset at Brook Pavilion—
drunk with beauty, we lost our way.
When the ecstasy faded, we turned our boat home,
but it was late and we strayed into a place deep
with lotus flowers
and rowed hard, so hard
the whole shore erupted with herons and gulls.

Li Qingzhao (1084–c. 1151)

Translated by Tony Barnstone and Chou Ping

Written on the North Tower Wall after Snow

In yellow dusk the slender rain still falls,
but the calm night comes windless and harsh.

My bedclothes feel like splashed water.
I don't know the courtyard is buried in salt.

Light dampens the study curtains before dawn.
With cold sound, half a moon falls from the painted eaves.

As I sweep the north tower I see Horse Ear Peak
buried except for two tips.

Su Dongpo (aka Su Shi) (1037–1011)

Translated by Tony Barnstone and Chou Ping

JOHN BALABAN

Translating Vietnamese Poetry

TONY BARNSTONE'S PHRASE "the poem behind the poem" offers a useful way of looking at translation. In the translation of a poem—as opposed to, say, a technical document—we are always looking for more than mere denotative equivalencies. We want to feel how the poem felt in its original. We want to inhabit the condition of its first reader or listener. Traveling in English, we seek to cross cultural borders and encounter the poem on native ground. To do this, we must hear "the poem behind the poem."

What lies behind, or even prior, to the poem depends on several things at once. First is the poem's historical tradition, including that tradition's habits of prosody, its abiding themes, its range of language, and its notion of what a poem is (and is not). Second, to hear "the poem behind the poem," we must consider the poet's unique operations within his or her poetic tradition. We must be able to feel the dialectical commerce, as it were, between the poem and the tradition it plays against. And finally, for the above to be working in a translation—for our incognito travel to take place—the translator must possess true talent in English poetry so that all prosodic possibilities seem alive and attendant. As Stanley Kunitz writes in the introduction to his and Max Hayward's beautiful translations of Anna Akhmatova:

> The poet as translator lives with a paradox. His work must not read like a translation; conversely, it is not an exercise of the free imagination. One voice enjoins him: "Respect the text!" The other simultaneously pleads with him: "Make it new!" He resembles the citizen in Kafka's aphorism who is fettered to two chains, one attached to earth, the other to heaven. If he heads for earth, his heavenly chain throttles him; if he heads for heaven, his earthly chain pulls him back. And yet, as Kafka says, "all the

possibilities are his, and he feels it; more, he actually refuses to account for the deadlock by an error in the original fettering."

The discovery of "the poem behind the poem" for a translator of Vietnamese is a long prospect. The literary poetry of Việt Nam began in the first century C.E. with poetry written in Chinese. From the tenth century and into the early twentieth, Vietnamese poets wrote in *nôm,* a calligraphic script devised by the literati for Vietnamese phonetics. This *nôm* literary tradition, with its characteristic forms, subjects, and allusions, was heavily influenced by the poetry of China (particularly the T'ang)—even more than the literary models of classical Greece and Rome influenced English poetry.

These literary poetries are only part of the Vietnamese landscape. Alongside and beneath the *nôm* and Chinese poetries, an even older poetry known as *ca dao* runs like a vast river or aquifer. This oral poetry, still sung in the countryside, originated perhaps thousands of years ago in the prayers and songs of the Mon-Khmer wet-rice cultures to which the Vietnamese are tied. The word-stock of *ca dao* is native, bearing few loan words from Chinese. It is a lyric poetry—not narrative—and its power lies in its allusive imagery and brief music. Its references are to nature, not to books; to delta fish and fowl, to creatures of the field and forest, to wind and moon, to village life. It belongs to the farmers of Việt Nam, which is to say that it belongs to most Vietnamese because eighty percent live, as ever, in the countryside.

This repository of images, melodic patterns, aspirations, and beliefs is the cultural center of all Vietnamese poetry. Even literary poets— whether they are working in *lü-shih* regulated verse (*thơ đướng luật* in Vietnamese), modern free verse, or the metrics of the oral tradition, like the great classical poet Nguyễn Du—seem always to be working in some relation to *ca dao. Ca dao* is the fixed foot of the literary culture's compass. Representing a folk culture resistant throughout the millennia to Chinese acculturation, it is an important aspect of "the poem behind the poem" in Vietnamese.

Vietnamese is a tonal language, which is to say that every syllable has a linguistic pitch that creates the semantic meaning. *Là,* with a falling tone, is the verb "to be." *Lá,* with a high, rising tone, means "leaf." *Lạ,* with a low, constricted tone, means "strange." There are six tones in the language, indicated in writing by diacritical marks. In prose, these tones fall at random. In poetry, these tones fall at certain places in the metrical line. In *ca dao,* as in the example below, the various arrangements of linguistic pitches give rise to patterns that easily become *musical* pitch patterns, that is, melodies or, more correctly, what the musicologist Trần Văn Khê calls "singing without song" or cantillation. It is just this singing that is *ca dao*'s chief delight to the Vietnamese listener.

How on earth does the translator convey this? One can approximate the rhyme scheme *(dạ/mạ, hàng/ngang/đàng* in the rove rhyme of the *lục-bát* couplet) with "heart/dart," "streaks/leaving/creek," but "the poem behind the poem" is essentially lost. To paraphrase the late critic Nguyễn Khắc Viện, this kind of translating "is like drawing a bucket from a moon-lit well at night and losing the silvery shine of its light." For it is the lone voice of the singer that makes one sad for the woman left behind in the field.

> Bước xuống ruộng sâu man sầu tấc dạ.
> Tay ôm bó mạ nước mắt hai hàng.
> Ai làm lỡ chuyến đò ngang.
> Cho sông cạn nước đôi đàng biệt ly.

> Stepping into the field: sadness fills my deep heart.
> Bundling rice sheaves: tears dart in two streaks.
> Who made me miss the ferry's leaving?
> Who made this shallow creek that parts both sides?

In the poetry of Hồ Xuân Hương, who wrote around 1800, near the end of the high tradition of *nôm,* we find poems behind poems behind poems. Almost all of her *lü-shih* or *chüeh-chu* poems, while apparently about natural landscapes or everyday activities, have hidden within them a complete, parallel second poem: a double entendre whose topic is sex. Sometimes, as in the poem below, the translator can succeed by finding words that are both true to the physical landscape she describes and suggestive of other things to the English ear: for example, "cleft," "bearded," "plunges," and "mount." Here, the translator's task is to also set up a double meaning with a single set of images.

ĐÈO BA DỘI

Một deo, một đèo, lại một đèo,
Khen ai khéo tạc cảnh cheo leo.
Cửa son đỏ loét tùm hum nóc,
Hòn đá xanh rì lún phún rêu.
Lắt lẻo cành thông cơn gió thốc,

Đầm đìa lá liễu giọt sương gieo.
Hiền nhân, quân tử ai mà chẳng...
Mỏi gối, chồn chân vẫn muốn trèo.

THREE-MOUNTAIN PASS

A cliff face. Another. And still a third.
Who was so skilled to carve this craggy scene:

the cavern's red door, the ridge's narrow cleft,
the black knoll bearded with little mosses?

A twisting pine bough plunges in the wind,
showering a willow's leaves with glistening drops.

Gentlemen, lords, who could refuse, though weary
and shaky in his knees, to mount once more?

As scholars have noted, the title "Đèo Ba Dội" ("Three-Mountain Pass") would probably suggest to a Vietnamese reader the range in central North Việt Nam called Đèo Tam-Điệp. But the poem's peculiar grotto would invite suspicion, and of course a literate Vietnamese reader would recognize immediately the pine and willow as male and female symbols, respectively. "Gentlemen" and "lords" (*Hiền nhân, quân tử*) are traditional terms for the elite, mandarin class. Yet Hồ Xuân Hương is anything but traditional. A woman writing in a male, Confucian tradition at the end of the decadent Lê dynasty, she only makes honorific references to men when she is being derisive.

The main aspect of the poem behind the poem (behind the poem) for Hồ Xuân Hương is that she is almost always working against tradition. Behind her traditional landscapes lies sexual dalliance. Behind her pagoda walls, irreverent fools. In the widow's funeral lament, she hears infidelity. Yet all her poetic subversions are launched in exquisitely made, regulated *lü-shih* and *chüeh-chu*: verse with traditional requirements for line length, rhyme and tone placement, and syntactic parallelism. But here too she is unique and surprising, often using the word-stock of *ca dao* and the aphorisms of the common people where her male contemporaries are content with flowery rhetoric and stock ideas.

In "Three-Mountain Pass," the double meaning is conveyed through the imagery; that is, the poetic manipulation of the landscape suggests the second meaning. For the translator—as Ezra Pound learned from his efforts with Chinese—this visual, or phanopoetic, aspect of poetry is a challenge, but an answerable challenge. More difficult to render are Hồ Xuân Hương's poems in which the second meaning is suggested through verbal puns, tonal echoes, and contemporary cultural detail. In the poem below, she makes allusions to the decadent state of the Amida Buddhist clergy.

VỊNH SƯ HOẠNH DÂM

Cái kiếp tu hành nặng đá đeo
Vị chi một chút tẻo tèo teo
Thuyền từ cũng muốn về Tây Trúc
Trái gió cho nên phải lộn lèo.

THE LUSTFUL MONK

A life in religion weighs heavier than stone.
Everything can rest on just one little thing.

My boat of compassion would have sailed to Paradise
if only bad winds hadn't turned me around.

The "little thing" that weighs down the monk and keeps him from entering the paradise of the Amida Buddha seems to be his penchant for sex. This is not said explicitly but rather with puns, some of them tonal: by changing the pitch of the words she's chosen, you get ones with obscene meanings. For example, in the last line of the original, *lộn* means "to confuse," "to turn about." *Lộn lèo,* then, means something like "to turn over" or "to capsize." But *lồn* with a falling tone means "vagina." *Lẹo* with a low, constricted tone means "to copulate." *Đeo* in the first line means "to bear" or "to carry." With a high, rising tone, it also means "to copulate," as does *trái* ("ill winds") if the pitch is shifted to the monotone, as in *trai gái.* It's not so much that this poem has a clear second line of argument or double entendre, as that obscenities unexpectedly seem to be trying to invade the poem—as if it expresses the tormented mind of the monk himself. Finally, balanced against this set of suggestions is the Buddhist notion of perfecting oneself, which is centered around the "perfection"—*paramita* in Sanskrit—of compassion. With the Buddhist symbol of the journeying boat of the spiritual self, we have a doctrinal echo from the very etymology of *paramita:* "to get to the other side," to the opposite shore.

This Vietnamese delight in covert verbal play reached its apogee in palindromes in *nôm,* with *lü-shih* that could be read forward *and* backwards to yield a second poem with a different meaning. There is a poem in *nôm* that, read in reverse, becomes a poem *in Chinese* about the same land-scape, but of course with a different point of view. Then there is the fabu-lous cyclical palindrome composed by Emperor Thiệu-Trị in 1848 and set in jade inlay in the imperial city of Huế. In this one sun-shaped *lü-shih*, there are concealed twelve perfectly metrical *lü-shih*. Each can be found by starting at any one of the calligraphic rays and going clockwise or counter-clockwise, from the inside out, or the outside in.

One of the last practitioners of poetry in the *lü-shih* style was Tản-Đà, the poet and patriot who ran a newspaper during French colonial rule in the 1930s. When informed that a more enlightened colonial administra-tion had lifted censorship, Tản-Đà lamented that a direct telling of the news would be too easy.

Two great traditions lie behind any Vietnamese poem: the oral folk poetry of the common people, and the *nôm* poetry of the literary elite. These two great and ancient streams of poetic tradition feed nearly every literary endeavor in Việt Nam, even today, and even in prose. Any effective translator of Vietnamese would have to have traveled some in these two realms of beauty and belief.

Đi ra một ngày, về một sàng khôn. "Go out one day," the proverb says, "and come back with a basket full of knowledge."

The Paper Fan

Seventeen, or is it eighteen…
ribs? Let me have it in my hands.

Thick or thin, opening its lovely angles.
Wide or narrow, inserted with a stick.

The hotter you get, the more refreshing.
Wonderful both night and day.

Cheeks juicy soft, persimmon pink.
Kings and lords just love this thing.

Hồ Xuân Hương (c. 1775–c. 1820)

Translated by John Balaban

Country Scene

The waterfall plunges in mist.
Who can describe this desolate scene:

the long white river sliding through
the emerald shadows of the ancient canopy

…a shepherd's horn echoing in the valley,
fishnets stretched to dry on sandy flats.

A bell is tolling, fading, fading
just like love. Only poetry lasts.

Hồ Xuân Hương (c. 1775–c. 1820)

Translated by John Balaban

Spring-Watching Pavilion

A gentle spring evening arrives
airily, unclouded by worldly dust.

Three times the bell tolls echoes like a wave.
We see heaven upside down in sad puddles.

Love's vast sea cannot be emptied.
And springs of grace flow easily everywhere.

Where is nirvana?
Nirvana is here, nine times out of ten.

Hồ Xuân Hương (c. 1775–c. 1820)

Translated by John Balaban

A Tiny Bird

A tiny bird with red feathers,
a tiny bird with black beak
drinks up the lotus pond day by day.
Perhaps I must leave you.

Anonymous *ca dao* (folk song),
collected twentieth century

Translated by John Balaban

Tao

Sad, I blame Mr. Sky.
When sad, I laugh. Happy, I cry.
Not a man, in my next life
I'll become a rustling pine
on a cliff in the sky.
Fly with the pines, cool and lonely.

Anonymous *ca dao,*
collected twentieth century

Translated by John Balaban

WILLIS BARNSTONE

How I Strayed into Asian Poetry

WHEN I BEGAN TO WRITE POETRY in 1948, I felt an affinity with the poetry of Spain, China, and India. I had studied Hebrew and knew Spanish and French. Then in 1949, near the end of Greece's civil war, I went to live and work a few years in Athens. There Greek joined the list, at first modern, then ancient. In 1952 I wasted a year at the School of Oriental and African Studies (soas) in London as a full-time student in Bengali. During that season I saw Sir Arthur Waley almost every day, standing about and talking to colleagues and students, dressed formally except for his bicycle clips, which he never removed from his striped trousers. His translations of the classical Chinese poets had first drawn me into the imagery and overheard poetry of China. Waley, who set his friend Ezra Pound on the path to *Cathay,* introduced Chinese and Japanese poetry to generations of English readers in his books. But I was timid and never dared speak to the wonderful man who had been the hermit of the British Museum's Oriental Sub-Department of Prints and Drawings and who was later remembered in the title of a book of tributes as "Madly Singing in the Mountains." I lost the chance of my life to enter Chinese poetry with the poet-scholar whose sensibility for China's poets and philosophers gave us a civilization. I chose wrong between India and China.

Although I felt closer to Chinese poetry than to any poetry I had been exposed to, it seemed futile to study the language, since it was then not possible to visit China and my notion was to get lost someplace in Asia, learn its ways, and translate its poets. So, as a result of the encouragement of Arun Mitra, a Bengali friend in Paris who had been my classmate at the Sorbonne, I went to soas, hoping it would get me to India. It would have been better to have gone directly to the subcontinent. Instead, I learned in London to read Rabindranath Tagore in his language and discovered that he was not an Edwardian-English misty poet, as he had translated himself to be, but a radically modern Indian poet, with mystical dimensions.

When I returned to the States after five years in Europe, I was soon drafted, classified by the U.S. Army as "an oriental expert," and sent to Fort Devins, Massachusetts, where I was to enter a radio spy outfit (they never told me more than the group's initials). However, being married to a Greek national during the McCarthy period, I couldn't pass the purity clearance, and so they shipped me back to France for two more years. Bengali faded and so too the hope of a romantic immersion in India.

But back in early 1949 in Paris, I had a major Chinese experience that was to nudge me for the rest of my life. I met Robert Payne, a prolific English novelist, biographer, and translator who had spent five years in southwest China during World War II. He had just returned from China, full of stories. He was especially excited about a talented poet whose poems he was the first to translate. The poet had been living in a cave, holed up with his army in Shensi province after the disastrous Long March. It was Mao:

WRITTEN ON A PHOTOGRAPH OF THE CAVE OF THE GODS

At bluegreen twilight I see the rough pines
serene under the rioting clouds.
The cave of the gods was born in heaven,
a vast wind-ray beauty on the dangerous peak.

But Robert spoke not of the war nor of the politics—though later he was to do an inclusive biography of Mao Zedong—but of the poet. At the same time, he urged me to translate the poems of the Spaniard Federico García Lorca (actually, as a result of his prodding, I worked on the poems of Antonio Machado), and so I had my first experience of burying myself in a poet by translating the poems. Translation is the best way to read and to know a poet.

Twenty years later, in 1972, the ping-pong diplomats had begun to crack the door into silent China. Late one afternoon while walking through a parking lot near my office at Indiana University, I remembered Robert's enthusiasm for Mao's poems, all written in the classical manner. I turned on the spot, headed for the library, and took out a book published in Beijing of his thirty-seven poems. Behind the bombastic Chinglish, I saw the work of a major poet. I then asked my Chinese graduate student, Ge Jingbo, whether he would like to collaborate with me on retranslating them. We did the thirty-seven poems in a month. From Jingbo I requested literal, dictionary meanings—not equivalents or interpretations—for each word. I did research and wrote a lengthy introduction with helpful apparatus for a manuscript that I sent to Harper & Row that September.

THE GODS

on the death of his
wife, Yang Gaihui

I lost my proud poplar and you your willow.
As poplar and willow they soar straight up into
    the ninth heaven
and ask the prisoner of the moon, Wu Gang,
    what is there.
He offers them wine from the cassia tree.

The lonely lady on the moon, Jang E, spreads
    her vast sleeves
and dances for these good souls in the unending
    sky.
Down on earth a sudden report of the tiger's
    defeat.
Tears fly down from a great upturned bowl of
    rain.

    Since Harper was already doing a book of my own poems, I didn't push them when they responded with nothing other than a letter confirming that the manuscript had been received. Then in late December, I got a frantic phone call from Fran McCullough, my editor, saying Nixon was leaving in two weeks for Beijing and asking why I hadn't sent the Mao book to her earlier. I told her I had sent it four months before and that she herself had signed the letter saying I'd hear from her shortly. "That was my assistant's letter," she told me. In short, they wanted to do it, and the book appeared in a record eleven days with Chinese text, a photograph of the new ruler in his long, black coat on the ocean beach, an ink drawing I did of him for the frontispiece, and six pages of his grass calligraphy—all in time for Nixon to have it before his trip to Beijing, where he would toast Mao with one of the poems. It was selected as a Book-of-the-Month Alternate Feature, and poems were extracted for the editorial page of the *New York Times*. That spring I was invited to impenetrable China as "a friend of China."

    The May and June I spent there occurred during the depths of the terrible, murderous Great Proletarian Cultural Revolution. In a book of memoirs I later published, there is a picture of a Chinese novelist and me at the Beijing Foreign Language Press. This was Ye Zhunzhan, a writer I had been told to contact. He was also the translator of a volume of Hans Christian Andersen's fairy tales. In the photo he has a book in his lap and is smiling benignly at me. Twelve years later, I went to China to teach for a year at Beijing Foreign Studies University. Ye Zhunzhan and I became good friends, and he invited me often to his house. One day after a long lunch he said, "Willis, do you remember the day we first met at the press?"

"Of course," I answered.

"I was actually not working at the press then."

"Where were you?"

"I was in jail. I'd been denounced by the Red Guards, and my job was scrubbing prison urinals. I couldn't let you know in any way that I had been let out for the day because you were there to see me."

"You put on a perfect show," I said.

In the Soviet Union after the war, Paul Robeson had gone back to Moscow after some years' absence. He wanted to see a close literary friend. They met in an elegant restaurant and had a fine meal. In this case, the friend was actually in a KGB prison, severely maltreated, but couldn't let the American in on his plight. Robeson was furious when he discovered the deception.

After my return from Cultural Revolution China, I spent three months immersed in Chinese at Middlebury College's summer intensive language school, took a year at Indiana University, and tried hard to acquire as much Chinese as I could during my year in Beijing. Though I love Chinese, learning its characters, tones, and speech was not like picking up Italian after knowing Spanish. But for reading classical Chinese I did dedicate two evenings a week during my year in Beijing to work with my son Tony and Xu Haixin, a student of mine from the university, on a translation of the poems of the T'ang-dynasty poet Wang Wei. Wang is a Taoist/Buddhist landscape writer and my favorite Chinese poet (Li Zhingzhao and Li Bai are also favorites).

MY COTTAGE AT DEEP SOUTH MOUNTAIN

In my middle years I love the Tao
and by Deep South Mountain I make my
        home.
When happy I go alone into the mountains.
Only I understand this joy.
I walk until the water ends, and sit
waiting for the hour when clouds rise.

If I happen to meet an old woodcutter,
I chat with him, laughing and lost to time.

Wang Wei's lines are fresh, said as if for the first time because of the subtle changes in syntax and thought, yet the vocabulary is not immense. I was able to learn the characters for virtually all the one hundred sixty-eight poems we translated. The book that resulted, *Laughing Lost in the Mountains: Poems of Wang Wei,* was first published in an English edition in Beijing as a Panda Book (1989), and later appeared with the University of New England (1991).

WRITTEN IN THE MOUNTAINS IN EARLY AUTUMN

I'm talentless and dare not inflict myself on this
    bright reign.
Perhaps I'll go to the East River and mend my
    old fence.
I don't blame Shang Ping for marrying off his
    children early;
rather, I think Master Tao Yuan-ming left office
    too late.
With a cricket's cry autumn abruptly falls on
    my thatched hall.
The thin haze of evening is saddened with the
    old whine of cicadas.
No one calls. My cane gate is desolate.
Alone in the empty forest, I have an appoint-
    ment with white clouds.

What do I think of translating from Chinese poetry? It is a tremendous pleasure. Is it possible? Of course not. Therefore let it be done. It cannot be done if by translation one means duplication. But one can come relatively close from any language into English, which is extraordinarily flexible. I don't wish to elaborate on method and philosophy (I did a book on the subject, and that's enough), but if I could say one thing in a few words, it would be this. When I began to translate, I believed, as I do now, that fidelity to the poem meant creating a poem in English, a good poem, one that a poet (or, at the very least, one who is a poet in the act of re-creation) translates. To do this requires freedom, perhaps a lot of freedom. But as I have gotten older, my view has changed. I think now that one should try to be as close as possible to the literal meaning, but not in a clumsy way. Within that closeness, and aided by an immense amount of information provided by the fullest knowledge of that literal meaning (with all its connotative elements and music), one can operate with great artistic privilege. Like reproducing formal prosody, to be close is hard but saves one from being seduced by the obvious. Therefore, one is obliged to come up with ten or twenty solutions for each linguistic enigma, one must take greater imaginative leaps, and in the end, I believe, this allows the original poet to talk. Perhaps to talk well. In the prison hospital of St. Elizabeths in Washington, D.C., Robert Fitzgerald came to ask Pound about translating Homer. Pound said, "Let Homer speak."

Chinese is a particularly good language to translate from, and as a result of felicitous versions in English, Chinese poetry has had a major impact on many American poets—from Amy Lowell, Ezra Pound, Wallace Stevens, and William Carlos Williams to Robert Bly, James Wright, Gary Snyder, and Allen Ginsberg. Despite the tones and the parallel rhymes, which have no equivalent in English, what makes Chinese poetry so striking in English is that Chinese verse is highly imagistic and its clear imagery translates well. One may miss allusions (annotation will compensate for that), but the picture, as in surrealist poetry, finds a picture in English. The Chinese poets, especially in the T'ang and Sung periods, "dance in chains"—meaning that despite strict forms, the voice comes through as natural, confessional, and candidly conversational—and this overheard quality is especially appropriate to modern American poetry.

When my son Tony, my student Haixin, and I worked together on those vibrant evenings in our Friendship Hotel apartment, the rule was that there should be no translation by way of explanation or interpretation. Robert Alter, in his extraordinary introduction to his version of Genesis, speaks about the heresy of explanation. Make the word in English a specific word, a thing and not its idea. Explanation is for the critic, not for the poet-translator. So, as when three decades earlier I had worked on the poems of Sappho, our method now was to translate, to tinker, to become the inspired poet who wrote the original until suddenly, as with all good epiphanies, the poem found shape and art in English and was a poem.

Apart from the Chinese experience, I have frequently translated from languages in which I had an imperfect knowledge of the tongue—or from languages, as in the case of fifteenth-century Indian poet Mirabai, whom I did with an Indian novelist, in which I could read nothing of the original. In working from so-called exotic languages—ones far from Western roots—it is unusual to find a poet with a proficiency in the more remote language. The alternative has been academics who are not dedicated poets, and they are usually bad translators of poetry. Most of the leading poets in America have translated one or more books of poetry from a European language. But when the language is exotic, it is usually necessary, *faute de mieux,* to put a good poet together with a faithful informant. It is too much to hope that an academic whose main credential is a knowledge of the original tongue—or worse, a native speaker whose English is secondary—will give us anything we should read. And we should not read inferior translations, since they traduce the work of the author. Having made these painful but realistic observations, I wish to add quickly that ignorance of the original tongue is never desirable. We should hope that generations of poets will arise with a knowledge of exotic tongues so that a better artistic partnership can be formed. Now, the quality and fidelity depend on the cleverness of the informant and poet to keep to their informational and creative roles, to pass on and receive information so that the word will pass from original poet to poet-translator.

I return to an original thought in these reflections on converting poems from tongue to tongue. Is translation of poetry possible? Is translation of Chinese poetry possible? Of course not. It is impossible. And it should be understood that only the difficult, the elusive, and the impossible lines are worth translating.

Escaping with the Hermit Zhang Yin

My brother Zhang has five carts of books.
A hermit, he reads endlessly.
Whenever he soaks his brush with ink he surpasses the sage of grass
    calligraphy.
When he writes a poem it makes a classical verse seem like a throwaway.
Behind closed doors under Two Chamber Mountains,
he's been a hermit for more than ten years.
He looks like a wild man
pausing with fishermen.
Autumn wind brings desolation.
Five willows seem taller as their leaves drop.
Seeing all this I hope to leave the peopled world.
Across the water in my small cottage
at year's end I take your hand.
You and I, we are the only ones alive.

Wang Wei (701–761)

Translated by Tony Barnstone, Willis Barnstone,
and Xu Haixin

Seeing Zu Off at Qizhou

Only just now we met and laughed
yet here I'm crying to see you off.
In the prayer tent we are broken.
The dead city intensifies our grief.
Coldly the remote mountains are clean.
Dusk comes. The long river races by.
You undo the rope, are already gone.
I stand for a long time, looking.

Wang Wei (701–761)

Translated by Tony Barnstone, Willis Barnstone,
and Xu Haixin

Magnolia Basin

On branch tips the hibiscus bloom.
The mountains show off red calices.
Nobody. A silent cottage in the valley.
One by one flowers open, then fall.

Wang Wei (701–761)

Translated by Tony Barnstone, Willis Barnstone,
and Xu Haixin

Snow

The scene is the north lands.
Thousands of li sealed in ice,
ten thousand li in blowing snow.
From the Long Wall I gaze inside and beyond
and see only vast tundra.
Up and down the Yellow River
the gurgling water is frozen.
Mountains dance like silver snakes,
hills gallop like wax bright elephants
trying to climb over the sky.
On days of sunlight
the planet teases us in her white dress and rouge.
Rivers and mountains are beautiful
and made heroes bow and compete to catch the girl—lovely Earth.
Yet the emperors Shih Huang and Wu Ti
were barely able to write.
The first emperors of the T'ang and Sung dynasties were crude.
Genghis Khan, man of his epoch
and favored by heaven,
knew only how to hunt the great eagle.
They are all gone.

Only today are we men of feeling.

Mao Zedong (1893–1976)

Translated by Willis Barnstone and Ko Ching-po

MARK BENDER

Hunting Nets and Butterflies: Ethnic Minority Songs from Southwest China

THE BROKEN UPLANDS OF SOUTHWEST CHINA range from the dry, pine- and rhododendron-covered hills of northern Yunnan province to the fantastic limestone karst peaks nestled along the green river valleys of Guangxi and Guizhou. In these uplands live millions of members of some of China's fifty-five ethnic minority nationalities. Arriving in China in 1980, I was hardly aware of these culturally and linguistically diverse peoples, who make up about nine percent of China's population and live mostly in the country's extensive border areas. My perceptions changed when a student, who happened to be a Zhuang from the Guangxi Zhuang Autonomous Region near Việt Nam, wrote a short paper on folk songs from her area. This led to a search of the local People's bookstore, where I found a number of Chinese-language versions of songs and narrative poems that had been collected from minority groups in the 1950s and were being republished in the early 1980s. I wanted to discover more about how these texts had been collected and produced, so I made it my goal to visit the areas where some of them had originated, find the original collectors, and, if possible, collaborate on translations into English.

Eventually, as my knowledge of China (and my personal connec- tions) increased, I was able to relocate to Guangxi. In between my teaching duties at Guangxi University, I began to work with a number of the compilers, who turned out to be a colorful group of folklorists, singers, and poets who had for decades shown an intense dedication to collecting, translating, and editing the local folk traditions for presentation to the larger Chinese audience. This task was greatly complicated by the Cultural Revolution (1966–1976) and other periods of political chaos, when com- pilers were often forced to "revise" their texts for ideological reasons. Many of them had participated in the nationwide folklore surveys in the 1950s, which had produced a large body of ethnic-minority folklore texts that became a new genre of Chinese literature: ethnic-minority oral perfor- mance in translation.

My guides and teachers included Li Zixian of Yunnan University; Li Shizhong (Ruohai'asu) and Meng Zhiren of the Yi Nationality Culture Institute in Chuxiong, Yunnan; Yi singer Yang Shen of Chuxiong prefecture; Guo Sijiu of the Nationalities Publishing House in Kunming, Yunnan; Nienu Baxi of the Honghe region in Yunnan; Jin Dan of the Nationalities Publishing House in Guiyang, Guizhou; and Chen Ju at Guangxi University. They carefully went over texts with me—sometimes pointing out passages that had been left out or modified for various political or editorial reasons—spent a great deal of time answering correspondence, and accompanied me and my fiancée, Fu Wei, on many field excursions, helping me to gain access to folk festivals, song meetings and singers, and "unopened" villages in their locales. I was allowed to live in some of these villages for short periods, which gave me a greater understanding of and feel for the many local customs, articles of material culture, and flora and fauna that regularly appear in the songs.

Everyone I worked with readily understood this concept of "going down to the country" to get a feel for the local area and lifestyle when making a translation. The notion of *cai feng,* or collecting folk songs to gauge the people's feelings, goes back to the age of Confucius. During the 1950s, it was standard procedure for groups of young researchers, many of them university students, to live among the people from whom they were collecting songs. Although quite different from a lengthy anthropological survey, this method proved very useful to me in the translation process.

I eventually focused on translating selections from what I felt to be the most accurate and least-edited collections, which for the most part were in Chinese or the local language, accompanied by Chinese cribs. These texts included ethnographic introductions, the names of the singers and other data, and, sometimes, original-language transcriptions. On the occasions when I was actually able to collect oral materials, I worked with native speakers to translate the texts, much as I have done with texts from local Han Chinese oral traditions. In several instances I was able to get part of the text, or witness an actual performance, in the native language. This greatly helped to mitigate the difficulty of working through what Victor Mair has called the "filter" of Mandarin Chinese. In the following discussion of two representative texts—one from the Yi in northern Yunnan and one from the Miao in southeast Guizhou—I will concentrate on how I dealt with understanding the cultural context of the songs.

My first example is a Yi folk song entitled "Hunting Song," which comes from the Chuxiong Yi Autonomous Prefecture in northern Yunnan and was probably sung in Chinese to a Yi tune, as is often the case among the more acculturated groups of Yunnan Yi. The text was included in

Yunnan Yizu geyao jicheng (Folk songs of the Yunnan Yi), published by the Yunnan People's Publishing House in 1986. Although the language was not difficult, and there were no obscure terms or loan words from Yi, some deeper understanding of the context was needed to give me the confidence and vision to render the song in English. I have found that one of the greatest dangers to a translator is in reading processes or feelings into a text that would not have been part of the "traditional referentiality" (to use John Foley's term) of the native audience. Although love lyrics have given me the most problem in that area, it was also a concern with this song. I felt that because hunting in the hills at night had been a part of my youth in Appalachia, I had special insight into the subject matter. Though this was to some extent true, the methods, attitudes, and social matrices in which Yi hunting activities and songs were situated differed from those of my own experience.

The song refers to the use of hunting nets, which are woven from hemp rope made by pounding long hemp stalks with a foot-operated mortar and pestle and then twisting the coarse strands together. After the nets are woven—some songs speak of this being done by daughters in the family—hunters string them around the hillsides and wait for game to be driven inside. I was shown pictures of such nets, and I observed the long stalks being processed into rope. Several times I met hunters on the hills, armed with muzzle-loading muskets and accompanied by their dogs. On one occasion, I attended a festival in which Yi women from different villages displayed their beautifully embroidered costumes as they danced in huge circles before a panel of judges. The local men displayed their hunting skills with musket and crossbow in a target shoot in which I was allowed to participate. During the festival, I also attended a traditional Yi banquet in which everyone sat in circles on layers of fresh pine needles, sharing a communal repast. These and other experiences helped me to understand not only the material culture represented in the songs, but also such customs as sharing a catch with anyone met on the road home:

HUNTING SONG

Carrying the hunting tools,
Leading the roving dogs;
Arriving at the forests,
Nets and snares are set.
With bows and crossbows readied,
Men hide about in the wilds,
Waiting for beasts to come.

As the sun sets into the hills,
The wild things roam the forests:
On the eastern hills the deer run,
On the western hills the boars call:
Roars come from the east,
Screeches from the west.

Wild boars are shot with arrows,
Deer enter nets and snares;
Then everyone gets busy,
Carrying the game away.

Anyone met on the road
Is given a share of the catch.

One of my biggest projects has been the translation of a cycle of antiphonal creation epics from certain subgroups of the Miao nationality in southeast Guizhou province who go by the local ethnonyms Hmub and Hmong. In preparing for this translation work, I was accompanied by Jin Dan, a Miao researcher who in the 1950s had collected the epics with the well-known linguist Ma Xueliang. After the Cultural Revolution, the pair was forced to re-collect much of the material because some of the manuscripts had been lost in the chaos. The printed Chinese version—which included an unusual number of valuable endnotes and lines in Miao transcription—was published in 1983 under the dual Miao/Chinese title *Hxak Hmub/Miaozu guge* (Ancient Miao/Hmub songs). (The *k* in Hxak and the *b* in Hmub are examples of unpronounced tone markers; these markers have been dropped from the Miao words used below.)

During the translation process, I had come up with a list of over one hundred terms that neither I nor my colleagues at Guangxi University could define. With list in hand, Jin Dan methodically guided me around the region where the songs were collected: the mountainous Taijiang region of southeast Guizhou province. I was shown homes, metal and cloth workshops, food stalls, markets, shrines, ferry crossings, boat-storage places, rice fields, groves, river bottoms, unusual hills, and local government offices. We also attended song festivals and participated in one impromptu antiphonal song exchange in a restaurant. Jin lectured me on various aspects of the local culture and language, demonstrated epic singing, shared his insights on singing practices, and played me recordings of several parts of the cycle. I also watched as Jin's wife and daughter showed Fu Wei how to wear the traditional indigo clothing, how young women lengthened their locks with extra hanks of hair, and how to cook meals of sticky ricecakes and pickled vegetables.

I also discovered certain things about the text I was translating. I found that for some reason Ma and Jin had decided not to present the text in antiphonal form. In performances of the song cycle, a pair of men will often sing opposite a pair of women—the exchange back and forth facilitated by the raising and answering of questions. In some instances, the same pair will raise and answer the questions, but in other instances the other will respond, displaying their knowledge of that section of the song. This may continue all night. I felt that this feature was a very important part of what Alan Dundes has called the "texture" of the song. Later, I worked with Jin to revive the antiphonal nature of the song exchange, which was not very difficult since the questions were retained even in the written version. Because the original had no rhyme and the tones of neither Miao nor Chinese can be reproduced in English, these aspects of the texture were not an issue.

One of the most challenging problems was identifying the numerous trees, shrubs, and aquatic plants common in the song cycle. An entire section describes how one of the early creators, Butterfly Mother (Mai Bang), emerges from the giant sweet gum as she ends her cocoon stage. With the help of various insects and birds, she gets out of the tree:

As the Sweet Gum was transforming into myriad beings,
Butterfly was forming within the heartwood.
Who opened the door to let her out?

The King of the Moth-borers opened the door
To let Butterfly out.
As the door opened,
Butterfly lightly turned her body, then raised her head.

Who flew from the East?

Woodpecker flew from the East.
His bill was thick as a leg.
He pecked at the wood, then ate the Moth-borers.

"Peck all you want on the roots and trunk—
But don't peck in the center.
Don't hurt Butterfly's hands and feet!"

After another day, Butterfly was strong enough to come out.
When Butterfly Mother was born, her face was mottled;
Her tangled locks were like balls of hemp.

What did she use to wash her face?
What did she use to comb her hair?

Her fingernails grew long and sharp—
She used them to comb her hair;
Rainwater washed the spots from her face.

The original text used a rather vague and colloquial term for the sweet gum that could also have been translated as "maple." It was not until conferring with Jin Dan that I was able to find the Latin term and positively identify the tree as a sweet gum (*Liquidambar formosana*), common to the hilly areas of much of southern China. Near some Miao villages in southeast Guizhou, groves of these trees are still maintained and worshipped as the home of Butterfly Mother.

A whole host of shrubs, herbs, and small trees appears in the passages about the mythic age when the land was cleared and the first fields were tilled. For instance, a certain type of wood was used to make the nose halter for the ox; another type was used in the making of the drums for the water-buffalo sacrifices. Other passages reflect a knowledge of local alchemy. One type of herb is mixed with rust from hillside seeps to produce brown dye; the carambola fruit (*Actinidia chinensis*) is used to brighten silver. On one hike Jin Dan showed me a small shrub called a horse-mulberry (*Coriaria sinica*), which in mythic times had been a giant tree. The story goes that there were ten suns burning in the sky, and the archer Hsang Xa stood in the top of the highest tree to shoot down nine of them. As punishment for the tree's complicity, the remaining sun turned it into a shrub.

A major challenge in translating the Miao epics was trying to access a worldview that treated such things as hoes, lead weights, plows, and drums as animate beings born sometime in the mythic past. Even elemental metals were born, were raised by their parents, married, and had their own children:

Iron's husband was called Pipe-bellows.
And who gave birth to Pipe-bellows?

In very ancient times, old Bang Xang Ye died—
His belly was left behind, and later changed
    into Pipe-bellows.
Iron married him,
And Iron was content.

Silver wanted children.
What were the names of her offspring?

Her children were called Neck Rings.
Gold also wanted offspring.
What were her children called?

Her offspring were called Golden Flowers.
Copper also raised children.
What were the children called?

They were called Flute Reeds,
And they live inside reed-pipes;
When oxen were slaughtered, the reed-pipes
Were taken out and played.
Lead also raised children.
What were her children called?

Her children were called Net Weights;
Net Weights that people used to catch fish.

When I examined firsthand many of the items that play in the transmutation process, things began to make more sense, at least on a literal level. I learned that pipe-bellows are a type of tubelike bellows used by blacksmiths and silversmiths in the region. Silver neck rings, huge silver crowns and lockets, and golden flowers are the most prized possessions of young women in the Taijiang area. At huge song gatherings attended by thousands of people of all ages, and at ritual buffalo sacrifices, many young people still play a kind of bamboo instrument called a *gi* (*lusheng* in Chinese). The instrument has several free reeds inside pipes, which vibrate when it is blown.

The portion of the epic concerning the birth of the metals and the creation of the suns and moons includes many other references to the tools of the metalsmiths. There were so many that Jin took me to a fully provisioned silversmith shop, where I was able to examine a forge, the porcelain crucibles placed in the coals to melt silver, and various hand tools. Once identified, these items further revealed the workings of the traditional Miao imagination. My favorite image from the entire cycle concerns a pair of tongs used to hold hot pieces of metal. In the song, the tongs were transformed from the claw of a tiny freshwater crab still found in the local rivers. The rivet that was used to hold the two pieces together was transformed from a leech, often found in rice fields. Grasping a pair of iron tongs in my hands not only brought back memories of my own short stint as a blacksmith, but also convinced me that a leech was a clever image to employ. Having no bones, a leech can contract or stretch, just as a piece of metal becomes malleable in the coals and is subject to the shaping blows of the hammer. Only a people with an intimate experience of the natural landscape and a sense of wonder at the art of metallurgy could create such an apt image.

Though several of my guides and teachers have passed away, their encouragement, patience, and generosity are not forgotten. Through them I realized that visiting or living in the places where the songs were born and nurtured is crucial to understanding the many social and physical contexts of texts based on oral performances. The challenge of transferring that understanding into another language's reality is great and, like so many things in the song of Butterfly Mother, involves transmutation of form through an extension of essence.

The Last *Bimo* in the Village[1]
(*Saizili zuihou yiwei bimo*)

From between lips and teeth grow countless words of bush and tree,
bushes and trees whereupon perch countless wise birds and beasts.

And though today hunters go to the city
(where the streets are heavy with fat game)
you stay alone in the village.

When guiding the soul of the last dead
you did not forget the way,
continuing to chant
even when
two teeth, whiter than jade,
flew from your thick lips
to pierce through
your sacred book.

Ancestor, ah
I will use my two old teeth
to exchange for your two new teeth.

Aku Wuwu (Luo Qingchun), 1995

Translated by Mark Bender

Ornaments[2]
(*Shoushi*)

A host of ancient white ants
leaps
from the wooden pedestal bowl
to enshroud the woman's headdress,
engaging in joyful rebirth.

Hunting dogs
or is it wild game,
padding along with
           sounds like autumn birds.

Pleated skirts,
full of stories strung together;
naked threads now break apart
in crazy shadows
as delicate ornaments are tread
into clay.

Those heads, soaked too long in pearls, jade, and agate
almost like wild fruits, overripe
falling toward the earth
snatched by a flying vulture
hungrily stealing its sustenance
leaving only this vivid portrait against the sky
to become a work of art that could
predate a history.

Aku Wuwu (Luo Qingchun), 1995

Translated by Mark Bender

"Heavenly Maiden Hxiyo'amei"[3]

Heavenly Maiden Hxiyo'amei
Arose so early one day,
And in a jade basin, washed her face,
And with golden water, rinsed her hands,
And with a silver comb, combed her locks,
And with a fine gold comb, combed her tresses.

She then flew quickly down to earth, going to Shawojjijji,
Buying there a rare and wonderful thing,
Buying a treasure box, tightly locked,
A treasure box that couldn't be opened.

She placed it one day in the ruler's hall,
And the ruler wished to open it,
But the ruler had no key,
And the lock would not come open,
The lock bar wouldn't loosen,
Thus, the ruler couldn't open it.

She placed it one day in a minister's court,
And the minister wished to open it,
But the minister had no key,
And the lock would not come open,
The lock bar wouldn't loosen,
Thus, the minister couldn't open it.

She placed it one morning in a *bimo*'s hall,
And the *bimo* went to open it,
But his hand held no key,
And the lock would not come open,
The lock bar wouldn't slide,
Thus, the *bimo* couldn't open it.

She put it once on the singing grounds,
And sister wished to open it,
Her hand held the key,
And the key unlocked the lock,
And the lock bar slid open.

Sister unlocked the precious box,
Opened it for brother,
And brother was so lucky!

Qugu folk song, collected 1996

Translated by Mark Bender

1. "How much do you two really know?"[4]

How much do you two really know?
I'm afraid I'm old, my body's weak,
As my teeth fall out, my cheeks grow hollow.
As my cheeks cave in, my lips stick out,
And the notes of my songs are not so round.
Were I young as you,
My Mandarin would flow like yours,
And one by one would my Miao songs ring.
This one singer could outsing ten,
Making them cry for their pa and ma,
Causing their tears by the hundreds to stream,
Stream like rivers to float a boat
Clear to Shanghai, that far-off port,
Clear to a big official's door;
That's what I call singing.

Sung by Gang Yenf Eb Ghob,
collected 1998 by Xenx Jenb Eb Ghob

Translated by Mark Bender

11. "Don't weave cloth without a loom"

Don't weave cloth without a loom,
Don't sing songs without the rules,
Follow the song-path when you sing,
Sing them all from head to toe,
Without missing anything in between;
If anything in between is missed,
Then we'll not sing in harmony.
If you want to sing a new song,
That we two haven't learned,
We'll have a hard time following sister.
We'll have to owe sister a little favor,
But don't feel bad over a favor owed,
Don't be sad on account of brother.
As teachers, companions, walking a familiar road,
Since we're so close, let's be friends,
Become dearest kin for life.

Sung by Fuf Nix Khat Gad,
collected 1998 by Qenf Dangk Khat Ged

Translated by Mark Bender

1 A *bimo* is the traditional ritualist who specializes in reading the ancient books of knowledge and conducting the complex Yi funeral ceremonies. In some areas these rituals still include cremation. A major portion of the ceremonies is guiding the soul of the deceased to the land of the ancestors. According to custom, a child's teeth are "exchanged" for new ones by tying the lost teeth to bits of black charcoal and throwing them on the home's roof.

2 A central image here is that of an ancient, wooden pedestal bowl, or compote, painted with designs and used to store objects such as silver ornaments. The image of the white ants emerging from their feast on the old bowl is transformed into that of the tiny silver ornaments that customarily decorate women's black cloth headgear. The ornaments and parti-colored pleated skirts are markers of tradition and belie the life experiences of individual Yi women and the people as a whole. The skirt images are especially rich in cultural nuance because, according to legend, three drops of an eagle's blood fell on the young woman Purmo Hniyyr (or Pumoniyi in Mandarin Pinyin romanization) while she was weaving, one drop staining her skirt and making her pregnant with the future culture-hero, Zhyge Alu (Zhige'alu in Pinyin romanization). The images of the disintegrating skirts and the simile of the falling fruits suggest both the breakdown and the constraints of the "old ways."

3 This courting song, rich in metaphor, was collected in the Bijie region of western Guizhou province. Hxiyo'amei is one of many female celestials in the local oral and written folklore. Singing, especially of love songs, has long played a major role in the traditional dating activities between young singles, though the tradition is in rapid decline in many areas. By convention, singers refer to each other as "brother" and "sister" while singing a variety of styles of love songs, which progress according to conventional themes as the couple gets to know each other.

The lyrics allude to a number of powerful figures. In centuries past, Yi overlords controlled areas of the Yi territory in a strict caste system. The five-rank system included rulers, ministers, priests (ritual specialists called *bimo,* or *bumo* in the Bijie region), artisans, and common folk. Later, local Yi rulers were empowered with rank by the Chinese imperial government.

According to Yi scholar and poet Bamo Qubumo, many Yi lyrics (like the present one) have three parts: a scene of the heavens, a scene concerning the situation on earth, and a more immediate, personal scene.

The translation is based on a bilingual Yi/Mandarin text collected and compiled by Aluoxingde (Wang Jichao), a well-known scholar of Guizhou Yi traditional texts in the Bijie area of Guizhou. The language of the original is semiliterary and similar to versions of such songs recorded in the ancient Yi script. (As texts from the Guizhou region are usually transcribed only in the International Phonetic Alphabet, the Yi words in this poem have been rendered in the standard Liangshan Yi romanization from neighboring Sichuan province.)

4   In the course of singing the Miao epic poems, the two competing pairs of singers (usually men versus women) intersperse lyrical asides with passages of the epic narrative. These lyrics use the same tunes as the epic passages, but the content and feeling is closer to other styles of folk-song singing, especially the rich antiphonal courting-song traditions. The examples here are "song flowers," used by one pair of singers (though they sing as if one person) to taunt or tease the other pair about their knowledge of epic content, their singing ability, and their stamina during the all-night sings.

WILLIAM I. ELLIOTT

A Poem Should Mean *and* Be:
Remarks on the Translation of Japanese Poetry

THE CLOSING LINES OF Archibald MacLeish's "Ars Poetica" are so
telling that a few moments may pass before one realizes just how problem-
atic those lines are:

> A poem should not mean
> But be.

Yes. It is what a poem *is* and not what a poem *says* that counts. But was
there ever a poem more "meaningful" than MacLeish's own handful of dis-
arming lines? Indeed the poem's meaning is so powerful that the "being" of
the poem is in danger of being overlooked. A parable comprises nothing if
not meaning(s).

Perhaps a distinction should be made here between meanings as
cerebral content and meaning-as-being. Apart from paraphrase or irre-
ducible ideas or conclusions that may be abstracted from the words of the
poem, the identity of the poem is askable. What is its "soul"? How is it dif-
ferent from what it is not? Do its constituent parts cohere? Do they work
together to form a wholeness? Does the poem exhibit internal integrity?
Such questions as these are ultimately referable to the distinct being of the
poem that constitutes its fundamental meaning. Whereas a poem's intellec-
tual meanings may be moot, its identity should not be.

Substitute the word "translation" for MacLeish's "poem":

> A translation should not mean
> But be.

The questions that apply to the poem apply equally to the transla-
tion. It is at this point that the poems of a poet such as Shuntarō Tanikawa
become, surface evidence to the contrary, difficult to shepherd into English.
Because his language is largely colloquial, delivered preponderantly in the

hiragana syllabary, it would appear that translation of his work should be transparent and fairly problem-free. To the contrary, his poems are written on the assumption that the poet does not entertain the composition of his poems as a primary goal; neither does Tanikawa intend to coddle words or cultivate language. He is searching for a way—poetry happening to be *his* way—of establishing, recognizing, and maintaining human bonds:

> I want to make something I can share with other
> people. This happened to be poetry rather than cars,
> academic essays or asparagus.

This was written later in his career, in 1987. But at the outset of his career, in 1956, he wrote in an essay entitled "Deviations":

> I've always considered that it is something other
> than poetry as such that matters to me… What does
> really matter to me is the relationship between life
> and words.

Central in Tanikawa's experience are the feelings that people hold or may hold in common. So far so good. When, however, it comes to rendering the work in English, the translator faces the challenge of making a coherent poem out of a colloquial Japanese that may lean on clichés and/or consist of otherwise flat language. Much is asked of translator and reader of either language. The task is to look beyond meanings for emotions emergent from the poet's deeper selfhood, to look for the poem's meaning-as-being; in mainstream Western poetic traditions, however, the quest for meaning(s), philosophic and otherwise, has often obscured the question of meaning-as-being. This has been the case, in part, because while meaning-as-being is hard to discern, meanings are comparatively easy to ferret out.

Whether meaning-as-being or mere meanings alone, the translation trek is so pocked by chuckholes and frustrated by blind curves that no translator works without assistance. There are, for instance, one's predecessors, from whom one learns by positive or negative example; there are living informants upon whom one relies (and it is unconscionable when their aid goes unacknowledged). I have never worked and would not willingly work in the absence of a native informant, for I do not possess sufficient knowledge of any subject that would be relevant to translation, including the Japanese language. My knowledge needs supplementing, my errors correction. There are such matters as the historical meanings of words, their varying careers and reputations, slang, idioms past and present, social history—what have you. In fact, a single native informant may not be sufficient, and even the poet whose work one is translating, if one is fortunate enough to have him near, may prove less than very helpful as a resource person.

Nor can all this save one from mistranslating. Even broad meanings can have escaped a translator—not to mention nuances and other teeming niceties, so teeming that they cannot possibly be tracked by one or two educated contemporaries reading a certain passage in a single poem. Social and linguistic processes form a complex welter of associations, all the details of which no one can perfectly, readily comprehend.

If one is interested and lucky, long and sustained immersion in the culture may lead, not unnaturally, to the capacity to ease and escort Japanese feelings into an English that yields similar feelings, even though this sometimes means schooling an English-speaking readership in what those feelings are. When a poem is successful, that success hinges at least as much on a reader's willingness and ability to enter into the poem as it does upon the poet's having made the poem accessible. A failed poem, I. A. Richards wrote some six or seven decades ago, may fail because of an irresponsible reader. Poet, translator, and reader form, if you will, an equilateral triangle.

Whatever Coleridge may have meant by the Secondary Imagination and Fancy, it is not these facets of consciousness that conduce to the writing of good poems or good translations. "Success" is not the right word, but when it occurs, it does so because another language (say, Japanese) has passed through a self (the translator's) that has absorbed Japanese sensibility enough to suggest with some confidence what one decent English rendering might be. The translator aims to pass on to the reader an opportunity to participate in emotions emerging from the poem. This is not quite Tanikawa's understanding, for I think he would be less insistent than I am about the handling of prosodic techniques as part and parcel of the poem's meaning-as-being. Prosody is not a cosmetics kit.

Meanings, meaning-as-being, and techniques are inseparable. Let one example serve: a *tanka* from the *Kinkafu* manuscript whose song version suggests that it preceded the *tanka* itself.

[1]	*Michi no be no*	[4]	Imagine:
[2]	*hari to kunugi to*	[2]	oak and hazel
[3]	*shinameku mo*	[1]	beside the road
[4]	*iu naru ka mo yo*	[3]	whispering:
[5]	*hari to kunugi to*	[5]	oak and hazel

When Noah S. Brannen and I put this into English, we tried to suggest one historical possibility: gossips, lovers, or prostitutes. Nature poems per se are unusual in ancient Japanese poetry. We settled on gossiping prostitutes upon whom some scorn is being heaped. Our version reads:

> See how supplely
> Side by side beside the road
> Oak and hazel sway
> Away the lazy hours,
> Oh, wagging their long, loose tongues.

Assonance, consonance, and alliteration honor the phonetic repetitiveness of the Japanese. As for meaning(s), our version is embroidery of a sort, but in the realm of *jōdai kayō* (ancient songs), all translation is interpretation: *jōdai kayō* are written in a Chinese that is used more for its phonetic value than its ideogrammatic sense—this in order to approximate the sound of Japanese. Thus the *kayō* are—one might even say wonderfully—open to various interpretations. At times even Japanese scholars are reduced to making educated, and contradictory, guesses. No translation is ever the final word.

To these remarks, however, I would add this final word. When Coleridge, conversant in German philosophy, set himself on locating the origin of a poem, he involved himself in a discussion of the creative process. He wanted to account for where a poem comes from, and that "place" he termed "the infinite I AM" within the poet. That is to say, he ultimately located the origin of a poem in the poet's basic creative energy: the poet's (or the translator's) act is imitative of God's (or the poet's) in creating the universe (or the poem). It is out of the selfhood that a poem and a translation come, and so I conclude that Coleridge was speaking about what has here been called meaning-as-being—the poet's, the poem's, and the translator's—*and,* we should add, the reader's.

Secret

Someone is hiding something.
I don't know who.
I don't know what.
If I knew that I'd know everything.
I hold my breath and cock my ear.
Rain patters on the ground.
It must be hiding something.
It falls to let us know its secret
but I can't decipher the code.
I sneak into the kitchen, peer around
and see my mother's back.
She's hiding something, too,
minding her own business while grating a
radish. I'm really curious about secrets
but no one tells me about anything.
When I look at the hole in my heart
all I see is the cloudy night sky.

Shuntarō Tanikawa (b. 1931)

Translated by William I. Elliott and
Kazuo Kawamura

Bare Ground

When I lay my head on a pillow, the earth strongly pulls me earthward.
The force is far fiercer than gravitation.
I flatten out like a flounder at the bottom of the sea.
Though my eyeballs keep rolling, I see very little.

If I were being pulled toward hell, there'd be some future pleasure.
But the bare ground has no intention of allowing such a luxury.
All it wants to do is stick me to its surface,
lest I forget that I am made of dust.

Yet I soon fall asleep
and dream that I keep on leaping toward the sky.
I happily kick the street's asphalt with my Reeboks
and evade the electric poles to the accompaniment of someone's requiem.

I called the model plane I made as a boy "Tottering Angel."
It used to zigzag up, spin and plummet nose-first to earth.
Ever since, the earth has been my teacher,
telling me that I have no place to live or die except on the bare ground.

Shuntarō Tanikawa (b. 1931)

Translated by William I. Elliott

Listening to Mozart

The person listening to Mozart curls up like a child,
his eyes following the curled wallpaper as if it were the blue sky,
just as though his invisible sweetheart were whispering in his ear.

The melody annoys him in the shape of a question
which he cannot answer,
because it easily answers itself,
leaving him behind.

The lover's words so vulnerably spoken to the whole world...
a caress too tender to survive this earth...
a prophecy too cruel to be realized...
the "Yes" which rejects every possible "No"!

The person listening to Mozart stands up.
He shakes off the caress of mother-music
and walks downstairs toward the street, looking for an answerable question.

Shuntarō Tanikawa (b. 1931)

Translated by William I. Elliott

OK-KOO KANG GROSJEAN

The Way of Translation

One of the *kongan* (*koan* in Japanese) that *sŏnsa* (Zen masters) frequently assign their students is "What is your original face?" Would it be far-fetched to think that poets too should question the ground of their poetry? Because the ground will determine the essence of their poetry.

As there are countless ways to enter truth, there are also countless ways or reasons a poet writes poems. I enter the world of poetry as a trav-eler on the Way, and I have always thought that my poems are signposts on my journey toward the unknown or the absolute, which cannot be named or described but only grasped intuitively. Poems come to me as a gift mostly when I am at work in the garden, taking a walk, or meditating, and I am like a midwife who delivers poems from the quiet heart. So each poem I receive tells me where I am and how far I have to go on my jour-ney. My teachers or guides in this travel are those sentient or insentient beings who quench my thirst or who awaken my longing for the state in which I am free from the world of discrimination.

What would this mysterious ground of poetry be? What makes any creation or creative activity possible? I thought about this for a long time, and one day an answer came to me: the ground of all creation is imperma-nence. Our life, which is the result of creation, and our creative activity depend on impermanence. Why didn't I think of such an obvious answer before?

What is the significance of impermanence as the ground of poetry? Impermanence means that nothing is unchanging, including time. It frees us from self, which is the product of time. Without impermanence, no-self is not possible. Impermanence is the world of the Flower Garland Sutra, where, as Blake said, we can perceive the universe in a grain of sand, and each moment becomes eternal, because eternity is only possible in the absence of time. Time is the territory of the known, and we are able to see the unknown only when we go beyond time. That is why the poems that come from this unknown territory cannot but be wild, fresh, and alive, like a leaping carp. Perhaps this state is what Gary Snyder calls "the practice of the wild."

In his essay "On the Path, Off the Trail," Snyder writes that "There are paths that can be followed, and there is a path that cannot—it is not a path, it is wilderness. There is a 'going' but no goer, no destination, only the whole field." He also writes that "'Off the trail' is another name for the Way, and sauntering off the trail is the practice of the wild. That is also where—paradoxically—we do our best work. But we need paths and trails and will always be maintaining them. You must be on the path, before you can turn and walk into the wild." After reading this essay, I realized that I am a traveler on the pathless path, where, as Dōgen said, "practice is the path," and I have chosen the way of poetry as my practice. Although this essay is about translation, I feel that how I happened to make my choice influenced the way I translate poems into English.

When I was growing up in Korea, I wanted to become a poet. I was deeply inspired by the lyric beauty of *hyangga* of the Three Kingdoms period and *kayo* of the Koryŏ period. The longing of the women in these *hyangga* and *kayo* for their lovers, and of monks for Amida Buddha, touched my heart deeply. And reading modern poems by Seo Jung Ju, the most accomplished living lyric poet in Korea, and Kim Nam Jo's devotional poems, I also wanted to become a poet.

Not being sure about my ability as a poet, I studied chemistry instead and came to America to pursue graduate work in pharmacy at Columbia University in New York in 1963. However, I didn't give up my desire to be a poet and continued to write.

On my way to New York, I stopped in Berkeley to see my sister and, during that visit, met my future husband at the university when I audited his English class for foreign students. Later, when I was disillusioned by the aggressive and competitive atmosphere of Columbia, my future husband sent me a copy of *Education and the Significance of Life*, by Krishnamurti, and said that the book might help me the way it helped him. The book indeed helped me. It changed me radically. It awakened me from my comfortable and conventional belief system.

Before I came to America, I was a very devout Presbyterian who was taught that Buddhism was an idol-worshipping religion. I felt guilty whenever I had to visit temples on school excursions because I was entering a territory where I should not put my foot. But, reading Krishnamurti, I began to understand the difference between religious organizations and the religious mind, and to understand that the truth cannot be contained in any religious organization because, as Krishnamurti said, "Truth is a pathless land." In this pathless land, there are infinitely many gates we can enter.

Krishnamurti's book also showed me how futile it was to try to learn and perfect the technique of writing poetry. He writes that one doesn't need to learn a style to be a writer. If one truly has something to say, the content will decide the way to express it. As I examined my desire to be a poet, I realized that I had nothing to say that was so urgent and so original. I gave up on being a poet and instead decided to translate good books into Korean. My first project was translating *Education and the Significance of Life*. I introduced Krishnamurti to Korea in 1980.

At that time, interracial marriage was greatly frowned upon in Korea, and no doubt still is. However, Krishnamurti said in his book, "with love everything is possible." I married my husband after eighteen months of agony, and as a result, I was disowned by my family until our son was born eight years later.

As Snyder said, "You must be on the path, before you can turn and walk into the wild." My initial path was Christianity, which gave me the opportunity to turn and walk into the wild, where I was exposed to many kinds of spiritual teachings, as well as the poetry of Eastern and Western poets. In that wilderness, I came to understand that the essence of all religious teachings is the same. In Linda Hess's translation of *The Bijak of Kabir,* Kabir beautifully expressed this idea in his poem: "The Vedas show many ways / to cross the sea." Ibn Arabi in his poem "I Follow the Religion of Love," translated by Andrew Harvey, says,

> My heart has become capable of every form:
> It is a pasture for gazelles,
> And a monastery for Christian monks,
> And a temple for idols,
> And the Ka'aba of the pilgrims,
> And the tablets of the Torah,
> And the book of the Koran.
> I follow the religion of Love:
> Whatever path Love's camel takes,
> That is my religion and my faith.

Didn't the Buddha say that there are 84,000 gates to the Dharma? If so, everyone has the freedom to choose a kind of practice that matches one's inclination and understanding. In this wilderness, I saw many wonders and beauties, and I started to record my experience. I wanted to share it with someone who might find the same pleasure as I do. My favorite *hadith* says, "I was a hidden treasure and I longed to be known." Beauty wants to be known and shared, just as a flower blooms to make its beauty available and to spread its perfume. In this beauty, nothing is excluded. Every thing and every action are equally beautiful in the world of non-doing or in the eye of Amida Buddha. The act of a cook is as beautiful to watch as the act of a dancer performing. I happen to express this beauty in the form of poetry, and my poems are those wonders I see and want to share with others.

There are many different schools of poetry translation. One school advocates a faithful and literal translation (*Übersetzung*); the other end of the spectrum is the school that insists on a creative translation (*Überdichtung*). I feel both schools have their merits. However, for me, the most important thing in the translation is not to lose the *rasa,* or flavor, of the poetry in the process. I call this way of translation the middle way. I learned something about *rasa* while reading the book *Dance of Shiva* by Ananda K. Coomaraswamy late in the sixties. Coomaraswamy, as quoted by Vishwanath S. Naravane in his biography, said that "the essential element in art is the flavor (rasa) which determines the aesthetic emotion. This is a transcendental experience and is of the same type as the mystical experience of the Divine." Any translation devoid of the flavor of the original is like the clay form of Adam before God blew His breath into him. The translator must love poetry so much that the poems become part of his breath.

I began to translate my poems into English while taking a course given by Richard Silberg at the University of California. We were to submit our own poems for each class, but at that time I wrote poems in Korean. While living in this country over thirty years, I kept my Korean fluent by translating books into Korean and writing essays and publishing them in Korea. However, my English needed help. My husband helped me translate my poems into English. He was not only knowledgeable about Chinese and Japanese classical poetry, but also English and American poetry. It was he who introduced me to the California poetry of Robinson Jeffers, Gary Snyder, and Kenneth Rexroth, as well as the *haiku* of Bashō, Issa, and Buson. My husband, who is more Oriental in his way of life than I, knew exactly what I was trying to express.

As poems come to me as a gift, sometimes it takes ten or twenty years to write a poem; "Beauty Only," although it has only six lines, is one that took that long. The core of Krishnamurti's teaching is "choiceless awareness." What does that mean? Intellectual understanding of that statement didn't satisfy me. I wanted to taste the state of choiceless awareness, as well as the state of direct seeing, which Zen talks about. The answer came to me as a poem during an illness in 1986. When I was nine years old, I had become a vegetarian after seeing a dead cow's head in the cellar, a cow that was killed for a wedding festival. Later, in my job as a biochemist, I had to be involved in killing rats. I couldn't do it and yet I couldn't quit my job, and I was in such torment that I became gravely sick. During my illness, death was friendlier than life, and I began to appreciate each moment as though it was the last. I became very sensitive to my surroundings. One day I felt better and went out to take a short walk. I saw a tiny yellow flower, and as I did not know anything about the flower, I had to look at it as it was. The beauty of the flower sparkled, and I realized that during most of my waking time I don't see things as they are. I look at things through my prejudices and preconceptions. So I wrote "Beauty Only." The poem in Korean is:

산보하다
한 송이 들꽃을
보았네 .

이름을 모르기에
그 고움만
보았네.

I translated it into English as:

Taking a walk
I saw
a wildflower.

Not knowing its name
I saw
its beauty *only.*

As you see, it is a very easy poem to translate. However, the position of "only" is very important for me. The Korean could be translated as "I saw / only its beauty," which is perfectly correct. But for me, "I saw its beauty *only*" is very different from "I saw *only* its beauty." "I saw only its beauty" indicates that there was something else besides beauty in that flower that I either missed seeing or deliberately did not see. However, what I wanted to say was that at the moment I saw the flower, there was nothing but beauty: the beauty that is revealed to the heart devoid of any discriminating thoughts, prejudices, or preconceptions. I would be very disappointed if someone translated it otherwise because the poem's flavor of urgency could be lost by mispositioning *only.*

Around the late sixties, I read *Journey to Ixtlan,* by Carlos Castaneda. In the book, there is a poem by Castaneda's teacher, Don Juan, with a line about walking a road with a heart. I fell in love with that line without knowing the meaning, and I struggled with the hidden teaching of it for over twenty years. One day in the early nineties, I understood it in my own way while watching a hummingbird's dance in my garden: that to walk a road with a heart is to live life with the great compassion that comes with the knowledge of the oneness of all things. In order to realize the oneness of all beings, we have to understand that emptiness means there is no such thing as a self that divides "I" from "you." There is a Buddhist expression for this, 同體大悲 (동체대비), which I learned from my teacher, Chung-Hwa *sŏnsa*. But how could I translate 동체대비 into poetic words? I realized that I could translate the term as "the dance with a heart" because it refers to the same thing. Perhaps someone might say that I was not being faithful to the original, but as a poet I feel my translation of 동체대비 as "the dance with a heart" is justified. The translated poem, "A Hummingbird's Dance," is:

> Whenever I water flowers
> somewhere
> a hummingbird appears
> and dances.
>
> For a long time
> I've watched that dance
> not knowing
> what moves me so.
>
> Today
> I see.
>
> In a hummingbird's dance
> there is no bird
> only movement.
>
> The dance
> danced without "I"
> is the dance with a heart.

Imagine if I translated the last line as "is the dance of great compassion from seeing the oneness of all beings."

I think the ideal condition for translating poetry is for the translator to work with a native speaker. However, in most cases this is not possible. In these cases, translators of poetry should be those who have fallen in love with the writing and the life of the poet so that they are able to look at the world with the poet's eyes. Otherwise, the translation may lack the essence or the flavor of the original poems.

Another poem I want to talk about is "Autumn Leaves." The mood of this poem is like dancing. However, if I translate it very faithfully, it reads like this:

Leaves the color of red wine
fall one by one
in the autumn rain.

That fleeting *dance*
quickens my heart
and tightens my throat.

Beauty never stays
but memories linger,
the *dancers* whisper to me.

The dance I will dance
when I die
will that be beautiful too?

In this other translation, my husband and I translated the rhythm and urgency of sorrow differently without losing the essence of the poem.

Red as wine
leaves fall
one by one in the autumn rain.

These fleeting *dancers*
quicken my heart
and tighten my throat.

Beauty never stays
but memories linger,
the *leaves* whisper to me.

When I dance my death
will that be beautiful too?

In this translation, I condensed the first stanza to capture the movement more vividly and changed "dance" to "dancers," and "dancers" to "leaves." The changes were more pleasing to our ears, and in the last stanza, the freer translation actually emphasized the immediacy of the moment more effectively. Translating is like choosing wine or food. It is a very individual matter and depends on personal taste. How can we cultivate a pleasing taste? That comes from rigorous practice: the practice of reading, writing, and translating in order to develop the knack to do it well. Translating is like preparing a dish by following a recipe. Just as it is critical to use the right herb or flavoring, choosing the right word or expression decides the success of the translation.

One of my poems has the title 천진하게. I chose this title deliberately. I entered Zen through D.T. Suzuki's writings. In the book *Zen and the Birds of Appetite,* by Thomas Merton, there is a dialogue between Suzuki and Merton on "Wisdom in Emptiness," which was important to my understanding of original sin in Christianity and of emptiness in Buddhism. Suzuki quotes a poem by Kyogen Chikan and a statement by Meister Eckhart to illustrate emptiness and the state of innocence. The poem is:

> Last year's poverty was not yet perfect;
> This year's poverty is absolute.
> In last year's poverty there was room for the
> head of a gimlet;
> This year's poverty has let the gimlet itself disappear.

Meister Eckhart's statement is, "He is a poor man who wants nothing, knows nothing, and has nothing." Suzuki defines ignorance as loss of innocence; to regain innocence is to be poor. I thought about this and wrote "Innocently":

> From the backyard
> came the sound of laughter.
> Going out I found
>
> husband and son
> laughing
> feeding pistachio nuts
> to a baby squirrel who
> not yet knowing fear
> had climbed the steps to the deck.
>
> Innocently
> before darkness and light
> were divided
> the squirrel is cracking nuts
> and husband and son
> are laughing.

In this poem, the title is most important because I wanted to express the state of innocence the way I experienced it. If I look up the English words for 천진하게, there are several: *innocently, artlessly, naively,* and *simpleheartedly.* But for me, there is only one correct translation here, and I used it for the title.

Writing poems and translating them are the way of my practice. However, without daily living, writing is not possible. So my activity at every moment is my way of practice. I want to perform whatever I do impeccably, with a heart.

Sound of a Falling Plum

for Gary Snyder

Sweet sound from the plum tree,
leaves swaying in the gentle wind
so different from the sound
of a squirrel dashing on young branches
looking for ripe plums.

I stop reading,
watch the baby squirrel, hungrily
eating nonstop
one, two, three plums.

Nothing stands still in nature.
Nature is dance,
each dance
like the wind, never caught
by leaves.

　　　　　Plop,

Squirrel in the tree
tree in the garden

　　　　　Where am I
　　　　　in the sound of
　　　　　no nature?

　　　　　Ok-Koo Kang Grosjean (1940–2001)

　　　　　Translated by the poet

Birthday Song

On the morning of his birthday
he said
"I wanted to see the ocean."

So we went
through the valleys
across the mountains
to the ocean
up the coast
past Jenner
past Fort Ross
past Gualala.

Coming home
along the Russian river
still drunk with the beauty
of the Pacific ocean,

I felt like embracing
a bouquet
of all beings.

Ok-Koo Kang Grosjean (1940–2001)

Translated by the poet

"My garden is my temple"

My garden is my temple.
Tending my garden,
my practice.
Today's dharma talk is
the smiles of flowers,
the attention of young squirrels
dashing from branch to branch
after ripe plums,
the sound of a falling plum.

These are true teachings
coming from the garden
where each path is no path.

Ok-Koo Kang Grosjean (1940–2001)

Translated by the poet

The Most Beautiful Color

for Glen

At Inspiration Point
around six o'clock,
the wind is soothing,
the sky is cloudless
and strangers smile to
each other when passing.

"I like those tall white flowers
very much" he said.
"Why don't you write a poem
about them?"

Looking at the flowers,
their gesture of abandonment
                          to the wind
reminded me
of a passage in the sutra
I read last night.

The Buddha said
that the most beautiful color
is the color of shyness.

Like the luminous color of those flowers?

In mutual delight
we laughed
feeling light and happy.

January 22, 1997

Ok-Koo Kang Grosjean (1940–2001)

Translated by the poet

I

The I in the mirror
is not I.

The I outside the mirror
is not I.

The body is just a bowl
which holds I.

As the bowl can't see
the water it holds,
my body can't see me.

The I which I can't see
I see in the sky
in the cloud
in the flower
in the birds
and momentarily
in whatever else I see.

The bowl and I
are inseparable but
they are not the same.

Still,
when I am not sought after,
I become
sky, cloud, a flower, a bird,
and even a bowl.

Ok-Koo Kang Grosjean (1940–2001)

Translated by the poet

SAM HAMILL

Sustenance: A Life in Translation

I WAS INTRODUCED TO CLASSICAL CHINESE POETRY by Kenneth Rexroth and the Beat poets in the late 1950s, especially by Rexroth's immensely popular *One Hundred Poems from the Chinese,* which included thirty-odd poems translated from Tu Fu, whom Rexroth called "the greatest non-epic, non-dramatic poet in history." I drew inspiration from what I learned of Han Shan in Jack Kerouac's *The Dharma Bums* and Gary Snyder's translations, and from the poets in Robert Payne's *The White Pony,* Witter Bynner's translations, and of course those of Arthur Waley.

Later, after four years in the U.S. Marine Corps, two of which were spent in Japan, where I began Zen practice and learned some rudimentary Japanese, I came to Ezra Pound's adaptations of the notebooks of Ernest Fenollosa, published as *Cathay* in 1915. In an essay in the second edition of *A Poet's Work,* "On the Making of Ezra Pound's *Cathay*," I discuss the origins and development of this little volume of only fourteen poems, claiming it to be the single most influential volume of poetry in this century. Here, I'd like to elucidate a few of this book's problems because they present some of the dangers of translating without knowledge of the original.

Fenollosa knew little Japanese and almost no Chinese. His informants were two Japanese professors, Mori and Ariga, neither of whom was fluent in classical Chinese, and thus Li Po became known in the West by his Japanese name, Rihaku. This trilingual effort sometimes produced strange results, as in the poem "Separation on the River Kiang." Pound retains Fenollosa's Japanese pronunciation, *ko-jin,* which means simply "person," mistakenly treating it as a personal name rather than recognizing the two Chinese characters *ku jen.* The *kiang* in the title means "river." So Pound's title becomes "Separation on the River River" rather than "Separation on the Yangtze River." Nevertheless, *Cathay* opened the doors to American modernism. More than any other volume, it is responsible for the personal tone of much of this century's shorter lyrical, imagistic verse.

When I began translating Tu Fu in the mid-1970s, I looked up each character and annotated each poem before attempting my own draft, and then turned to translations by Florence Ayscough, William Hung, Rexroth, and others for comparative readings. What I found was often surprising.

Here is my translation of Tu Fu's "New Year's Eve at the Home of Tu Wei":

> Seeing the year end at a brother's home,
> We sing and toast with pepper wine.
> The stable is noisy with visitors' horses.
> Crows abandon trees lit by torches.
> Tomorrow morning I turn forty-one.
> The slanting sunset shadows lengthen.
> Why should one exercise self-restraint?
> I may as well stay drunk all the days of my life.

Rexroth, who is very good at locating the personal voice and situation of Tu Fu in his translations, makes no effort to recapture the formal end-stopped couplets of the original, even though the couplet is the fundamental unit of classical Chinese poetry and Tu Fu its greatest master. Choosing in its stead a typically loose line that may be a run-on, Rexroth's version ends:

> In the winter dawn I will face
> My fortieth year. Borne headlong
> Towards the long shadows of sunset
> By the headstrong, stubborn moments,
> Life whirls past like drunken wildfire.

Sometimes relying too heavily on Ayscough or the French translations of Hervey de Saint-Denys or Georges Margoulies, Rexroth is clearly led astray by the former in this instance. Ayscough's translation reads:

> At bright dawn my years will bridge four tens;
> I fly, I gallop towards the slanting shadows of sunset.
> Who can alter this, who can bridle, who restrain
>   the moments?
> Fiery intoxication is a life's career.

While Rexroth's version makes a fine poem in English, Ayscough's version carries considerable Victorian baggage. Neither poem, I believe, captures the spirit of Tu Fu very successfully. Tu Fu's poem is not about "fiery intoxication." It is not about life whirling past or about the pathetic fallacy "drunken wildfire." Hung's version:

To see the year depart at a brotherly home,
To participate in the songs and toasts with the
      pepper-wine,
I can hear from the stable the noisy horses of the guests,
I can see the crows leaving the trees because of
      the torches.
By tomorrow, I shall no longer be forty;
The evening of life will be fast coming upon me.
Of what use is it to be cautious and to exercise restraint?
Let me forget it all by being utterly drunk.

Even if Hung is wordy, he is closest to the original. However, if his penultimate line is far too prosy, the ultimate line is far too generalized. He also inserts an intrusive "I can hear" and "I can see" where none exist in the original; sometimes a first- or second-person pronoun needs to be added in translation, but one should do so only when essential. Elsewhere, Hung also contributes to general misunderstanding, as when he translates this line in what is probably Tu Fu's last suite of poems: "Such is indeed the shining grace of God." Tu Fu had no concept of a monotheistic god. The principal religions of China in the eighth century were Taoism and Buddhism, neither of which accommodates any notion of a monolithic god. Master Tu was a good Confucian in many respects, but not a deeply religious man. Rather he demonstrated a decidedly existential turn of mind. Hung allowed Western civilization to intrude upon Eastern art in a notably ugly translation.

Tu Fu's joy in joining his brother is shaded by deep resignation as the poet considers the conditions of his life. What is implied in the original, and what should appear in English, is the notion that somehow, being Tu Fu, he will *not* waste away sitting before the wine jug. The great poet-out-of-office, unsung in his own time, asks the question every poet asks under such circumstances: Why do we do it? Why not give up and submit to despondency or the numbing effects of wine? The Chinese poet is not embarrassed by direct expression of this conflict.

Another way translators sometimes go wrong is by investing too much in the pictographic elements of characters. Although an excellent essay, the Pound-Fenollosa "Chinese Written Character as a Medium for Poetry" leads many a Westerner to forget that Chinese is a spoken language and that its poetry, like our own and others', aspires to the conditions of music. One of the things immediately lost in translation is the play of pictographic elements, but if we remember that Chinese poetry was chanted, then we can remember how important is the ear in poetry.

There is not much we can do in English with a basically monosyllabic, rhymed five- or seven-character line. Attempts to translate classical Chinese into rhymed metrical structures in English have largely resulted in academic doggerel. In translating Tu Fu, I sought formality enough to represent the couplet-by-couplet construction of the original, including the syntactical parallelism where possible, and also sought to interpret or interpolate within the poem only where I deemed it essential. Chinese has an almost infinitely larger capacity for rhyming than does English. I therefore sought to pay particular attention to assonance and consonance, and to slant and implied rhymes, while struggling to be true to what I perceived the poet said and to the spirit in which his poem was given—meaning the general tone and stance.

I learned early to rely on scholars whose knowledge of classical Chinese was far greater than mine. After nearly ten years of studying Tu Fu, I completed a first-draft manuscript of about one hundred of his poems. A university press editor asked Irving Yucheng Lo to evaluate my work. Professor Lo was kind enough to comment on each poem, noting exactly where I had misread a Chinese character or misinterpreted a line. His generous offering of time and scholarship was encouragement enough for me to revise the manuscript.

Here is one of Tu Fu's last poems, "Heading South":

南　征

春岸桃花水， chūn àn táo huā shuǐ

雲帆楓樹林。 yún fān fēng shù lín

偷生長避地， tōu shēng cháng bì dì

適遠更沾襟。 shì yuǎn gèng zhān jīn

老病南征日， lǎo bìng nán zhēng rì

君恩北望心。 jūn ēn běi wàng xīn

百年歌自苦， bǎi nián gē zì kǔ

未見有知音。 wèi jiàn yǒu zhī yīn

Spring returns to Peach Blossom River
and my sail is a cloud through maple forests.

Exiled, I lived for years in secret, moving on
farther from home with tearstains on my sleeves.

Now old and sick, at last I'm headed south.
Remembering old friends, I look back north a final time.

A hundred years I sang my bitter song,
but not a soul remembers those old rhymes.

I am perhaps guilty of stating too much by adding "living in secret" where the original suggests simply "refugee." In addition to wanting to do more than just call up the image of the refugee, I needed to fill out the line musically, so I interpolated here. I think "Heading South" is an important poem and have been surprised that David Hinton and other recent translators of Tu Fu have ignored it. After years in exile, the old poet thinks he is about to return home, though still virtually unpublished and unknown but to a few poet friends. The resignation and frustration articulated in the poem have been given a deeply ironic turn by the judgment of history. Tu Fu died shortly thereafter, never dreaming that he might one day be declared the greatest poet in the history of Chinese.

While completing work on Tu Fu's *Facing the Snow,* I translated a small selection of the Tzu Yeh songs and poems by Li Ch'ing-chao, *The Lotus Lovers;* about fifty poems by Li Po, *Banished Immortal;* and Lu Chi's *Wen Fu.* I found *Wen Fu* to be particularly helpful, not only as a translator's handbook but also as a writer's: "When studying the work of the masters," Lu Chi says, "watch the working of their minds." Among the first poets to discuss poetic form and content, Lu Chi lays out an elegant tradition, a good deal of which may be applied directly to our practice two centuries and another language later. In each instance, my translations were corrected, improved, and clarified by being passed under the eyes of such knowledgeable scholar-translators as J.P. Seaton, with whom I recently translated *The Essential Chuang Tzu.*

I was fortunate to receive a Japan–U.S. Fellowship in 1988 and spent much of that year following Bashō's famous route through Japan's northern interior as I began to translate his *Oku no hosomichi* (*Narrow Road to the Interior*), now included in the much more comprehensive *The Essential Bashō.* When I began studying Bashō, I had thought *haiku* was something I would study for perhaps a year. Ten years later, when I finally saw my book in print, I realized that I would continue to be Bashō's student for the rest of my life. The work is never finished. Every translation is a provisional conclusion.

While I knew that my studies in Chinese would be helpful in translating Bashō, just how helpful became clear almost immediately. Bashō's poems and prose are loaded with paraphrases and quotations and echoes of Chuang Tzu, Tu Fu, and Po Chü-i. All during his twenties and thirties, Bashō studied Tu Fu. He claimed to have carried a copy of *Chuang Tzu* with him wherever he went. To know the working of his mind, it is helpful to read what he read, to understand as much as possible about his Zen practice and the social conditions and traditions within which he came to flower.

Japanese poetry flows from two forms, the *chōka* (longer poem) and *waka* (shorter poem). Over a century of aesthetic discussion and development, the *waka* evolved into *tanka,* both written in syllabic lines of 5-7-5-7-7. Unlike Chinese, Japanese is polysyllabic, and its sounds are much closer to those of Western languages. The Japanese language combines *kanji,* Chinese written characters, with a phonetic syllabary, *kana,* of forty-odd characters. Translated literally, *tanka* and *haiku* usually come out a few syllables shorter in English than in Japanese. Consequently, most Western translators have simply ignored the Japanese syllabic structure, thereby sacrificing the musicality that may be achieved by adhering to form.

Another, and to my mind much more egregious, mistake on the part of many translators is to rearrange the order of perceptions in a poem, often with the intent of creating a kind of formal closure. From R.H. Blyth's renowned scholarship of the thirties to that of recent times, one sees this unfortunately common practice. *Haiku* often opens at the end, rather than closes, as in Bashō's most famous poem:

> *Furuike ya*
> *kawazu tobikomu*
> *mizu no oto*

> At the ancient pond
> a frog plunges into
> the sound of water

How this poem has suffered in English! I can't remember whose version it was, nor can I locate it now, but years ago I read one that went:

> An old pond.
> A frog leaps in.
> Kerplop!

The "translator" wanted a punch line at the end. If we may assume that he knew what the original actually said, perhaps this final line is a poor attempt to achieve onomatopoeia. The result may be economical, but completely misses the whole point Bashō is making. While the translation remains true to the order of perceptions, it ruins the poem by creating artificial closure. *Mizu* is water, *no* is postpositional, and *oto* is sound: "The sound of water." Every translator who has put this frog (*kawazu*) into water has missed the poetry. The frog *plunges*—a word I chose because of its onomatopoeic quality in the context of leaping into water—into pure sound. I wanted to stay close to the original form and remain true to Bashō's final line, which, I propose, is followed by a fourth, unwritten line of silence. The poem opens at the end, leaving the reader-listener listening.

Some say that *haiku* is indebted to the four-line Chinese *chüeh-chu* and that, by leaving out the third line, an imaginative leap is made. I doubt the accuracy of such a theory, but there are some structural similarities. Bashō, like his Chinese predecessors, often sets a scene in the first line; however, he uses the Japanese "cutting word" *ya* to create a kind of emphasis: "At the ancient pond, yes, / a frog." The *chüeh-chu* also makes use of an imaginative leap, usually between the third and fourth lines. But there, similarities end. The Chinese poet has no cutting word.

Another example:

> *Fuyuniwa ya*
> *tsuki mo ito naru*
> *mushi no gin*

> A winter garden—
> the moon also a thread,
> like the insect's song

What does that *mo* ("also") in the second line refer to? If the moon (*tsuki*) is "also a thread," what is the first thread? The insect's song (*mushi no gin*)? Chuang Tzu often speaks of "running out the string of our days." Perhaps Bashō means here the thread of his own life. The ambiguity is in the original, and to fail to represent that complexity is to fail in the service of poetry. One implication might be that the moon is the thread stitching the winter garden to the insect's song. Where there is a deliberate use of ambiguity in the original, I try to create a parallel in the translation.

Sometimes the translator must make shifts, as in this poem:

> *Uki fushi ya*
> *take no ko to naru*
> *hito no hate*

which literally means:

> A sad confluence—
> young bamboo shoots
>> [literally, *take no ko,* "children of bamboo"]
> to become
> everyone in the end

A revised version reads:

> A sad confluence—
> everyone in the end becomes
> young bamboo shoots

In the end, what is any poem in translation except another blade of grass in the field—not a conclusion but a provisional entryway into the vast ecology of the poem within its greater tradition? It is best to have two or three translations of any classic text: one a strictly scholarly, literal treatment, and one a more imaginative, more interpretive translation, preferably by a sympathetic and knowledgeable poet.

But of course there can be no such thing as a literal translation since even individual nouns and verbs often have no exact equivalents in other languages. Even when they do have acceptable equivalents, we still find problems of translation. When the Chinese or Japanese poet writes of "clouds and rain," he or she may mean only clouds and rain or may mean sexual congress since "clouds and rain" has been a fixed epithet or *makura kotoba* ("pillow words") for two millennia or more. In the hands of a good poet, the weather and the personal experience become interlocking parts of a compound metaphor. Since we don't have equivalents in English, we must learn to read the translation as well.

Horace was among the first to warn against *verbo verbum* translation. Octavio Paz notes, "Every poem is a translation." With roots in Greek, Latin, and German, and with an admixture of foreign terms that have become Americanized through common usage, the English language itself is a translation.

My practice as a poet and a translator is really one work evolving as much from my Zen practice as by any wish to "make" a poem. Translation has been for me a simultaneous learning and making. There are few stupidities I have not committed. But since I am an *unsui,* a perpetual beginner in the temple of poetry and along the dharma path, I understand that there is no perfect prescription and that we are all students together. In the company of Chuang Tzu, Tu Fu, Bashō, and Issa, my practice is refined, but perfection remains an elusive ideal rather than an attainable reality, and translation a provisional conclusion.

When Bashō advises his students, "Don't merely follow in the footsteps of the masters, but seek what they sought," I number myself among his students. I feel a solidarity with Tu Fu in his exile, despite the fact that we are no longer living in a time of war and I have been fortunate enough to have published more than thirty books while he died an obscure poet. I translate because I want to be in the company of these poets—to comprehend their art, to learn what they learned, and to be shaped by their learning—and because I want to make them available to others.

When an otherwise notable translator like Stephen Mitchell muddies the waters with something as irresponsible as his wild interpretation of Lao Tzu, passing it off as translation, it is like a computer virus that begins to invade other programs. Mitchell writes that he felt no compunction to study the original Chinese because he got the transmission directly from his Zen master and thus felt free to interpret Lao Tzu's *Tao Te Ching* as he wished. In at least a couple of chapters, there is not as much as a single word from the original. The problem here is that the naive reader might assume that the English bears some resemblance to the original, which all too often simply isn't so. Or as Chuang Tzu would say, "Not quite *there* yet, eh?"

To truly understand Lao Tzu, Chuang Tzu, or most classical Chinese poets, we would need a large scholarly apparatus to clarify the allusions and explain the characters, and to explicate the cultural-philosophical contexts and linguistic differences. Bill Porter's recent translation of *Tao Te Ching* is brilliant—in part because it is accurate and in part because he includes insightful commentaries unknown to previous translators.

Chuang Tzu to Tu Fu, Lu Chi to Bashō, the Taoist and Zen literary masters are the very foundation of my practice as both poet and Zen Buddhist. When I say I "practice" the arts of poetry or translation, I mean as a doctor or lawyer "practices" his or her profession. Poetry in America is not a profession, but an avocation. Nevertheless, one is a *practicing* poet, a *practicing* Buddhist or Christian or Jew—or, in my case, Buddhist atheist. (Buddhism is generally nontheistic.) I've always been moved by Gary Snyder's remark "As a poet, I hold the most archaic values on earth." What Tu Fu valued, I value; what Bashō sought, I seek. The human condition remains relatively unchanged over a millennium. And I agree with Stanley Kunitz that poetry "has its source deep under the layers of a life, in the primordial self."

We are fortunate to live during the greatest time for poetry since the T'ang dynasty. While academicians bemoan the decline of "the canon," the canon is expanding exponentially. One can't really begin to understand the East Asian canon without knowing Confucius, *The Lotus Sutra* (the foundation of Buddhism), Chuang Tzu, T'ao Ch'ien, and the T'ang poets. Anyone who believes for a minute that Confucius is not as important as Plato is suffering from tunnel vision. To understand something about Tu Fu and Bashō is to establish kinship with a great and powerful tradition.

American poetry has flowered precisely because we have brought these and many other masters into English. When I survey the great literary influences on the poetry of the last fifty years, I must include beside the many East Asians such poets as Rilke, Akhmatova, Rumi, Trakl, Odysseus Elytis, George Seferis, Yannis Ritsos, Valéry, Neruda, García Lorca, Cavafy, Sappho, and Paz. Their influences have provided sustenance, inspiration, and models for hundreds of our poets. There are more terrific poets writing in America today than have lived here in the past two hundred years, and much of what they create—from surrealist to language poetry, sonnets to "organic verse"—is a direct or indirect result of translation.

Kunitz writes in his *Passing Through:* "Through the years I have found this gift of poetry to be life-sustaining, life-enhancing, and absolutely unpredictable. Does one live, therefore, for the sake of poetry? No, the reverse is true: poetry is for the sake of the life." I sit at the feet of the great old masters of my tradition not only to be in a position to pass on their many wonderful gifts, but to pay homage while nourishing, sustaining, and enhancing my own life.

Returning to My Fields and Gardens

When I was young, my world was disharmonious
at root, fields and mountains were my nature.

Nevertheless, I lived in the dust of the world
for more than thirty years,

a caged bird longing for remembered groves,
a pond fish dreaming of deep seas.

Clearing brush along a southern trail:
living simply returns me to gardens and fields.

My three small acres hold
just a thatch-roofed hut

with willow and elm behind for eaves,
and peach and plum besides.

The memory of village life grows dim,
passing like smoke on gentle winds.

A dog barks down the road.
A cock crows in a mulberry tree.

I've swept the dust from my dooryard.
My empty room is a pleasure.

Thirty years locked in a cage,
but now I return to my own true nature.

T'ao Ch'ien (365–427)

Translated by Sam Hamill

Visiting Pai-an Pavilion

Beside this dike, I shake off the world's dust,
enjoying walks alone near my brushwood house.

A small stream gurgles down a rocky gorge.
Mountains rise beyond the trees,

kingfisher blue, almost beyond description,
but reminding me of the fisherman's simple life.

From a grassy bank, I listen
as springtime fills my heart.

Finches call and answer in the oaks.
Deer cry out, then return to munching weeds.

I remember men who knew a hundred sorrows,
and the gratitude they felt for gifts.

Joy and sorrow pass, each by each,
failure at one moment, happy success the next.

But not for me. I have chosen freedom
from the world's cares. I chose simplicity.

Hsieh Lin-yun (385–433)

Translated by Sam Hamill

Moon, Rain, Riverbank

Rain roared through, now
the autumn night is clear.
The water wears a patina of gold
and carries a bright jade star.
Heavenly River runs clear and pure,
as gently as before.

Sunset buries the mountains in shadow.
A mirror floats in the deep green void,
its light reflecting the cold, wet dusk,
dew glistening,
freezing on the flowers.

Tu Fu (712–770)

Translated by Sam Hamill

Night Thoughts While Traveling

Thin grass bends on the breezy shore,
and the tall mast seems lonely in my boat.

Stars ride low across the wide plain,
and the moon is tossed by the Yangtze.

What is fame and literary status—
the old and infirm should leave office.

Adrift, drifting: what is left for the lone gull
adrift between earth and heaven.

Tu Fu (712–770)

Translated by Sam Hamill

JANE HIRSHFIELD

from The World Is Large and Full of Noises:
Thoughts on Translation

MY OWN EXPERIENCE AS A TRANSLATOR dates from 1985, when dur-
ing a year as a Guggenheim fellow I started collaborating with Mariko
Aratani on a translation of the poetry of Ono no Komachi and Izumi
Shikibu, the two foremost women poets of Japan's classical period. I had
first encountered a handful of their *tanka* in English as an undergraduate
taking courses in Japanese literature in translation. The Japanese women's
concerns—love and transience—paralleled my own, and despite the pas-
sage of a millennium since its composition, their poetry held for me an
immediacy and power that was life-altering. Not only did it affect my own
writing, it led me three years later to undertake the study of Buddhism; in
1979 I was lay-ordained in the lineage of Sotō Zen.

I first realized the need for a larger selection of Komachi's work in
1971, and I waited almost fifteen years for someone to make it possible for
me to read more. Then a fortunate introduction to Mariko—a weaver, jazz
pianist, and native speaker of Japanese who also loved the classical-period
poets—led to our translating a dozen poems together for a journal. We
quickly decided to continue working toward a book-length selection of the
two poets' work, eventually titled *The Ink Dark Moon*. Although in this
account I will say "I" in describing the way a few poems from that book
traveled from literal to final versions, Mariko Aratani's contribution at
every stage was indispensable to the finished work. Her expertise went far
beyond skills of language.

The poems appear here first as they did on the worksheet Mariko
and I devised. During weekly meetings over the course of a year, we creat-
ed such a sheet for each poem we considered for the book. Along with the
original and rough translations were Mariko's comments covering back-
ground information, grammatical uncertainties, the nuances of certain
words, and so on. I wrote down each Japanese poem in *rōmaji* (the
Roman-alphabet transliteration of spoken Japanese). The core English

meaning (or meanings, if more than one were possible) appeared below each corresponding word, and the metrical line-units of the Japanese were separated by a slash mark. Through this system, Mariko could give me access to both the sound of the original poem and its original syntax, something that even the most literal rough translation cannot do. I would then take the sheets away and work toward finished translations, returning them always to her for rechecking.

Here is a first poem, relatively straightforward to translate, by Izumi Shikibu, the greatest of Japan's women poets:

> *Nadote kimi / munashiki   sora ni / kienikemu /*
> why   you   empty   sky   in   disappear did(?)
>
> *awayuki   dani mo / fureba   furu   yo   ni*
> frail snow even   !   when falling falling world   in

A prose headnote—not uncommon in Japanese poetry—offers more information about the poem's background: "Around the time Naishi (Shikibu's daughter) died, snow fell, then melted away."

> Why did you vanish
> into empty sky?
> Even the fragile snow
> when it falls,
> falls in this world.

The finished translation is quite close to the literal, with only minor adjustments of word order and a few changes in word choice: "vanish" for "disappear," "fragile" for "frail." Japanese does not use articles before nouns, and so in bringing the poem into English, I might have also chosen to say, "Why did you vanish / into *the* empty sky?" Why didn't I? One reason was rhythmic—the extra syllable seemed to my ear to clutter the poem. But more important, there was the difference in meaning. Without the article, Shikibu's daughter not only rises amid her cremation smoke into the sky, she also becomes that emptiness and absence—an effect that the inclusion of the article the would have diluted.

The five-line free verse translation reflects but is not identical to the formal structure of the original. Japanese poetry's conventions for transcription onto the page are unlike those of English. Its columns do not use visual breaks to mark each metrical unit, and at least one translator from the Japanese, Hiroaki Sato, advocates forgoing them entirely. My own feeling, however, is that for Western readers the line break is the fundamental signal that they are encountering a poem: words to be met with the mind and expectations of poetry. Even had I followed strictly the Japanese *tanka*'s syllabic pattern of 5-7-5-7-7, the translation's fundamental "poemness" would not have been clear to American readers: English verse speaks a language of stresses rather than count, and American ears do not hear the pattern. Further, the two languages differ enough that metrically exact translations often are forced either to leave out parts of a poem's meaning or to add unnecessary words to fill the count. Both reasons affected my choice of form.

Another poem, one of Shikibu's most famous, required more extensive changes to bring the Japanese into English:

Kurokami no / midare   mo   shirazu /
black hair 's   messiness, tangling (obj) without knowing
                                          without caring

uchifuseba /   mazu   kakiyarishi /
when lying prone   first   stroked
                   clear

hito   zo koishiki
person   !   longing

This poem is one continuous sentence, and the first task in approaching it is to determine the grammatical clauses governing meaning. In Japanese, word order is often the reverse of that in English, and a syntactical break often appears after the first two or three line-units in a *tanka*. Using these principles, the poem's basic meaning quickly resolves itself: "While lying down without caring about black hair's tangling, longing for the person who stroked it first." This then became:

> Lying alone,
> my black hair tangled,
> uncombed,
> I long for the one
> who touched it first.

The largest change between the original and the translation is that the poem has been placed into a grammatical voice: the first person. Many *tanka,* like this one, do not specify their speaker or point of view. This reflects not only Japanese grammar but also a culture in which experience itself, not the subjective frame around it, is felt to be important; a few lightly sketched phrases evoke a situation in which the reader becomes an equal participant. English, however, demands grounding. To follow the original grammar too closely would only mute the impact and emotional immediacy the poem carries in its own language.

A second departure from the literal is use of the word *alone.* My after-the-fact explanation (in actual practice, this is simply how the poem spoke itself in my ear after I had immersed myself in it sufficiently long) is that it arises out of *shirazu*—"without knowing or caring." This woman neglecting her hair is surely in the solitary aftermath of a love affair. Finding herself alone, she has no reason now to attend to her physical beauty; but she remembers such a time—not the recent love, but her first.

Shikibu, we know, was disowned by her family and divorced by her husband (Naishi's father) after she began a love affair with an imperial prince, who soon died. Later in life she took many lovers, and the reputation of "floating woman" came to accompany her reputation as a poet of surpassing insight and lyrical skill. Shikibu apparently tried to reestablish communication with her husband many times; though he never replied to her letters, he is almost certainly the early love she recalls in this poem.

A last change from the literal is that for the one word *midare* I used two: "tangled, uncombed." "Uncombed" and the earlier "alone" probably arose together, the near-rhyme giving the poem a music satisfying to my ear and the sound of the long *o* holding the poem's resonant grief; the word also reflects the indifference to self contained in *shirazu,* "without caring." The textured physicality of the word works as well to bring Shikibu's presence vividly into the poem. This is true to the original's spirit: Japanese critics have long pointed out that Shikibu's tangled black hair is one of very few references to the details of physical life in all Japanese poetry.

I took more liberty still with this poem by Ono no Komachi, written around the year 850:

> *Ito   semete   / koishiki   toki wa /*
> very   extremely   longing   time —
>
> *ubatama no / yoru   no koromo   o /*
> hiougi   's   night 's   clothing   (obj)
> nut
>
> *kaeshite zo kiru*
> turned   ! wear
> inside
> out

Born roughly one hundred fifty years before Shikibu, Komachi was one of the first women members of the court culture to benefit from a newly developed system for transcribing spoken Japanese using Chinese characters. During this period Chinese served the Japanese court as the language of both writing and government, much as Latin functioned as the learned language of medieval Europe. Education in Chinese was reserved for men, however, so only with this new writing system could women participate fully in the literary life of a culture in which artistic skill was becoming a paramount value, and the exchange of poetry a central mode of communication.

Poems were written to express private feeling, but also to conduct a courtship, convey condolences, or demonstrate publicly (in frequently held official competitions) one's talent, learning, and refined sensibilities. Because the imperial court's women, unlike the men, wrote solely in the vernacular, they became the primary creators of the great literary flowering of that age. Komachi in particular, living at the start of the era, brought to the writing of *tanka* a fiercely passionate nature, technical mastery as a poet, and at times a profound insight into Buddhist teachings.

The poem above shows Komachi's explicit revelation of passion. It also makes use of a technical device specific to Japanese poetry, the *makura kotoba,* or "pillow word." A pillow word, much like a Homeric epithet, is an image that regularly accompanies its noun; the *wine-dark* sea is one familiar Homeric example. Like the cushion on which the round bowl of a temple bell is placed, a pillow word works both to elevate a poem and to increase its resonance. And as with the wine-dark sea, the meanings of pillow words are often so archaic as to be baffling, unless one somehow discovers that the ancient Greeks did in fact make a wine whose color was closer to purple-blue than to red.

The poem shows Komachi alone and missing an unnamed lover. Many of her poems are responses to seeing her absent lover in a dream. In one, she wishes she had never wakened; in another, she determines to commit herself to a life of dreaming; in a third, she mourns the cruel fact that even in their dream meetings she and her beloved meet in the fear of being seen. In this poem, however, we see Komachi before sleep, turning her nightgown inside out—a folk custom believed to make one dream of one's love.

Here is the version in *The Ink Dark Moon:*

> When my desire
> grows too fierce
> I wear my bedclothes

inside out,
dark as the night's rough husk.

To American ears, the opening phrase of the original might seem abstract rather than emotional, but the phrase *ito semete* ("very extremely") is rare in *tanka* and would have stood out; later in the poem, the word *zo* also functions as an intensifier. My response was to replace the usual translation of *koishiki*, "longing," with the stronger "fierce desire." Because Japanese readers would at least be aware of the folk custom explaining why one might reverse one's nightgown when feeling longing, I chose to begin the poem with "When," to indicate that a causal connection exists. I also tried to give my translation of "hiougi nut" an extra imagistic vividness and weight. Researching this pillow word for "night," I learned that the nut has a virtually black shell; I then made rather free with the image to create the last line of my version.

One thing translation teaches is that other choices may always be made. Here is an alternative translation, closer to the original in one way, more free in another:

> Longing,
> fiercely longing—
> To dream of him
> I turn my bedclothes inside out
> this dark-husked night.

For a final example of my own experience as a translator, here is another poem by Komachi. One of her most famous, it illustrates a different technical device of Japanese poetry, the *kakekotoba,* or pivot word: a word that can be read in two different ways, both intended to be part of the poem. (The pivot words below are indicated by an asterisk between the alternative meanings in English.)

> *Hana no iro wa / utsuri ni keri na /*
> flower 's color (subj) faded has alas
>
> *itazuri ni / waga mi yo ni furu /*
> uselessly my body world in aging
>   *
>   falling
>
> *nagame seshi ma ni*
> long rains doing while
>   *
> watching

Komachi here confronts transience in a manner quite different from that of Shikibu in her poem mourning her daughter. When she wrote these words, Komachi most likely was still in the midst of her life at court but would have been realizing that that time must be nearing its end. A single woman would not be welcome in a world so centered on love and beauty once her own beauty was gone.

> While watching
> the long rains falling on this world,
> my heart, too, fades
> with the unseen color
> of the spring flowers.

The heart of the poem is its complex and skilled interweaving of its various images of passing time. No translation can convey *kakekotoba* with justice, and it is possible that no one from a different culture can fully appreciate the depth of regret expressed in Komachi's image of uselessly fading spring flowers. Where a poet of ancient Rome responded to transience and mortality with the proud attitude of *carpe diem,* the poet of classical-era Japan acquiesced with a heart full of sorrow, believing that such deep feeling was the mark of being human. The adjacent pivot words *furu* and *nagame,* with their multiple readings, create between themselves a kind of harmonic resonance. The poet is watching her own aging, the long rains are falling, she looks out of her window upon a rain that causes flowers to fade without being viewed, she herself grows older without being known by her lover. It is the other side of Komachi's passionate dream life we see in this poem: the long hours of waking and solitude, the realization that human life is fleeting and the pleasures of youth and beauty even more fleeting.

Unlike most of the poems Mariko Aratani and I translated, this one exists in many different English versions; it was one of the poems that had first aroused my interest in Komachi and her work. Because it is much translated, and well, I felt a certain freedom (and a certain responsibility) to make it my own. In this version—one of eight or ten quite different drafts that I made—the idea of "aging" is implied by the fading spring flowers rather than stated; "uselessly" is clarified for the Western reader with "unseen"; and the word for "body" became "heart" in an effort to make a poetic statement that flowed as seamlessly as possible. A "heart," I think, can both "watch" and "fade"; for a "body" to do so would seem incongruous. I could as easily have simply used the pronoun "I," since the phrase "my body" is often used simply to indicate the grammatical first person. That is the choice made by Kenneth Rexroth, in his concise translation of this poem, and also by Burton Watson:

> The colors of the flower fade
> as the long rains fall,
> as lost in thought,
> I grow older.

> (trans. Kenneth Rexroth)

> The beauty of the flowers faded—
> no one cared—
> and I watched myself
> grow old in the world
> as the long rains were falling.

> (trans. Burton Watson)

From even this small sampling, it is easy to see the range of possible choices in bringing these thirty-two syllables into English. In yet another version, Rexroth allows himself almost complete freedom:

> As certain as color
> Passes from the petal,
> Irrevocable as flesh,
> The gazing eye falls through the world.

Though Japanese *tanka* are unrhymed, the varying sound of the words is part of their effect—much as it is in American free verse—and I would not want to close my description of working with these poems without touching on that part of the task. In my own version of Komachi's poem, the consonants and vowels shift as it progresses, culminating in the final "flowers," which contains most of the recurring sound elements of the poem; as in the opening line, especially, of the Japanese, the sounds of *o* and *a* preside. Japanese and English prosody are quite different, but my hope was that at least some of the effects of Komachi's music had found their way into the translation.

"How invisibly"

How invisibly
it changes color
in this world,
the flower
of the human heart.

Ono no Komachi (ninth century)

Translated by Jane Hirshfield with
Mariko Aratani

"Although the wind"

Although the wind
blows terribly here,
the moonlight also leaks
between the roof planks
of this ruined house.

Izumi Shikibu (c. 947–c. 1034)

Translated by Jane Hirshfield with
Mariko Aratani

"The way I must enter"

The way I must enter
leads through darkness to darkness—
O moon above the mountains' rim,
please shine a little further
on my path.

Izumi Shikibu (c. 947–c. 1034)

Translated by Jane Hirshfield with
Mariko Aratani

SUSIE JIE YOUNG KIM

Entering the Pale of Literary Translation

TRANSLATION IS A LITERARY PRACTICE that has been abused and mistreated in many ways. Literary translations have often been viewed as subordinate and inferior forms that straddle the line separating what is "literature" from what is not. They have often been kept out of standard literary histories because the translator didn't have the appropriate birthplace, and because translations have been plagued by a discourse of equivalence, which assumes that for any given word, there exists an exact equivalent in another language. For translation to operate in this artificial way, one would have to assume that language lacks any adaptability and flexibility and is therefore impervious to the influences of its cultural context; that the meanings of literary texts are fixed and therefore there is only one possible interpretation of every story, novel, play, or poem; and that a translator is able to suppress all the experiences she would normally bring to a text so as to be a sterile medium through which this mechanical process can take place. Literary translation is, of course, a bit more than a mechanical, formulaic, or clinical process in which one text is seamlessly transformed into its equivalent in another language.

In my own academic work, I have encountered translation in one of its most creative forms. In the early 1900s, translators were translating just about everything into Korean. Their creations transcended strict notions of "translation": some would technically be considered "adaptations," that is, liberal transformations in which only a skeleton of the "original" text remained. Translators wrestled with a multitude of foreign languages, and some did not even know in which language the text that they were translating had originally been written. Some translators based their work on previous translations done in Japanese, Chinese, English, and even Esperanto. These early translators understood the process as one of literary creation and went about their work with the freedom usually associated with more conventional literature. Rather than gain their rightful place in literary history, however, their role has been simplified to that of helping to introduce Western literature to Korea and thereby make Korean literature more "modern."

Besides the two languages and cultural traditions involved in the translation process itself, there are external factors that affect literary translations. The historical relationship of the two literary traditions also influences the translator's approach to or attitude toward the process. As a translator of Korean poetry and fiction into English, I am very aware of the uneven power relationship between Korean literature and its European and American counterparts that resulted from the cultural imperialism accompanying territorial colonialism in early-twentieth-century Korea. And of course, the translator's own position comes into play. Unlike some adherents of more standard notions of translation, I am very aware of the fact that my various identities as a Korean, as a scholar of Korean literature, and as a woman all leave their respective traces on my translations.

To restate, the act of translation is not merely a process of copying contingent on the linguistic principle of equivalence. The text is filtered and contaminated through the translator and thereby transformed, most obviously in its physical appearance and more subtly in its content. Literary translation, which for practical purposes is an arrested moment of such fluidity, also maintains a fluidity of its own. It is this aspect of the translation process that I aim to achieve in my own work.

What often occurs when I ask people to read drafts of my translations is that they assume the attitudes discussed above. The most frequent comment I get is some version of "We don't say that in English," "We don't have that expression in English," or "This doesn't sound right." Such comments are often justified. I have misread the original text, become myopic—as one inevitably does when spending too much time concentrating on a translation—or, more simply, mistyped. My reader then does her job as a reader: to point out a sentence or phrase that is incorrect. However, it is also often the case that the wording of a phrase or sentence is deliberate on my part, as when I purposefully retain the tensions arising from the translation process. Interestingly enough, I have found that I am given more freedom in this respect when I am translating poetry. This is partially aided by people's assumptions about poetry: poetry is *supposed* to be cryptic; it's *supposed* to make little sense.

In order to illustrate the thinking that underlies my own translation process, I offer my drafts of a poem by Yi Sŏng-bok. Yi Sŏng-bok's "1959" represents the political embodied in the lyrical. The sense of futility, mental paralysis, and despair aptly represents the poem's historical context: a turbulent era in Korean history when the Korean War was still vividly etched in people's minds, the cease-fire having taken effect only a few years earlier. Within the temporal context of the poem, it has been fourteen years or so since the nation regained its independence from the Japanese, but the people are feeling the strain of being trapped under yet another type of authoritarian rule. A year later, in spring of 1960, the social unrest would explode into nationwide protests encompassing people from all levels of society.

1959

Winter passed that year and summer arrived
But spring never came. Peach trees
Bore tiny fruit before efflorescing
And barren apricot trees withered away.
Pus oozed out of boys' genitals without reason
And doctors emigrated as far as Africa.
Friends going abroad for school bought us a round,
And we unexpectedly received a letter from an uncle
Who had been shipped off to the South Seas during
    World War II
But no surprise could lift us from the lethargy, our
    frigid state of being
We merely embellished our dismal routines more lavishly
    than the year before
Nothing created memories.
Though Mother was alive and my sister vigorous,
Their happiness would be quietly thrashed by these feet
Or crushed beneath a fly swatter.
Each time I saw a painting of spring it looked desolate
That year, winter passed and summer came
We did not fight with spring but morals and phony
    principles
Spring was not to come
So we voluntarily entered an imaginary prison

The translation above is a version I attempted several years ago. Being something of a perfectionist (like many translators, I suspect), I never question whether or not a translation is "complete." Rather, translation for me is an ongoing process. A hiatus usually appears in the form of an editor's nonnegotiable deadline; it also may come in the form of reaching a creative impasse. In whatever form the break manifests itself, it too is part of the translation process. Although such a break is not an unequivocal cure for such creative woes and frustrations, it is only through time spent away from the translation that one can approach it again with fresh eyes. Revisiting the above version of "1959" after having laid it aside for about four years has given me a fresh outlook on the original poem, as well as on my translation. The hiatus has allowed me to develop alternative readings of the poem that were unavailable to me at the time of my translation.

At times the process of translation involves imaginative negotiations. In general, the negotiations and compromises I was having to make with this version of "1959" had to do with questions of form versus content. Most of the liberties I eventually took were contingent on concerns of not adding too much information for the sake of comprehensibility. Related to this, I also recall, I spent a great deal of time struggling over the rhythm in English. The rhythm in this version is not too bad, partly because I attempted to make it smoother by inserting my own punctuation. With the exception of one comma in the middle of the line that is in the middle of the poem, Yi Sŏng-bok's original contains no punctuation. Also, because Korean does not use case to distinguish between words, Yi Sŏng-bok's poem flows in the natural rhythms of Korean without the pauses and stops created by case changes. In this more recent version, I experimented with the translation by leaving out the punctuation and rendering all the words in lowercase.

1959

winter passed that year and summer arrived
but spring never came peach trees
bore tiny fruit before efflorescing
and barren apricot trees withered away
pus oozed out of boys' genitals without reason
and doctors emigrated as far as africa
friends going abroad for school bought us a round
and we unexpectedly received a letter from an uncle
who had been shipped off to the south seas during
        world war ii
but no surprise could lift us from the lethargy our frigid
        state of being
we merely embellished our dismal routines more lavishly
        than the year before
nothing created memories
though mother was alive and my sister vigorous
their happiness would be quietly thrashed by these feet
or crushed beneath a fly swatter

each time i saw a painting of spring it looked desolate
that year winter passed and summer came
we did not fight with spring but morals and phony
    principles
spring was not to come
so we voluntarily entered an imaginary prison

I have not decided whether this works well in English, but one thing that I
can say is that I like the fact that the poem is not as cluttered as before.
Somehow, leaving out punctuation helps this version to remain much quieter than my initial one did.

Another challenge of this poem lies in Yi Sŏng-bok's line breaks.
Korean grammar is such that, more often than not, an English translation
must invert the order of a Korean sentence. Thus, the lines, "and we unexpectedly received a letter from an uncle / who had been shipped off to the
South Seas during World War II" reads in the original more like, "during
World War II to the South Seas [who was] shipped off the uncle / unexpectedly a letter received." Translating becomes tricky when determining
the line break in English, as emphasis will be placed on different things
depending on where I decide to make the break.

Rereading my initial translation of the poem, I feel the need to
attempt a few modifications. I ponder the word choice in line three: "bore
tiny fruit before efflorescing." I like the economy of "efflorescing" because
the word conveys the idea that peach trees were producing premature fruit
even before they had flowered. A more literal rendition of Yi Sŏng-bok's
lines reads something like the following:

spring did not come peach trees
before their flowers had bloomed bore very small fruit

To translate this line as "before the flowers had bloomed they bore tiny
fruit" seems incorrect because the translation is a bit too drawn out, interrupting the rhythm more than is necessary. However, "efflorescing" perhaps connotes a bit more than I would like it to here. It would sound better to say "flowering" rather than "efflorescing."

In line ten, "but no surprise could lift us from the lethargy our frigid
state of being," I made the opposite gesture: toward expansion rather than
compression. Yi Sŏng-bok's lines read:

from an uncle who was drafted to the South
    Seas during World War II
we received a letter unexpectedly but no

surprise could from the lethargy and frigidity
lure us, it was just that compared to the previous year

In my translation, I opted to elaborate upon "frigidity" and render it as "our frigid state of being" for the purposes of maintaining consistent rhythm in that part of the poem. I made a similar gesture in the final line of the poem, but for different reasons. Here is how Yi Sŏng-bok's lines read:

we were with moral principles and pseudo doctrines not
    with spring
fighting since it had to be that spring didn't come
we voluntarily went into a prison that could not be seen

"Moral principles" is interchangeable with "morals" in Korean, so I chose to be more economical in this case. With "pseudo doctrines," I wanted to convey the speaker's distrustful tone. "Pseudo doctrines" does not quite encapsulate the cynicism, so I chose "phony principles."

For "a prison that could not be seen" or "a prison that we could not see," I opted for a more liberal rendering. At the time I was working on this version, I was drawn to the notion of an "imaginary" or "imagined" prison: a prison constructed out of that period's oppressive social and political context. The sense of hopelessness and dejection is effectively captured in Yi Sŏng-bok's image of people blindly walking into such a prison. Pondering it now, however, I hesitate. The translation would perhaps work better if the image evoked in this line was emphasized in a more direct manner.

The following is my latest version of "1959":

1959

winter passed that year and summer arrived
but spring never came peach trees
bore tiny fruit before flowering
and barren apricot trees withered away
pus oozed out of boys' genitals without reason
and doctors emigrated as far as Africa for us
friends going abroad for school bought us a round
from an uncle who had been shipped off to the South
    Seas during World War II
we even received a letter unexpectedly but no
surprise could lift us from our lethargy or frigidity

we embellished our dismal routines more lavishly than
      the year before, that was all
nothing created memories
though Mother was alive and my sister full of life
their happiness would be quietly crushed by these feet
if not already smashed beneath a fly swatter
each time I saw a painting of spring it looked dilapidated
that year though winter passed and summer began
we were fighting with morals and phony principles not
      with spring
since spring was not to come
we voluntarily entered an invisible prison

Kyŏul kŏul II
(Winter Mirror II)

History is sorrow
History is fear
A fear one cannot elude
Ah
Standing atop its lingering snow
I stare into a field of stars
And observe the universe through history,
History through the universe
In the old snow
I stare into the enchanting field of stars again.

Kim Chiha (b. 1941)

Translated by Susie Jie Young Kim

Kyŏul sip'yŏn
(Winter Psalm)

The depth of my soul

Is like the winter sea

My outstretched shadow cast
Atop the asphalt
Between apartment buildings
Touches the sky

Imprisoned deep in the snow-covered mountain
My friend has fallen asleep
Having my dream
To the sound of falling snow

My body is like a pine tree
Here now, I am,
Yes
Immortal

Kim Chiha (b. 1941)

Translated by Susie Jie Young Kim

Ŏdum
(Darkness)

Someone calls
From the edge of darkness

Someone calls in the middle of the night from the bank of
    Pongch'ŏn stream
And has me stand beneath the poplar tree

As I light up a cigarette
And listen with bated breath
Darkness speaks
There is no darkness

How can that be
When it is so dark
And I am tormented so

From the edge of darkness
Someone keeps calling me

From the dark
Someone calls me
From the dark
A rusted crimson darkness
From beyond the prison bars facing me
Two eyes glaring in the dark
Oh, that silence calls
A phlegmy breathing sound calls me

As ashen skies softly sprinkle rain
Several times cut off by the sound of pigeons on the roof
Cut off again and again
By keys rattling, horns blowing, the sound of footsteps
It keeps calling without end
An old bloodstained undershirt hanging on the window
Bloodied soul writhing in a basement many nights
Every scream of the body broken

Shaking its head
Oh, shaking its head
That still silence calls me
Calls my blood
To reject
To reject any and all lies

In the darkness
As ashen skies softly sprinkle rain
From that deep crimson darkness of flesh
Those two glaring eyes

Kim Chiha (b. 1941)

Translated by Susie Jie Young Kim

Sarang
(Love)

Loves subdues winter
And knows to wait for spring
It waits, then
Tills the wasteland again
Grinding up its bones, scattering them like ashes
A thousand years' promise
Knows to plant a tree
Atop the hill of spring

Love
Stands amid the fields after the autumn harvest
And cleaves an apple in two
Knowing to share
As you and I, we
Gaze up at a star

Kim Namjo (b. 1927)

Translated by Susie Jie Young Kim

LEZA LOWITZ

Midwifing the Underpoem

I SEE TRANSLATION AS A KIND OF MIDWIFERY. I am responsible for the translation, but not for the original poem. How can this be? I did not create the child, yet I must ensure its safe passage into the world. In the *Oxford English Dictionary,* "to translate" means to "express the sense of (word, speech, book, etc.) in or *into* another language." Not the "meaning" of a word, but the "sense." What is a sense if not subjective? Translation is a presumption that one can deeply enter not only another language and culture, but also what Tony Barnstone calls the poem's "gestalt," the life force of the writer who created it. A translator must transcend her culture and step into the shoes of another person—sometimes one who has lived in another time—and enter the poet's "country." A translator is always in exile.

From a linguistic point of view, there are many difficulties in translating Japanese. One is what Edward Seidensticker calls "the rather tentative air" of Japanese, sometimes called ambiguity, vagueness, or even insubstantialness. In a language lacking subjects and prepositions, much is open to interpretation. On the other side of this ambiguity, Japanese can be rather wordy—ostensibly for clarity. When translated literally into English, this wordiness can appear as redundancy, or worse.

The following *haiku* by Nobuko Katsura (b. 1914) illustrates the potential for both ambiguity and wordiness:

> *Futokoro ni chibusa aru usa tsuyu nagaki*

Literally translated, the *haiku* would be "on chest bothersome have breasts rainy season long." *Futokoro ni* can be translated as "on (my) chest" or "on (my) bosom." It is easy to understand why this location word is designated in Japanese, as *futokoro* is a part of the anatomy where the tightness of a *kimono* and the subsequent discomfort would naturally be felt. But these assumptions don't translate. Westerners don't wear *kimono,* and breasts are by nature "on the chest." Discomfort would be obvious from the word *usa* ("annoyance," "bother," "nuisance"), so for the sake of the compression essential to *haiku,* my cotranslator and fellow poet Miyuki Aoyama and I rendered the poem as:

> The nuisance of breasts
> a long
> rainy season

Conversely, words that resonate with a multitude of deeply ingrained cultural associations abound in Japanese. To cite a common example, the word *kokoro* can mean "mind," "heart," "spirit," "mentality," "soul," "thought," "essence," "the heart of things," "feeling," and so on. In fact, definitions of this word and phrases containing it take up three-quarters of a very large page in *Kenkyusha's New Japanese-English Dictionary. Kokoro* is also the title of a novel written by Natsume Sōseki in 1914, two years after the Meiji emperor's death. In 1957, the novel's translator, Edwin McClellan, wisely chose to leave the title in its original language. (The title's meaning becomes clear after reading the book.) Another difficult word to translate is *furusato,* which means "native place," "spiritual homeland," "hometown," "birthplace," "country of one's birth," "home country," "home," even perhaps "heartland." Many Japanese left their villages to seek their fortunes in large cities, and typically looked back on their hometowns with longing, nostalgia, and sometimes even disdain or regret. Depending on the context, this attitude is embodied in the Japanese word but not the English synonyms.

When we translated Ainu poetry, Miyuki Aoyama and I chose to leave several words in the original language, explaining them in footnotes. Footnotes pose other problems, but are often the best option when it comes to "untranslatable" words. Think what a translator might have done with *sushi* (in the dictionary defined as "vinegared fish and rice") before this food became popular in the West as a cultural transplant.

Czesław Miłosz has written that "The three major problems of translation are: Familiarity with the language of the original, the skill in the language into which we translate, and limitations imposed by our belonging to our time." The last is the most difficult problem to overcome. How to capture the soul of a poem, what Tony Barnstone calls "the poem behind the poem"? How to translate the fact that poetry is something *lived,* not just written?

First there is the skein of language that must be unraveled. Then there is the cultural framework that surrounds the poem. Then there is the body of the poem itself: structure, syntax, lineation, rhythm, word choice, and so forth. Within this body is an essence, spirit, aura, a kind of "underpoem." The translator must connect to the emotional essence before attempting to "decode" the poem's language. If I cannot find some common ground in my own experience that connects me to this emotional essence, I can't transcend myself enough to navigate into the poem, and then to find a path back out of the poem and into a different culture and language. I might give up. But if I stick with the struggle, I inevitably face two choices: one is to translate for literal, dictionary meaning; the other is to attempt something that is less concrete, more intuitive, that approaches the poem's "soul." Often, when I can find no perfect word, I must bridge the gap between these choices. My partner and I negotiate, coax the English poem out.

Christopher Drake, a wonderful translator of modern Japanese poetry, said at the First International Japanese-English Translation Conference in Hakone, Japan, in 1990:

> I'd like to suggest that until now there's been a law
> of diminishing returns in the translation of Japanese
> poetry. It is that people who've studied it the most
> generally come up with the least interesting literary
> translations. I suppose there are two reasons for this.
> One of them is that the study requires such a great
> deal of effort that you hate not to display or at least
> utilize your scholarship. It's also taken many years,
> and you've become numbed to the original emotion-
> al response and intuitive approach that you had
> before you began studying. So all this scholarship
> has also acted as a kind of superego or ideological
> machinery, pushing on the translations quite heavily.

This does not mean that there are no excellent academic translators of Japanese literature, as Drake acknowledges. His key point is that "original emotional response" and "intuitive approach" are central to any good translation.

Painstakingly choosing each word when I am cotranslating has made me pause when writing poems of my own; the process is not unlike that of writing an original poem. In both activities, the initial impulse from thought/image to word arises as a gift, almost like the presence of the muse. Then the delicate process of choosing, wavering, discarding, discovering, honing, tightening, and repeating all this many times over begins. When the right word is found, a synthesis of language, meaning, and art begins. Then I must find another right word, and another, until the poem itself is "right."

Like many Westerners of my generation, I was led to Japan and Japanese poetry through an interest in Zen Buddhism and a fascination with the Beats. In 1980, when I was a freshman in the dramatic writing program at New York University, my teacher gave us Kenneth Rexroth's *One Hundred Poems from the Japanese* as the basis of a discussion of filmic perspectives (close-up, long-shot, montage). That same year, when I was seventeen, I studied Okinawan martial arts, meditating, and chanting the Heart Sutra and the Lotus Sutra from romanized texts. Although I did not know what each word meant, the chanting led to a familiarization with the Japanese language on a gut level, and the rhythms of the words stayed with me as a means of *transporting* myself. Later, in an undergraduate writing workshop with Robert Hass at University of California, Berkeley, I encountered Japanese verse again—this time *haiku*. On my second trip to Japan, in 1989, I began to cotranslate poetry for an anthology of contemporary Japanese women poets.

I lived in Japan for five years, learning more of the language and more about the culture. My romanticized, outmoded notions of Japanese aesthetics gave way to a more realistic view of contemporary Japanese society. I saw a *geisha* only once in Kyoto, scurrying to work after midnight in the Gion district. When I encountered people in *kimono,* it was usually on formal occasions or at traditional cultural events, like tea ceremonies or the *kabuki.* During the cherry blossom festival, people got drunk and rowdy during *hanami* ("flower viewing")—singing, stumbling, and vomiting. Was this the *mono-no-aware* ("awareness of the pathos of things") I had been taught to appreciate in Japanese literature? I learned that there were many facets of Japanese culture that were seldom spoken about: the Ainu, an indigenous people; a deeply ingrained caste system; and third-generation Koreans in Japan, who were not given the benefits of citizenship. Where was the poetry that reflected this reality? It had not yet been translated.

Drawn to Japanese culture because of alienation from my family and my own culture, I studied Japanese literature, first by focusing on *haiku* and the great modern novelists Sōseki, Tanizaki, Mishima, and Kawabata. I read and admired the poets in the *Man'yōshū* and the Heian-era court poets Izumi Shikibu and Ono no Komachi, translated beautifully by Jane Hirshfield and Mariko Aratani. I married into a family where Japanese is the only language spoken (my father-in-law, who is a writer, critic, and professor of Japanese, British, and Russian literature, reads many languages but is not conversant in them—and, incidentally, he wears a *kimono*). But I wanted to try to translate contemporary Japanese women's poetry as a way of understanding the situation of Japanese women, and of joining that community *through its words.*

Having now cotranslated many Japanese poems and stories, it is difficult for me to single one out for discussion. Rather than choose a favorite one I think is particularly successful, I have decided on a poem that I feel best illustrates the vagaries of the translation process. The poet, Ibaragi Noriko, was born in Ōsaka in 1926 and was a founder of the influential postwar poetry group Kai, which later included the well-known poets Tanikawa Shuntarō and Ōoka Makoto. Her poem—translated by Miyuki Aoyama and me—is titled "When I Was at My Most Beautiful." Written in 1957, just over a decade after the war ended—after Nanking, Pearl Harbor, Hiroshima, and Nagasaki—the poem describes the impact of military conflict and personal loss on an *ordinary woman* with no political agenda living in an *ordinary town.* Deeply resonant in Japan, it became a kind of anthem for a generation.

In Japan, war was elevated to an art form (*bushido*). In feudal Japan, military glory in the ancient capital of Heian-kyo was second only to literary glory. And throughout the ages, the two were not always unrelated. In the caves of Okinawa, for example, where the Japanese Imperial Army hid from the onslaught of American troops, death *tanka* were written on the walls by generals before they committed *seppuku.* Poems have also saved lives. In the sixteenth century, Lord Tameakira was about to be tortured into confessing a rebel plot, but the *tanka* he composed was so impressive that his captors released him unharmed.

In this cultural context, in which Japanese citizens were taught to believe in the supreme power of the emperor and the rightness of war, Ibaragi Noriko's poem opened a window into the sensibility of a young woman for whom war had no glory:

WHEN I WAS AT MY MOST BEAUTIFUL

When I was at my most beautiful
town after town came crashing down.
I caught glimpses of the blue sky
from the most unexpected places.

When I was at my most beautiful
people were dying all around me
in factories, at sea, on islands without names.
I lost my chance to make the best of myself.

When I was at my most beautiful
none of the young men brought me tender gifts
all they knew how to do was salute
and set out for war, leaving only their glances behind.

When I was at my most beautiful
my head was empty
my mind obstinate
but my arms and legs shone like chestnuts.

When I was at my most beautiful
my country lost the war
how could all that have happened?
I rolled up my sleeves and marched around my
    humiliated town.

When I was at my most beautiful
jazz flowed from the radio
I devoured the sweet exotic sounds
the way I smoked my first forbidden cigarettes.

When I was at my most beautiful
I was so very unhappy
I was so very awkward
and so terribly lonely.

So I decided I'd live a very long time
like old man Rouault
who painted his most beautiful works in his old age
    if I could.

Ibaragi's title and refrain, *Watashi ga ichiban kireiidatta toki,* has been translated as "When My Beauty Was at Its Best" by James Kirkup and "When I Was Prettiest in My Life" by Naoshi Koriyama and Edward Lueders. *Kirei* usually means "pretty," but prettiness in English signifies physical beauty only. By contrast, "beautiful," the word we chose, can signify physical, spiritual, and emotional qualities.

The second line of this stanza, *Machimachi wa garagara kuzureteitte,* contains the words *machimachi* and *garagara,* which are onomatopoeic in Japanese. Miyuki Aoyama and I tried to capture this quality by translating *machimachi* as "town after town" and following it with the rhyme "came crashing down"—a rhyme that echoes the haunting repetition in the nursery song "London Bridge Is Falling Down." Fumiko Horikawa and Peter Robinson rendered the same line as "Towns came clattering down," while Koriyama and Lueders translated it "The cities crumbled down."

The last line of the second stanza, *Watashi wa oshare no kikkae o oto-shiteshimatta,* is equally problematic, and some of the weight of the "poem behind the poem" hangs on it. Horikawa and Robinson's translation, "I did miss my chance to be well dressed," does not capture the fullness of the speaker's loss. Koriyama and Lueders's translation, "I lost the chance to dress up like a girl should," implies a certain imperative. Kirkup's "I had no chance to make the best of myself" comes closest. Still, having "no chance" is not the same as losing the chance completely, which is what the poem is about. There is something about *otoshiteshimatta* (past tense of "lost") that captures the poet's resignation, so we rendered it "I lost my chance to make the best of myself."

Obviously, this poem is about more than "putting on nice clothes." It is about the freedom of going out at night, being young, alive, and full of the possibilities of the future. Stanza six also proved problematic and has been rendered in various ways. Horikawa and Robinson's:

> jazz poured from the radio.
> Dizzy, like smoking again when you've stopped,
> I devoured the exotic sweet music.

Koriyama and Lueders's:

> jazz music streamed from the radio.
> Feeling dizzy, as if I'd broken a resolve to quit smoking,
> I devoured the sweet music of a foreign land.

Kirkup's:

> I heard jazz streaming from the radio,
> and I plunged myself as rapturously into its
>   sweet melodies
> as when I first knew the forbidden pleasure of
>   smoking.

After many attempts at absolute faithfulness to the original, we couldn't find a way to make the line poetic and keep the rhythm, so we took a bit of license:

> jazz flowed from the radio
> I devoured the sweet exotic sounds
> the way I smoked my first forbidden cigarettes.

The last stanza of the poem was perhaps the most difficult:

> *Dakara kimeta dekireba nagakisuru kotoni*
> *toshi tottekara sugoku utsukushii e o kaita*
> *furansu no ruō jī san no yō ni*
>
>   *ne*

The difficulty was largely caused by the simple declarative *ne* at the end, a little affirmation—akin to "hmmm," "right," "yeah"—that has a certain wistful quality none of the English words convey. Kirkup's:

> That's why I've decided to live a long time if I can,
> like Monsieur Rouault, the dear old man who
> painted those marvelously beautiful pictures in his
>   old age.
> —Yes, in his old age.

Koriyama and Lueders's:

> Therefore I decided to live a long time, if I could
> like old Rouault of France,
> who painted magnificent pictures in his old age.

Horikawa and Robinson's:

> So I decided, if possible, I'd live a long life
> like that French artist grandpa Rouault
> who painted in old age outrageously fine pictures,
>   wouldn't I?

Aoyama and I rendered it this way:

> So I decided I'd live a very long time
> like old man Rouault
> who painted his most beautiful works in his old age
>   if I could.

Some of the digression in this essay reflects the process of how I midwife a translation into American English after a native speaker and poet has done the initial translation. The poem becomes a part of my daily life: I dream about it, read supplemental texts, meditate on the process, learn all I can. The translator must first be a medium between the natural and human worlds, between the living and the dead, and among cultures, languages, and peoples. The translator of poetry must also be a historian, a linguist, a magician, a composer, an intuitionist, a lover, and a midwife; but most of all, he or she must be a poet.

Tree

Within a tree
there is another tree that does not yet exist
now its branches tremble in the wind.

Within the blue sky
there is another blue sky that does not yet exist
now a bird flies across its horizon.

Within a body
there is another body that does not yet exist
now its shrine gathers new blood.

Within a city
there is another city that does not yet exist
now its plazas sway where I am heading.

Rumiko Kōra (b. 1932)

Translated by Miyuki Aoyama and Leza Lowitz

Other Side River

Through many old souls of the dead
I push my way over to the other side river
The forest the once-living died and reached
I, this being who has never been born
Make my way.

At the womb's *dawn* I, smelling of chaos and blood
Wrapped in a pillow of flesh, almost transformed
Into the still-sleeping sun at the depths of the sea
Sleep
In the surging waves of nausea and giddiness
For millions of years since the moment of Creation
As an amoeba
Through the season of floods
Up to the time of the dinosaurs
In an armor of a simple handful of flesh
I trembled, clinging to the placenta like a sponge

And I endured
Before I had a body
I was the liquid galaxy
Flying anxiously in the womb's low arc
Taking shape from the chaos again
In a hot muddy season
Without eyes, mouth or brain
My body was a shovel of the soul
Kneeling before the King of Blood, vomiting
I, still
Lacking eyes, nose or mouth
Neither amoeba nor fish
Become a man of the future.

Now or never, I
Am far away from my father (how many billions of light-years?)
And yet close to my father at the same time
I, who have not yet become a man
In the womb's chamber, create

Chaos and a life
Inside a soft, bloody womb that even this mother
Does not know
Brighter than the outside world, a universe
Flown by the tide
Now
Outside the womb, the tide begins to ebb in it
I see my father dragging the chains of death,
Carried on the passage of time
Swimming upstream like a fish
Caressing the sweetest hair
Of the wife of an unnamed seaweed.

That's why in the depths of the night's darkness
My father walks with invisible eyes
Groping and edging up
To the untouchable mother's heart.

In a desert in the moonlight
Two cacti, their bodies full of thorns
Tremble in the wind, talking of
An untouchable love
Or two sea turtles
Swimming out to sea very slowly
Eating the dark silence
Together.

They are my father and mother wet with an almost desperate
     Determination
Shining hot and muddy.

Before they inch toward their inevitable deaths over the years
I, passing outside their consciousness
In the valley of the unconsciousness
I, who have never been born before
Going through the womb's narrow throat to sudden death
Like dirty water running from a sewer
Forever unnamed

Having committed no crime
Not knowing even the sweetness of light and air
I will go.

Suddenly to the other side river
To a forest of old souls
I   this being   will go.

Kazuko Shiraishi (b. 1931)

Translated by Miyuki Aoyama and Leza Lowitz

DAVID R. MCCANN

Translating Korean Poets

MY BEST TRANSLATIONS FROM KOREAN POETRY are poems that I have memorized in Korean. I can recite them at the drop of a hat.

I wrote a poem once in Korean, about what it was like to go into town with the teachers at the school, get through a few bowls of *makkŏlli,* and then head out for home down those paddy field paths. How the pigs would wake up and start grunting when I came in range of their hearing. But I couldn't for the life of me translate that poem into English.

I translated a modern but early poem by the great Cho Chihun into *kagok,* a way to sing traditional Korean verse. This was an on-the-spot simultaneous translation from Korean poetry into Korean song, in the company of a number of Korean professors who were most indulgent of my efforts, by that point in the evening. They said, "Great job!" I also translated a different modern Korean poem into Korean writing on numerous occasions, when it was my turn to perform something at a wine house, more than thirty years ago. It was difficult for the others in the room to figure out what I was doing because I am left-handed and nobody else in Korea was.

Two days driving around the island of Cheju with the poet Ko Un, the novelist O Sŏngch'an, and a young writer who was our driver, listening to Ko's tales about life on the island thirty years ago, his getting arrested by the South Korean police, interrogated, led to a narrative poem that closed with Ko's advice to the young writer: *Send me only your very best. Anything less, I will blow my nose on it.*

For a writing assignment in a creative writing class, to write a poem about a work of art in some other medium, I translated Donatello's statue of David into Michelangelo's by way of a little story about Florentine guilds and their sexual politics.

There are a number of fine poets in Korea, most of them unknown outside of that country. And fewer still known from north of the 38th Parallel. Most of the poets I have translated are poets I have met, or to whose works I have been introduced by someone who was quite clearly nuts about them. How could anyone refuse the call of such work?

There once was a translation group, a circle, in Ithaca. The group called itself OSIP, for Osip Mandelstam, and as an acronym for the Organization for Singing International Poetry. The basic premise of the outfit was that the job's not done until the poem is read in translation to an audience. So we had readings, every once in a while, and thought about some day doing an anthology of our work. But in the interval, we went on having monthly meetings where we read and heard translations of modern Greek poetry, Serbo-Croatian poetry, Swedish and German poetry, Palestinian poetry, Korean poetry.

Another group in Ithaca, a bunch of poets, met every once in a while and read our poems, and less frequently, went downtown and did readings.

There's one fellow in Korea, named Brother Anthony. I think of him as Bad Ass (B.A.) because he once translated and published a poem by the famous early-twentieth-century writer Sowŏl six different ways! "Here," he wrote, "is the poem as a modern Korean poem. Here it is as the lyric to a pop song. Now here it is as a postmodernist poem. Or again..."

Outrageous!

There are at least fifteen distinct ways to read the famous poem by Sowŏl, so how could one ever be satisfied with any given translation? The poem keeps moving, turning aside, regressing, transgressing how you read it, how you did read it, what it was taught as meaning, what it was taught to mean. The only way to translate it is to memorize it, so how could a translator ever feel any special pride at some choice phrase, some felicitous turn of the linguistic lip? It's all just news. Somebody wants to get it on the broadcast at ten so it can make the current Nobel Prize committee pile of deliberations.

Chinese poems do seem to inspire deep thoughts. *Before the bed the bright moon shines.* Just try writing those five characters almost anywhere in Asia! Folks will be impressed, and they will be able to finish out the other three lines, and then they will say, "Oh, far from home, are you?"

Imitation is the highest praise? Bad translations are nothing but product. So why do we think so highly of Bashō on his peregrinations? Quoting other writers all the time, and stuffing the names of his sponsors into his books of travel verse. *Narrow Road to the Deep North* is an advertising banner, flapping behind the little two-footed entourage. "Here comes the poet. Whoa, we're gonna get cryptic tonight!"

Haiku translates the Chinese ideogram into syntax. For example, the famous one about *Old pond frog jumps water sound* could have been a Chinese character, the way "person" plus "tree" becomes "resting." (A person under a tree is resting.) Or "tree" plus "tree" becomes "forest." Add another "tree" and it is a "dense forest." But it takes three of "woman" to make "adultery."

The poet Sŏ Chŏngju published a book titled *Unforgettable Things*. I agreed to translate it and then discovered, well into the collection, a poem entitled "David McCann, Translator of My Poems, and the Town of Andong." The poet misremembered our first conversation, but in translating the poem, I didn't correct his mistakes about me, the translator of his poems. I also tried to preserve my somewhat stilted Korean:

> It was in 1974, summertime, when an American who seemed
> to be about thirty years old came out to my house by
>   Kwanak
> Mountain. When he introduced himself as someone who
> believed the most important thing he could do was to
>   translate
> my poems, I asked him why, with all the countries in this
> world, he happened to choose Korean poetry.
>
> "Well," he said, "I graduated from Harvard College, in the
> United States, and entered the Peace Corps. I hoped to go
> to Korea, and eventually was assigned as an English
>   teacher at
> the Agriculture and Forestry High School in Andong,
>   Kyŏngsang Province."

McCann had replied with reasonable fluency in our language, smiling as he did. He went on: "To speak frankly, I still didn't know then just what there was that could be called real literature in Korean, so I asked one of the teachers at the high school about it. Well, that teacher just blew up at me. 'Is that all you think of our country? Why, isn't there any good literature in Korea? Is that what you think? No more talking about it. I'll teach you, starting with the *sijo*. I want you to learn one of them every day.' For the three years I stayed at the school, I worked hard at studying Korean literature, and have come to comprehend the extent to which Korea is indeed a country with good poetry."

On another occasion, when I was translating another collection of Sŏ's poems, he read my translation of one of his early lyrics and said that I had a phrase wrong. But he liked it. "Leave it this way," he said. So I did.

It is amazing how many very well known poets have translated from so many different languages. And not just any old languages, the usual ones like French or Italian or German or Spanish. No. Polish. Chinese. Russian. Where do they find the time to learn those languages, read the poems, and work through the long process of translating? Where do they?

On the other hand, someone who is really good at poetry in a language like English probably can do an efficient and effective job of taking the rough translation that someone else has worked up from the original, turning it into a translation. There is an interesting letter from Ezra Pound to some Japanese pal of his in which Pound sends some lines from a poem, his idea of a Japanese-Chinese-Oriental-Asian poem of some sort, and then asks his correspondent to "ideograph it"—a technique that would collapse etymology into a kitchen-table crossword game, and turn it inside out into the bargain.

Tony Barnstone writes, "From a set of monosyllabic, largely pictographic characters calligraphed on a Chinese painting, fan, or scroll, the poem proceeds through a hall of mirrors, reappearing on the other side of time, culture, and speech as a few bytes of memory laser-etched on a white page in polysyllabic, phonetic language." I guess I could be coy and say I don't get it. Must be because he's writing about Chinese poetry, 'cause I've never hit a pile like that in Korean. But then, if I were going to be translating a Chinese scroll painting, I would think of translating it onto a scroll. Painting. The first time in public that I wrote out the line to that poem by Li Po, "Before the bed the bright moon shines," I was sitting in a restaurant in Seoul with a bunch of other people who had assisted Professor Kim Chong-gil with the preparation of the Korea University English-language edition of the course catalogue. Professor Kim treated us to dinner and plenty of delicious wine, and then introduced the very famous calligrapher who was there in our company. The calligrapher did a piece of calligraphy for each one of us. In preparation he took out his inkstone, poured some water, rubbed in the stick, wetted the brush, and then went at it. Someone suggested, *Why don't we give it a try, ha ha.* So of course we all were made to have a go at something with the brush. My turn came, *Oh no, Oh no;* but I had watched the way he would get the brush sopping wet with ink, slam it down onto the paper, draw down that first bold stroke, then the rest of the character, with a pause at each brushstroke end, a flourish of the brush at each resting place. It was a dance! Down the page, with the arm, the body, no wrist! Great, they all said. Not about my characters, but my dance with the brush. I really gave it my all, with a flourish, and for the interval while it was happening, I was translating the poem from ancient Chinese into the moment.

Midday

A path through a field of red flowers
that plucked and tasted bring dreaming death;

along the path winding like the yellow back
of an opium-stunned snake
my love runs, calling me after

and I follow, receiving
in my two hands
the blood flowing sharp-scented from my nose.

In the broiling midday, hushed as night
our two bodies burn.

Sŏ Chŏngju (1915–2000)

Translated by David R. McCann

Self-portrait

Father was a serf;
he never came home, even late at night.
The only things standing there were grandmother, withered
and pale as leek root,
and one flowering date tree.
Mother, unmooned, longed for green apricots, even one.
By the oil lamp set in the dirt wall's niche
I was mother's boy, with black fingernails.
With my large eyes and thick hair
I am said to take after grandfather on my mother's side
who went off to sea, the story goes, sometime
during the year of reforms, and never returned.
For twenty-three years it is the wind that has raised the better part of me.
Life has become more and more an embarrassment.
Some read a convict in my eyes,
some an idiot in my mouth,
but I repent nothing.

Mornings, at dawn, the drops of blood
mingle with the dew
of poetry fallen on my brow;
for I have come, tongue hanging out,
panting through sun and shade like a sick dog.

Sŏ Chŏngju (1915–2000)

Translated by David R. McCann

Snowy Night

On Cheju Island where I spent
Christmas night my sixtieth year
wandering about
and met that girl in a wine house
by the shore—
she had learned my poem
"Beside a Chrysanthemum"
from her high school language book
and still could recite it perfectly.
When some pesky drinking friend said
"Here, come meet the writer,"
she drew to my side and hid her eyes in the folds of my coat,
sobbing—that child:
Is she crying somewhere still as the snow falls this night?
Or have her tears dried? Has she learned to laugh out loud?

Sŏ Chŏngju (1915–2000)

Translated by David R. McCann

KEN MCCULLOUGH

Tuning In to the Poetry of U Sam Oeur

This essay is not about translating the Khmer language in general but about translating the poetry of U Sam Oeur in particular. I am neither a Khmer scholar nor a linguist; however, I am a poet myself and have been good friends with U Sam Oeur since 1966. For fourteen of those years, from 1970 to 1984, U Sam Oeur and I were not in contact; he was placed in, and managed to survive, six concentration camps run by the Pol Pot regime. Much of his poetry reflects that experience.

I first met U Sam Oeur when we were graduate students in the Iowa Writers Workshop, from 1966 to 1968. I liked the poetry that Sam wrote in English, finding it straightforward and often pastoral, but we never discussed his primary language. At the time, I was taking courses in Chinese painting, calligraphy, and poetry, all of which were taught by the noted Chinese scholar and artist Ch'eng Hsi. I took readily to the formulae of Chinese brush painting, eventually illustrating a chapbook, Gary Snyder's *Three Worlds. Three Realms. Six Roads.* I studied Frodsham and Ch'eng's translations, comparing them with the plethora of other translations. Nevertheless, I kept returning to Rexroth's versions as my touchstone. I was also reading a great deal of Japanese poetry in translation, was studying Buddhism and Hinduism intensively, and had begun practicing *zazen.* But I had no interest in studying Chinese, Japanese, or Khmer.

Sam told me that if I were to write a poem while traveling through almost any Cambodian village, the people there would build a small shrine and put my poem in it. He told me that they worshipped beauty. I looked through the magazines Sam received from home and was stunned by how physically attractive his people were. We made tentative and naive plans for me to go to Cambodia and work with him on translating his country's folk literature into English. I imagined, I guess, some kind of Lord Jim existence for myself.

Sam returned to Cambodia in 1968, and we corresponded until 1970, when civil war broke out in his country. We lost contact until the English department of the University of Iowa received a letter from him, fourteen years later, requesting a copy of his thesis, which he'd burned in 1975 because it was evidence of his literacy and therefore a potential threat to his life. The letter came through the Catholic Relief Services office in Bangkok. Through these circuitous channels, Sam and I resumed corresponding, and I began working with Clark Blaise, then director of the International Writing Program at Iowa, to find sponsorship for Sam as a fellow in the program. Because the sponsoring organizations only wanted big-name dissident writers, the process lasted eight years. It took them that long to appreciate the catch-22 of Sam's situation: if he had been a well-known dissident writer, he would have been one of the first executed by the Khmer Rouge; and if he had somehow avoided execution, as a well-known writer he would have been harassed—as he eventually was—by the succeeding Vietnamese regime.

The Lillian Hellman–Dashiell Hammett Fund for Free Expression finally agreed to sponsor Sam, recognizing that he had the potential to produce writing of consequence. In September 1992, Sam arrived in Iowa, and we immediately began transcribing and translating his poetry—most of which was in his head rather than on paper.

The little knowledge of Khmer I have has all been learned from Sam over the years we've worked together on his poems. I have read other Cambodian poets in translation (translated primarily by George Chigas); most of these are significantly younger than Sam, having been children during the Pol Pot regime. I have also read Sam-Ang Sam's thesis on the *pin peat* ensemble, which contains a section on the forms of traditional Cambodian poetry. Through these readings and by listening to Cambodian music, I have some sense of Cambodian poetry's sounds and rhythms.

Since the 1960s, when Sam and I were in school together, I have continued my studies of Eastern religions and philosophies, spent time in India, and incorporated several of the practices into my daily life. The philosophy in Sam's poetry is mainly traditional Theravada Buddhism, with a dash of Confucianism and Hinduism (which pervades traditional Cambodian mythology). There's also an element of *bhakti* (devotional) yoga in the poems, with which I feel quite at home. In short, for a long time I have been predisposed, in one way or another, to Sam's poems.

One difficulty for translators of traditional Cambodian poetry lies in the way it rarely speaks directly about sensitive subjects. This is reminiscent of what Leslie Marmon Silko says about Pueblo storytellers: they will tell an old, traditional story in order to illuminate a contemporary situation, but without explaining the connection. Similarly, a Cambodian poet might refer to myths from the Angkor era (tenth to fourteenth centuries), assuming that the reader will recognize parallels to an unnamed, present-day issue.

In addition to this kind of indirectness, Sam uses another strategy to criticize contemporary political figures and factions: he refers to them allegorically as animals with telltale traits. In "Intda's Prophecy 1," for example, Sam makes ten animal references in thirty-eight lines, the meanings of which are obvious to most Cambodians who lived during Pol Pot's regime; the rest of us would need a full page of footnotes to understand them. This is a familiar tactic in many cultures: poets clever enough to invent a "cover story" have always been able to get away with their barbs without being skewered in return by those they have targeted.

Secular Khmer consists primarily of one-syllable words. Some longer words have crept in from Pali, and these usually pertain to sacred subjects; additional words have crept in from French and other languages. In translating Cambodian poetry, it's frequently necessary, in order to get closer to the spirit of the poem—its duende, gestalt, or what have you—to use a polysyllabic word in English as the equivalent of several Khmer words. Take, for instance, a line from Sam's poem "The Fall of Culture":

ពាក្យ ពេចន៍ គវី   ចារ ទុក   ទូន្មាន

Phonetically, the line reads:

> *beak   bic   kawei   caa   tduk   tdounmean*

A literal translation of the line is:

> word—very important—poet—written—for—counsel

The way Sam and I agreed to translate the line is:

> O, quintessential words of poets!

Another difficulty for translators of Khmer poems lies in the complicated rhyme schemes: in order to conform, the poems sometimes lapse into abstractions that are, at least to my Western sensibilities, undesirable. Here is the first stanza of "Oath of Allegiance":

កាលនោរភ្លុងខ្ញុំ   ស្រុករកើតទុក្ខភ័យ
សង្គ្រាមឥស្សរៈ   រៀវកមិញលុកស្រុក
បារាំងអបលក្ខណ៍   ចាប់ខ្មែរដាក់ច្រវាក់
ខ្មែរសម្ងាប់ខ្មែរ ។

Phonetically, the poem reads:

kaal	*nauv*	*kmeng*	*khcei*	*srok*	*koeut*	*tduk*	*bhaiy*
sangraam		*isarak*		*Vietminh*		*luk*	*srok*
baramng	*apalak*		*cap*	*Khmer*		*dak*	*crawak*
	Khmer		*samlap*	*Khmer*			

Translated literally, the poem reads:

when was (is) childhood   country was hard to bear panicked
war for freedom   Vietnamese communists invade country
French bad   arrest Cambodians put chain
            Cambodians slaughter Cambodians

My original translation read this way:

Innocent peasants were tortured every day—
their heads held underwater,
fish sauce forced through their nostrils,
beaten to death by colonial authorities,
shot or butchered by Khmer Viet Minh.

You can see that I changed the stanza from seven "lines" to five. Later I compressed it further, making it four lines, even though the original has seven-line stanzas throughout. I also changed its abstract language into something more specific. As we readied the poem for publication, Sam and I agreed we should try to restore the form as well as the meaning. The stanza as it appears in *Sacred Vows* sounds choppier and less dramatic, but it is truer to the original. My first version specifies what happened at that time in Cambodia, but those details are *not there* in the original. Here is the final version, the one that appeared in print:

During my childhood   the country was in chaos.
It was the war of liberation   and the Viet Minh infiltrated.
The French colonialists   chained innocent Khmers
            while Khmers killed each other.

Another way Sam and I have dealt with abstract language in Cambodian poetry is to use a metaphor or image in place of the abstraction. The following is a line from "The Fall of Culture":

deung yaang naa loeuy longvek sahs khyawll

Literally translated, the line would read:

> no—what—[syllable added for rhyme]—space—empty—air

The final version reads:

> Ah, I can't see across those three wildernesses.

The line in the original refers to killing, disease, and starvation—the three voids that Cambodians faced during the Pol Pot years. The metaphor of wilderness Sam and I came up with became central to *Sacred Vows*. And now the working title of Sam's autobiography, on which we are collaborating, is *Crossing Three Wildernesses*.

Khmer poetry remains tied to Cambodian oral traditions; hence, almost all Khmer poets chant their work. Most chant in a fairly flat style, while Sam's style alternates between rhythmic narrative passages and emotional, operatic ones. Though I have a good ear for music, I do not read or write it and thus cannot transcribe Sam's melodies; neither does he chant a poem the same way each time. However, the following couplet from "The Fall of Culture" will serve as an illustration. The notation was done by Mark Bruckner, composer of *Krasang Tree*, a chamber opera based on Sam's poetry and performed in September 1998 in Minneapolis. This opera is done entirely in Khmer, except for one long poem, "Lunar Enchantment," which Sam recites in English near the end of the performance.

ឱ គេហដ្ឋាន បាន ផ្លាប់ មនោរម្យ
កេរ ឪពុក ខំ សន្សំ សាង សង់

O, gheathaan thaan dhluorpp manorom
ke auvpuk kham sansam saang sang

O home! Home! The sacred ground where we lived happily, the heritage built, bit by bit, by my father.

The music of Sam's work is quite dramatic, and one way I've tried to capture its spirit—without attempting to approach the work's musical scaffolding—is to use alliteration and assonance. Here is the opening stanza of "The Krasang Tree at Prek Po":

កាលចិតប្រាំ ក្រសាំងនៅខៀវខ្ចី
មនុស្សមូលមីរ ចោមសុំផ្ទៃក្រសាំង ។
ដល់ចិតប្រាំបួន ក្រសាំងក្រៀម
ដើមប្រឡាក់ឈាម មានសក់ជាប់ ។

kaal cit pram krasamng nauv khieu khcei
manuh mool mii com sii ple krasamng
dawll cit pram buon krasamng kriam
doeum pralak jhiam mean sak jeab

A literal translation would read:

when [past] '75 *krasang* tree was green
people congregate swarming eat fruit *krasang* tree
when [now] '79 *krasang* tree dry (dead)
trunk stain blood to have hair stick

In this case, the Khmer is in free verse; and my translation, in this odd case, is even more lyrical than the original:

In '75 the *krasang* tree was green,
bore fruit for the soup of all the villagers.
By '79, the *krasang* tree had withered, its thorns
adorned with the hair of babies, its bark bloodstained.

Half the poems in *Sacred Vows* are written in traditional forms, and the other half in free verse. Some of the English versions give the impression that they were conceived in English, which to some extent they were; these translations are true collaborations. Through my long friendship with Sam, I have come to be able to intuit his thoughts. An example of this occurred early on in our collaboration. The fourth stanza of "Nightmare" eventually came to be translated as:

I take off my shirt,
hide my face,

embrace a bamboo stalk,
hold my breath,
wish again:
"Oh, God, change their minds!"

As we worked on the translation, I could tell from his facial expression that there was something I wasn't getting that had to do with bamboo. I kept asking him questions about the properties of bamboo until, after forty-five minutes, it became apparent to me that bamboo was a metaphor—referring to the Indo-Chinese communists—specifically, the Vietnamese. The Vietnamese have a habit of planting bamboo wherever they settle; bamboo chokes out any plant growing in its vicinity, and like bamboo, Vietnamese communism stifles any ideology it encounters. Once you understand the metaphor, it's obvious that the poem expresses Sam's feeling about Vietnamese communism. Without that understanding, there's nothing in the poem to indicate that the references to bamboo are anything but literal.

Since Sam's arrival in the United States in 1992, we have been working on translating Whitman into Khmer. I'd like to close by quoting two passages by Sam that reveal his thoughts about the traditions of Cambodian poetry and Whitman's importance to him. In a press release for *Sacred Vows* Sam wrote:

> For the last thirty years I have managed to stay alive
> primarily to bring free verse to the younger genera-
> tion of Cambodians. I regard Walt Whitman as the
> ultimate poet of freedom and the poet of democracy
> and see in his philosophy and his exploding lines an
> antidote to many of the conventions of the ancient
> mummified past… While I love our traditions and
> pay homage to them in [my] poems, I attempt to
> break the aforementioned bonds to express the inex-
> pressible horrors of our recent history.

In the foreword to a chapbook that we translated and that includes parts of "Song of Myself" and "I Hear America Singing," Sam elaborates on his connection to Whitman:

> I still have not seen many poems which I think I'd
> be able to translate into the Khmer language, so that
> they would be meaningful to the Khmer people.

Whitman's work remains the only poetry which I believe they would be able to grasp; it contains universal thinking and is written in universal language, like the teachings of Buddha. When I recite the first few lines of "I Hear America Singing" in Khmer, it sounds so free, and it's about the ordinary daily life of the people—it is about them, it is related to their lives.

In addition to the language of the poems, they carry a spirit which is essential for the Khmer people at this time—the lines are infused with freedom and democracy—we have existed, for almost an entire millennium, in bondage of one kind or another. If I can publish a book of Whitman's work for the younger generation of poets, it will liberate them. They are all still writing in classical styles. While I myself am adept at writing in these forms and realize the beauty of them and the importance of preserving them, I also see that it is time to evolve. There are 49 traditional forms, including "the creeping snake," "the hopping crow," the three-syllable line, six-syllable, seven-, eight-, nine- and eleven-syllable lines. These new poets are fed up with the old style—it's as if two magnetic poles, south and south, have come up against each other—they are repelled by these restrictions. They want to express themselves freely; having access to Whitman's poetry would give them a way to do this, they wouldn't have to waste space and time looking for throwaway or sometimes even nonsense rhymes to conform to the classical style. You see this even in the epic poem *Tom-Teav*—meaningless sounds are thrown in on occasion when the poet can't come up with a rhyme which works—the younger poets are tired of this convention! This old-hat philosophy is reflected in the politics of Cambodia—they do the same old things over and over, permutations of the same mistakes; if a regime is installed by Vietnam, they conform to Vietnamese practices and standards, if a Thai-backed regime is in power, they conform to the Thai model. There has been no free expression in Cambodia; it's like living in custody. For the poets, regularized end-rhyme and internal rhyme are part of this trap. They are frustrated. Freeing the poets is my main goal in translating Whitman... Whitman is the ideal starting point, because the work is so expansive on the one hand, so concrete on the other. In my generation we had French classes with no books—nothing, empty space. We'd listen to the French teacher the same way a water buffalo listens to someone playing a flute; with no concept of what we were hearing. Then there were the Moger readers which were used throughout the country because someone had cut a deal with the French government and had a monopoly—a ten-line poem by Ronsard, one by Voltaire, one by Hugo, one by Baudelaire—we'd memorize this stuff, but it was meaningless to us. Whitman says "I too am untranslatable" but, to me, he seems to be the most translatable of poets for the time and situation in my country. He also says "after we start we never lie by again." That is how I feel about the possibility of his influence on Cambodian thought—once they hear his words they will embrace his work absolutely, and the deadening cycle, in so many areas of our life, will be broken forever.

Exodus

Once the Blackcrows had usurped the power
they started to evacuate people from Phnom Penh;
they threw patients through hospital windows
(women in labor and the lame), drove tanks
over them, then bulldozed them under.

The sun shone bright, as if it had come close to the earth.
The ground was dried and cracked.
Millions of panicked Phnompenhards jostled each other,
desperately overflowing along prescribed routes.[1]

Out! Out!!! *Phankphankphank!* My cousin's guts were hanging from
    his belly.
Over there! *pap—pap—*
The corpses floated face up, face down in the Bassac River—
those who refused to give up their Orient[2] wristwatches.

> Twenty meters a day
> for the first three days
> the journey without purpose;
> lost to wife and children,
> separated from your loved ones,
> repeated night and day,
> wandering in circles.
>
> There is crying and wailing
> and the elders are groaning—
> no one bothers with them;
> everyone stampeding
> to reach a destination,
> any destination
> away from Phnom Penh.

U Sam Oeur (b. 1936)

Translated by the poet and Ken McCullough

My Invisible Sisters and Death by Execution

The horde of prisoners
returns to the dam-building site
out near Prek Ta Kao
after *élection forcée,* April '76.

My twins! O my twins!
If you'd been allowed to live
I would have met great fortune—that's what
Sovanna Mealea, son of the Ta Trasak Phem,[3] told me.

I chop the ground, put it in two shallow baskets
balanced on a pole over my left shoulder,
and carry it to the dam,
which is getting high now.

"I'm a poet, member of the National Assembly,
member of the Steering Committee of the Social Republican Party,
which has political guidelines that
freedom, democracy, and the welfare of Cambodian society

must be born from private enterprises,
not from forced labor—"
these factors render my physiognomy suspicious.
Then one night a devil calls for a session of autocriticism.

The devil praises Angkar[4] as higher than God,
and asks why some of us are not satisfied
when it is clear that Angkar has been serving *sangkum.*[5]
"Even water buffalo take care of their own offspring!

That's all I have to say about it.
Now I shall offer my body and soul
before Angkar for judgment
so that I can be the best of servants."

After evening gruel,
Angkar orders me to join my family.
An oxcart is ready.
I jump on it, light-headed.

On the way to my shelter
the driver offers me a coconut shell of sour palm juice.
We start to chatter about Samdech Euv.
"Samdech warned us about this in the late '60s!"[6] I tell him.

When I reach my family
another oxcart is waiting—
Hurry, Ta! Load your stuff!
As in a whirlwind, we're taken somewhere else.

Base people, new people,[7] stand up startled
as we pass, knowing where we're headed.
The oxen gallop forward
through the dark across the jungle.

It's so dark I can find no bearings.
"Here you are, Ta—
bring your things to that house—
I built it myself before you arrived."

No talk, no thanks, I bring my belongings
to the new shelter, five meters by six meters, with open kitchen.
By starlight I can see a vast cornfield
spread behind it, the Mekong River in front.

"My wish come true: water, firewood, fish."
I tell my family,
"Mom, you cook rice, I'll go fetch water."
We've kept a twenty-liter bucket and a twenty-liter cooking pot.

We enjoy our summer resort for two weeks.
In the mornings I go to find fish.
Otherwise, we just sit around bewildered
at how our invisible sisters[8] have cared for us.

I hide my Buddha made of pagodite[9] on the roof
and my invisible sister[10] in the mosquito net by day
and out in the dew at night.
"I saw a naked man sitting on a termite mound,

one of his legs folded under him, the other bent at the knee,
and his penis big as a liter bottle,
and he said, 'Wherever you go, if you give us a green sour
tamarind fruit, grandchild's family will be safe.'"

My wife tells me this when we wake up the second morning
of our stay. "So we'll do it!" I tell her.
I climb into the tamarind and pick one fruit, and
put it on a nearby termite mound, praying for security.

The Angkar of the village doesn't know we're here.
I wander during the day, finding fish that we'll preserve.
At night, we sneak among the mosquitoes like snakes.
I'm invited to Phnom Penh for an extraordinary Congress:

I recognize some of my colleagues, but the majority
of the Congress is all strange—the Chairman is
two meters tall, dark skinned, strongly built;
twenty men of my size cannot budge him.

Each member of the Congress takes his turn
at the podium to speak about what I don't hear.
Finally, the Chairman raves: "Whoever ascends
to power by violence, he will be overthrown by violence!"

When I open my eyes, I'm in the mosquito net
at Boh Leav concentration camp.
I go outside to recover my invisible sister,
taking her inside to her hidden sanctuary.

New people are brought to my concentration camp.
"Who let you stay here, Ta?" Angkar asks me.
"Comrade Angkar of Prek Ta Am put us here two weeks ago,"
I say, without looking at their faces.

The Angkar of Boh Leav lists the names of my family.
We get thirty kilograms of unhusked rice a month.
Angkar divides us into groups of ten.
They put me to work again, gathering palm fronds.

My partner is Nuth Dara, English teacher, Sisowath High.
We clear swamps, plow fields, transplant rice
during the day, pedal water mills at night.
We both enjoy humming in English.

"Samoeurn! Samoeurn! Does Samoeurn live in this house?"
"No, Ta Gold lives here. No Samoeurn here."
My wife dreams that Angkar shouts:
"Pack your stuff! Angkar orders this family forward."

The moon shines brightly over the swamps.
It's midnight when the screams break the silence—
"Ta Gold! Ta Gold! Heh, Ta Gold!
Get up and pack your stuff, Ta."

By now our stuff is perpetually ready.
We load it onto the same oxcart, it seems.
The driver takes off to another camp,
leaving the fruits of our labor for Angkar.

U Sam Oeur (b. 1936)

Translated by the poet and Ken McCullough

Autocriticism Meeting (1987)

The secretary of the Regional Party of Industry
opens the meeting by addressing us from the podium:
"Respected vice-ministers, leaders,
beloved comrades, dear friends!

Today we have a great honor—
to have our respected vice-ministers
and leaders share with us
our great afternoon session of autocriticism."

One vice-minister jumps up and begins:
"Our Revolutionary Peoples' Party of Kampuchea
wholeheartedly acknowledges our beloved comrades
who sacrifice spiritually as well as in body

to squash imperialism and hegemony.
There are two deadly enemies:
hegemony is the immediate enemy, China;
and the indirect enemy is the United States.

The Party shall ever acknowledge
our comrades' sacrifices, devotion, and dedication.
In the 2,000 years of our existence, our people
are finally masters of their own destiny."

Each comrade preaches the same praise.
When it's my turn, first, I apologize to the Party.
"I thank the Party for granting people the right
to till the soil, raise livestock for the Party,

and to stay awake all night on sentry duty
so that freedom and democracy, the enemies of the Party,
many not sneak into our base, but I'd rather be a complete
slave of the people, in order that I might have villas, a Lada,"

special rations, and the position of vice-minister,
than to be a master with so many rights

that I can hardly carry out any of them;
I'm just not the type to be such a master."

U Sam Oeur (b. 1936)

Translated by the poet and Ken McCullough

I Try to Survive for My Nation

Silver, gold, rubies, sapphires, diamonds,
apartments and villas innumerable,
but I'm not interested; I regard them as booty.
Tables, beds, radios, TVs, cameras…the list goes on—
Aren't they the common property of the state?

My family is small—
why should I bother with those things?
Why should I be a slave to material?
I'd rather be destitute than abandon my vows.

Bursting with hope
I have worked from dawn to dusk
restoring factories, gathering machinery, spare parts,
warehousing them for safekeeping.

Even though there is not much to eat,
still I am proud like Grandpa Kleang Moeung,[12]
hoping the country would soon be happy and prosperous.

My hairline recedes, my skin thickens,
time slips by without fanfare.
After thirteen years of service to my country
my savings are gone; my pension, poverty.

I'm afraid of evil deeds
and I'm ashamed of sin.
I have no bribes to offer my superiors—
that's why poverty prevails over me.

The trees growing on the banks of lakes
are lucky, but if they grow
on the Mekong in Cambodia,
they are washed away every monsoon season.

The heart of Grandpa Dek[13]
never shrinks from responsibilities
alive or dead—I have taken vows:
serving people and the Triple Gem.

Even though these ghouls look down
on me, trample my intellect,
insult me and send me to the fronts,
I try to survive for my nation.

U Sam Oeur (b. 1936)

Translated by the poet and Ken McCullough

1   The population of Phnom Penh numbered 2.5 million to 3 million. The
    evacuees could only travel by government-prescribed routes, which were so
    narrow that the people crowded against each other, trampling the young,
    the sick, the dying.

2   Orient: Southeast Asia's equivalent of Rolex.

3   Ta Trasak Phem: Sweet Cucumber Dynasty, presided over by T. Jey, who
    became the king Indravaraman III in A.D. 1295.

4   Angkar: Khmer Rouge's name for its organization.

5   *Sangkum:* society.

6   Samdech Euv: reference to Prince Sihanouk; literally means "Prince-
    Father." In a 1967 speech, Prince Sihanouk said the following: "*Kone chauv*
    [my compatriots—literally, my children and grandchildren], you should
    not side with the Red [Communism]. If my *kone chauv* wish to side with
    the Red, Samdech Euv must precede you. I can do that for I am already
    intimate with their leaders. But Euv will grant the rights to the Blue [free
    world and intellectuals] and the Red together to find peace for Cambodia.
    Wait to see how they are going to save our people. *Kone chauv* will see this
    come to pass."

7   Base people, new people: local peasants and urban transplants, respectively.

8   Invisible sisters: Pido Mean Roeudhi, a princess from the Heavenly Realm,
    and the herb *prateal,* found on Sharp Mountain in Kompong Speu.

9   Pagodite: soft mountain clay used for making statuary.

10 Invisible sister: the leaves of the *prateal.*

11 Lada: a Russian-made car regarded as a status symbol.

12 Grandpa Kleang Moeung: sixteenth-century warrior who was chief of the
    subdistrict of Kravagn Mountain, Pursat. He gave his life to save his nation
    by helping the king fight against marauding warlords.

13 Grandpa Dek: sixteenth-century nobleman. His faithful fiancée died from
    grief because she loved Grandpa Dek deeply, but her parents would not
    allow her to marry him. Her grave became a termite mound. People worship
    her spirit in order to have their wishes come true, especially to get stolen cat-
    tle back. The story goes that one night her spirit came to tell Grandpa Dek
    that in the morning an elephant owned by the king would fall dead as it
    passed in front of the altar erected in her memory. She said, "You should not
    save the elephant—if you do, you will die." But Grandpa Dek had taken
    vows to serve his people and the Triple Gem. He knew that without the ele-
    phant the king would have a poorer chance of defending his people and his
    country; so he saved the elephant, sacrificing his life in the process.

W.S. MERWIN

Preface to *East Window: The Asian Translations*

THESE POEMS, taken from *Selected Translations 1948–1968, Asian Figures, Selected Translations 1968–1978,* and *Sun at Midnight,* represent my attempts to make poetry in English out of poems originally written in Asian languages, over a period of more than three decades. I cannot remember when I first encountered Asian poetry, but it was in translation, of course, because I know no Asian languages. When I was still a child, I found, in the Harvard Classics, Edward FitzGerald's version of the *Rubáiyát of Omar Khayyám*—the original language not, according to some definitions, strictly Asian, and the rendering, I am told, a distant approximation, but I have remained fond of it ever since, as a great piece of Victorian poetry. By the time I was sixteen or so I had found Arthur Waley's Chinese translations, and then Pound, and was captivated by them both. Their relations to the forms and the life of the originals I will never be able to assess. But from the originals, by means and with aspirations that were, in certain respects, quite new, they made something new in English and they revealed a whole new range of possibility for poetry in English. Poetry in our language has never been the same since, and all of us are indebted to Waley and Pound whether we recognize and acknowledge it or not. Their work suggested, among other things, that the relation between translation and the original was more complicated and less definite than had often been assumed. But in fact the notion of what translation really was or could be had been undergoing change all through the nineteenth century, partly as a result of efforts to bring over into English a growing range and variety of originals. The assumptions inherent in the word "translation" had shifted radically since the early eighteenth century.

When Pope set out to translate Homer, almost everything (as it appears to us) was known beforehand. He knew who most of his immediate readers would be: they had subscribed for the translations. They, in turn, knew—or thought they knew—who Homer was, and they knew the text, in the original. Both the subscribers and the translator took it for granted that the proper form for heroic verse, in English, must be the heroic couplet. Pope's work was expected to display the wit, elegance, and brilliance with which he could render a generally accepted notion of the Homeric poems in a familiar English verse form.

Since the eighteenth century, and especially since the beginning of modernism, more and more translations have been undertaken with the clear purpose of introducing readers (most of them, of course, unknown to the translators) to works they could not read in the original, by authors they might very well never have heard of, from cultures, traditions, and forms with which they had no acquaintance. The contrast with Pope's situation is completed by the phenomenon, which has appeared with growing frequency in the past half century, of poet-translators who do not, themselves, know the language from which they are making their versions and who must rely, for their grasp of the originals, on the knowledge and work of others.

New—or different—assumptions mean different risks. New assumptions about the meaning of the world "translation," whether or not they are defined, imply different aspects of the basic risk of all translation, however that is conceived. Which is no risk at all, in terms of the most common cliché on the subject: that all translation is impossible. We seem to need it, just the same, insofar as we need literature at all. In our time, an individual or social literary culture without it is unthinkable. What is it that we think we need? We begin with the idea that it is the original— which means our (as scholars, potential translators, or readers) relative conception of the original. At the outset, the notion is probably not consciously involved with any thought of the available means of translation. The "original" may even figure as something that might exist in more forms than one, just as it can be understood by more than one reader. But if we take a single word of any language and try to find an exact equivalent in another, even if the second language is closely akin to the first, we have to admit that it cannot be done. A single primary denotation may be shared, but the constellation of secondary meanings, the moving rings of associations, the etymological echoes, the sound and its own levels of association, do not have an equivalent because they cannot. If we put two words together and repeat the attempt, the failure is obvious. Yet if we continue, we reach a point where some sequence of the first language conveys a dynamic unit, a rudiment of form. Some energy of the first language begins to be manifest, not only in single words but in the charge of their relationship. The surprising thing is that at this point the hope of translation does not fade altogether, but begins to emerge. Not that these rudiments of form in the original language can be matched—any more than individual words could be—with exact equivalents in another. But the imaginative force that they embody, and that single words embody in context, may suggest convocations of words in another language that will have a comparable thrust and sense.

By "rudiments of form" I mean recognizable elements of verbal order, not verse forms. I began translating with what I suppose was, and perhaps still is, an unusual preconception about the latter: the fidelity in translating a poem should include an ambition to reproduce the original verse form. Besides, I started translating partly as a discipline, hoping that the process might help me to learn to write. Pound was one of the first to recommend the practice to me. I went to visit him at St. Elizabeths in the forties, when I was a student. He urged me to "get as close to the original as possible" and also to keep the rhyme scheme of the poem I was translating, if I could, for the exercise as much as anything else. He was generous. And eloquent about what the practice could teach about the possibilities of English. He recommended that I should look, just then, at the Spanish *romancero,* and I did; but it was almost fifteen years before I actually made versions of many of the *romances*—and without the original rhyme schemes. I kept to his advice, at the time. When I did come, gradually, to abandon more and more often the verse forms of the poems that I was translating, I did not try to formulate a precise principle for doing so. Translation is a fairly empirical practice, usually, and the "reasons" for making particular choices, however well grounded in scholarship, are seldom wholly explicable. I would have recognized, probably quite early, a simple reluctance to sacrifice imagined felicities of the potential English version, to keep a verse pattern that was, in a sense, abstract. The preference seems to me practical, at least. I think I began to consider the subject more systematically when I was trying to decide on the best form for a translation of the *Chanson de Roland.* I had before me versions in blank verse both regular and more or less free, and one that contrived to keep not only the metrical structure of the Old French but the rhyme scheme: verse paragraphs known as *laisses,* sometimes many lines in length, each line ending with the same assonance. The result, in English, struck me as nothing more than an intellectual curiosity; unreadable. The word order of the lifeless English was contorted, line by line, to get those sounds to come out right. As for the virtues of the original that had moved hearers for centuries and contributed to the poem's survival over a thousand years, there was scarcely an indication of what they might have been. It's easy to multiply examples of this kind of translation. And yet it must be true that in translating—as in writing—formal verse, exigencies of the form itself occasionally contribute to the tension and resonance of the language. But I realized at some point that I had come to consider the verse conventions of original poems as part of the original language, in which they had a history of associations like that of individual words—something impossible to suggest in English simply by repeating the forms. Verse conventions are to a large degree matters of effects, which depend on a familiarity that cannot, of course, be translated at all. The effects of the convention in the new language can never be those the convention produces in the former one. This is true even with forms that have already been adopted. There would be certain obvious advantages in retaining the sonnet form in English, if translating a sonnet from Italian, but however successful the result, the sonnet form in English does not have the same associations it has in Italian; its effect is not the same; it does not mean the same thing. And sometimes an apparent similarity of form can be utterly misleading. The *Chanson de Roland,* again, for example. The original is in a ten-syllable line, and an English-speaking translator would naturally think, at first, of iambic pentameter. But if the poem is translated into any sort of blank verse in English (leaving aside the question of the relative vitality and brightness of that form in our age), the result is bound to evoke reverberations of the pentameter line in English from Marlowe through Tennyson—echoes that drown the real effect and value of the Old French verse.

The whole practice is based on paradox: wanting the original leads us to wanting a translation. And the very notion of making or using a translation implies that it will not and cannot be the original. It must be something else. The original assumes the status of an impossible ideal, and our actual demands must concern themselves with the differences from it, with the manner of standing instead of it. When I tried to formulate practically what I wanted of a translation, whether by someone else or by me, it was something like this: without deliberately altering the overt meaning of the original poem, I wanted the translation to represent, with as much life as possible, some aspect, some quality of the poem that made the translator think it was worth translating in the first place. I know I arrived at this apparently simple criterion by a process of elimination, remembering all the translations—whatever their other virtues—that I had read, or read at, and set down, thinking, "If the original is really *like* that, what could have been the point of translating it?"

The quality that is conveyed to represent the original is bound to differ with different translators, which is both a hazard and an opportunity. In the ideal sense in which one wants only the original, one wants the translator not to exist at all. In the practical sense in which the demand takes into account the nature of translation, the gifts—such as they are—of the translator are inescapably important. A poet-translator cannot write with any authority using someone else's way of hearing.

I have not set out to make translations that distorted the meaning of the originals on pretext of preserving some other overriding originality. For several years I tried to maintain illogical barriers between what I translated and "my own" writing, and I think the insistence on the distinction was better than indulging in a view of everything being the (presumably inspired) same. But no single thing that anyone does is wholly separate from any other; and impulses, hopes, predilections toward writings as yet unconceived certainly must have manifested themselves in the choices of poems from other languages that I preferred to read and wanted to translate, and in the ways that I went about both. And whatever is done, translation included, obviously has some effect on what is written afterward. Except in a very few cases, it would be hard for me to trace in subsequent writings of my own the influence of particular translations that I have made, but I know that the influences were and are there. The work of translation did teach, in the sense of forming, and making available, ways of hearing.

In the translations in *Asian Figures,* I let the sequence of the ideograms (which in most cases I had in front of me, with their transliterations) suggest the English word order, where that could be done without destroying the sense. The series of translations from Ghalib—made from literal versions, scholarly material, and direct guidance supplied by Aijaz Ahmad—were part of the same impulse. My first drafts remained close to the original *ghazal* form, and both Aijaz and I thought them papery. As he planned to include in the eventual publication the original texts, literal versions, and his own notes on vocabulary, the whole point of the enterprise was to produce something else from the material: poems in English, if possible. The rule was that they were not to conflict with Ghalib's meaning, phrase by phrase, but that they need not render everything, either. Translation was viewed as fragmentary in any case; one could choose the fragments, to some degree. Considering the inadequacy of any approach to translation, I had been thinking of Cézanne's painting the Montagne Sainte Victoire over and over, each painting new, each one another mountain, each one different from the one he had started to paint. I imagined that in translating a poem something might be gained by making a series of versions bringing out different possibilities. I still think so, though I realize that versions, however many, from a single poet-translator are likely to sound like variants of each other, and echo the translator's ear at least as clearly as they do the original.

The Ghalib translations are among those made without any first-hand knowledge of the original language, as I have explained. I don't know that such a procedure can be either justified or condemned altogether, any more than translation as a whole can be. Auden, for one, thought it the best possible way of going about it. I suspect it depends on the circumstances: who is doing the work, and the collaborators' relation to each other and to the poetry they are translating. I have had my doubts about working this way, and have resolved several times not to do any more translation of this kind (as I have resolved not to translate any more at all), but I have succumbed repeatedly to particular material.

I should make it clear that the only languages from which I can translate directly are Romance languages, and that I am less familiar with Italian and Portuguese than with French and Spanish. All the translations in this collection were based on someone else's knowledge. I continue to go about this in different ways, certain that no one translation will be absolute, for the obvious reason that it cannot be the original, and the original, as long as anyone is interested in it, will be heard in ways that gradually come to differ more and more among readers who use the second language in changing ways.

After 1978, my principal attempt at translation from an Asian language was the collaboration with Sōiku Shigematsu on the poems of Musō. I met Shigematsu-sensei in 1976, and we began talking about Musō, as I remember, almost at once. For years I had been interested in what I had read of Japanese poetry from the earliest period through Bashō and his disciples, and in the relation between much of the poetry and Buddhist insight. Shigematsu-sensei is a Rinzai priest and a professor of American literature (particularly the Transcendentalists) in Japan, who had been working on literal versions of Musō's poems for years and was looking for a poet with whom he could collaborate in English. We worked together on Musō's poems, mostly by correspondence, for over a decade.

When I look back at the various attempts to make in English something whose life seemed to me to suggest what was alive in the original, I am not sure that "translation" is the right word for some of the ways of trying to do that, but no other term seems adequate either, and the restless search for one becomes part of the practice of translation—an enterprise that is plainly impossible and nevertheless indispensable. The fond hope that has led me is fed by the same spring, I think, that sustains poetry and language itself.

Free Old Man

His original way
    is plain and simple
        not caught up in things
He preaches the dharma
    at liquor stores
        and fish shops
He pays no attention
    to sacred rituals
        or secular conventions
Thick white eyebrows
    in his old age
        signs of enlightenment

Musō Soseki (1275–1351)

Translated by W.S. Merwin and
Sōiku Shigematsu

Reply to Bukkō Zenji's Poem at Seiken-ji

I remember that once
    my dharma grandfather
        was happy to visit here
I feel ashamed sometimes
    to be inferior still
        to the seagull he saw then
But I'm lucky
    to hold in one phrase
        all the words of all the ages
Above the sea
    the full moon
        is shining on the shore

Musō Soseki (1275–1351)

Translated by W.S. Merwin and
Sōiku Shigematsu

159

No Gain

Virtue and compassion
  together make up
    each one's integrity
Nothing that comes through the gate
  from outside
    can be the family treasure
Throwing away
  the whole pile
    in your heart
with empty hands
  you come
    bringing salvation

    Musō Soseki (1275–1351)

    Translated by W.S. Merwin and
    Sōiku Shigematsu

For Ko Who Has Come Back from China

A brief meeting today
      but it seems to gather up
           a hundred years
We have exchanged
      the compliments of the season
           that's word-of-mouth Zen
Don't say that
      your wisdom and my ignorance
           belong to opposing worlds
Look: China and Japan
      but there are not
           two skiess

Musō Soseki (1275–1351)

Translated by W.S. Merwin and
Sōiku Shigematsu

For a Monk Going West

For many years
     our friendship
          has ripened
One morning
     you say goodbye
          and start down to the west
Stop trying to find the secret
     of succeeding
          as head priest
Look the sharp ax
     has been in your hands
          since the beginning

Musō Soseki (1275–1351)

Translated by W.S. Merwin and
Sōiku Shigematsu

SHOGO OKETANI

Some Thoughts on the Meaning of Translation

TRANSLATION OF A POEM begins in the reading of it. But the reading of a poem is not necessarily an easy task.

The poet's work of finding the first word or phrase can be compared to the work of a miner who digs for a lode he may or may not find. The reader's task can be like trying to arrive at the center of that lode through the holes bored by the poet's pen. The reader must rely on the faint light of a lantern. In other words, the reader has to regenerate, reconstruct, and accept the voice, images, and ideas the poet has uttered and acquired in the process of digging.

This act is a creative process imposed on the reader. This is the only way a poem can be read.

I don't want to reject the idea that reading or appreciating poetry should be a simple activity. But the emotional impact on the reader of a great work is the result of this internal process of reconstruction, whether it be conscious or not.

The act of translating a poem is premised on the act of reading a poem, of reconstructing the poet's words. Though reading a poem is an individual process of reconstruction, the act of translating requires some kind of collaboration. Through the process of reconstruction, the translator has to reflect on the cultural and social forces that have shaped him, because the basic purpose of translation is to convey the meaning of the original to those who speak the same tongue as the translator. By its nature, then, this process can no longer remain in the realm of the individual. Translation is not merely the transferring of a work to a language with different words, grammatical structures, or features. It is also the task of understanding and reconstructing the original in a different language *system*.

We can't deny that language reflects a culture's particular "way of see-ing," just as the "way of seeing" of a culture is defined by its language. When a work constructed in a language born of a particular climate, histo-ry, and nationality is translated into another language, the new language has a kind of convulsion because of the impossibility of understanding the core words of the original, which were created in a different historical framework or were influenced by a particular natural environment. Generally, this convulsion may seem to symbolize the difficulty of translation, but it is this very convulsion that shakes the translator's conventional perceptions of the foreign culture that is the foundation of the original work. This convulsion acts as a catalyst for people to destroy their old frame of reference regarding the foreign culture, which was originally formed by a different belief system. This ultimately leads to changes in cultural and social perceptions necessary to support the creation of new words and terms that come from subliminal acceptance of the different culture. This is where translation finds its meaning and mission.

For example, the basic reason the Beat poets were fascinated by the world of *haiku,* symbolized by Bashō's *Genroku Haikai,* or by Zen was not because they were looking for "new and unusual" things. Rather, faced with the rise of the Civil Rights Movement and the advent of the Cold War, they were forced to acknowledge deception in their social and cultural background, which had supported a highly developed consumer society monopolized by white people. They needed new values to replace the materialism and commercialism on which their society rested. One alternative was the world found in the *haiku* written by Bashō, which saw the self as having an uncertain place in nature. The Beat poets' inner need led them to this world.

I have written such a long and somewhat self-evident definition of translation because of my dissatisfaction with the state of the translation of Japanese literature in America. I have felt this way since moving to California three years ago. For the past two years, Leza Lowitz and I have been translating the work of the Japanese postwar poet Ayukawa Nobuo. Our process is as follows: I translate the original into English; Leza reworks my Japanese-English translation into more "natural" English; I explain the nuance of each word I want to change and discuss with her the words she has changed; we decide which word is best; finally, she edits each line of the poem again until the whole poem is complete. (This essay has gone through the same annoying process of me writing the first draft in Japanese, translating it into English, and then asking Leza to rewrite it in natural English.)

Given the above definition of translation, someone like myself— whose mother tongue is Japanese and who thinks in Japanese—is the most unsuitable and, in a sense, gratuitous person to translate work from Japanese to English. I have no choice but to be a foreigner in the American cultural and social environment, and I don't intend to close this distance. For a translation to have a relationship with the cultural and social environment of the country into whose language the translated words are to be accepted, this process should be completed by someone who has *interiorized* this environment.

The reason I began to translate Ayukawa's work is because of Leza's answer to my question "What do you think of Ayukawa's poetry?" She replied, "Who is Ayukawa?"

At that time, Leza was living in Japan and translating modern Japanese women's poetry into English. When I asked the same question of her American friend, an editor and translator who was interested in modern Japanese poetry, she also said, "Who is Ayukawa?" You can easily understand my surprise if you imagine an American encountering some Japanese talking about modern American poets without knowing who Ginsberg is.

Ayukawa was a founding member and leader of the postwar Japanese group Arechi (Waste Land), which played a leading role in postwar Japanese poetry. His works examined his own war experience and the reality of postwar Japanese society. In the late 1940s and 1950s, he was the only poet who acknowledged that those who wrote poems after the war about the atomic bomb or revolution (almost all such poems were superficial) should admit their own responsibility for what they did during the war. Even writers whose poetics differ from Ayukawa's acknowledge their indebtedness to him and to his influence; his lyrical poems contain great tension, and he is always included among the list of major postwar poets in Japan.

In addition to the high esteem in which Ayukawa is held in Japan, the power of his most important works, particularly the long poem "America" (1947), led me to assume that his poetry had been translated into foreign languages. "America" is a 200-line poem full of literary quotations from the works of Mann, Dostoyevsky, Kafka, Pound, Valéry, and Eliot, all of whom had a major influence on twentieth-century literature. In this poem, the meaning of "America"—which symbolizes twentieth-century world history—is brought into relief through Ayukawa's despondency over the reality of his defeated country. It is no surprise that the poem is considered a major work in twentieth-century modern poetry.

However, only a few of Ayukawa's poems have been translated into English, Italian, and Korean. Most of his important works, including "Morning Song at the Moored Ship's Hotel," "The Man on the Bridge," and "Soldier's Song," have not been translated at all. It was as if the poet Ayukawa Nobuo had had no hand in the development of modern Japanese poetry. If modern Japanese poetry wasn't considered excellent by global standards, this oversight might be understandable. But Japanese postwar or modern poets who are not as important as Ayukawa have been readily discussed and translated—and sometimes overrated—in the West.

The same tendency, to a lesser extent, can also be seen in the way Japanese novels are picked for translation in the West. The best-known novelists outside of Japan are Tanizaki, Kawabata, and Mishima, with the recent addition of Ōe. Although their work is not necessarily to my taste, it cannot be denied that these four novelists are good writers. Still, some people in Japan can't help but be cynical about the reason for their wide acceptance outside the country. These people wonder if it is because Tanizaki, Kawabata, and Mishima—who skillfully used traditional Japanese aestheticism as a backdrop in their novels while not being limited by it—satisfy readers with a thirst for exoticism. The work of Ōe, which deals with the horrors of the atomic bomb among other things, is attractive to foreign readers who wish to see postwar Japan primarily in relation to Hiroshima and Nagasaki. Basically, many of these works offer an easy-to-understand image of Japan that can be summarized as Fujiyama (Mount Fuji), *geisha, samurai, genbaku* (the atomic bomb). Unfortunately, these novels by themselves prevent foreigners from recognizing the existence of a more radical postwar Japanese reality.

For example, if I say that *Shirei* (*Dead Spirit*), the long, unfinished novel of Haniya Yutaka (1910–1997), is the most important novel of postwar Japan, those who understand contemporary Japanese literature wouldn't disagree with me. Haniya started writing this novel in 1946 and continued until his death in 1997. An attempt to reproduce the notion of Kant's antinomy in the field of literature, this novel is full of philosophical dialogues about consciousness, revolution, the cosmos, death, and darkness. Had it been translated in the 1950s or 1960s, Japanese literature would have generated an entirely different influence on global literature. As far as I know, not a single chapter of *Shirei* has been translated into a foreign language.

Similarly, it is strange that Takeda Taijun's novels—whose themes are sex, revolution, and Buddhism—and Takahashi Kazumi's novels about revolution and defeat have not been translated. Takeda Taijun (1912–1976) became a Buddhist priest (*jodo shinshu*) after being arrested as a communist. He lived in China during World War II, first as a conscripted soldier and later as a scholar of Chinese literature. He wrote about the twisted reality of postwar Japan from many perspectives: a defeated communist, a priest, and a witness to the Japanese invasion of China. Takahashi Kazumi (1931–1971), whose novels were enthusiastically read by students in the 1960s and 1970s, depicted the fall of Japanese postwar radicalism. Some Japanese might say of these two, "They are forgotten novelists," but since

Ōe's early novels were translated, it would have been natural for their novels to have been translated as well. There are many, many more Japanese novelists, poets, and critics of the modern period whose work deserves to be translated.

As for Japanese poetry, from what I have seen I can say that the bulk of Japanese poems that have been translated and discussed are traditional, short, fixed forms of verse like *haiku* and *tanka,* as well as modern poems that deal with phenomena like the atomic bomb. Poets who have received attention from the media, for whatever odd reason, also tend to be translated.

Of course, there are translators who work according to their own taste, keeping a distance from conventional concepts of Japanese literature. Yet as I consider why Ayukawa's work has never been widely translated, the thought occurs to me that the logic and ethics of his poetic worldview were constructed by completely dispensing with traditional Japanese notions of beauty or aesthetics. Perhaps this puzzled translators who tried to understand his works. Perhaps they had some prejudice against this kind of writing and felt a disenfranchisement from it. Despite having written many poems attacking totalitarianism, Ayukawa never wrote about Hiroshima or Nagasaki. For him, most so-called anti–atomic bomb poems lacked an awareness of Japan's responsibility for the war, and the anti–atomic bomb movement in Japan was merely another facet of anti-American sentiment.

> Oh, I need the rain, street and night.
> Only at night can I
> completely embrace the whole of this weary town.
> From the window,
> I stick out the grimacing face of the ideologue
> born in the valley of two world wars
> between West and East—
> a failure in revolution and in love,
> quickly corrupted.
> The town is dead.
> A fresh morning wind
> sends the cold razor blade to my throat,
> debased by the collar.
> For me, the shadow by the canal
> becomes a wolf with a gouged-out chest
> never again to howl.
>
> (trans. Shogo Oketani and Leza Lowitz)

This is the last stanza of "Morning Song at the Moored Ship's Hotel," which was written in 1949 and is one of Ayukawa's most important works. Since there are no traces of traditional Japanese aestheticism here, some people might consider it to be a mere imitation of European forms. Yet it is not so difficult to read between the lines and feel the sense of futility and desperation that followed World War II. By 1949, the possibility of a social revolution had already evaporated. The following year, the Korean War broke out. The peace that had come with the defeat of fascism had gradually become banal, and the world began to divide along ideological lines: West and East, capitalism and communism. People were starting to realize that the dream of communism (which was still seen as a kind of salvation) would be crushed by the realities of a socialist system.

Moreover, when considering why Ayukawa rejected traditional Japanese aestheticism, one cannot ignore the historical fact that this tradition, based on nature, started to lose its place in the lives of ordinary people at the end of the nineteenth century because of the process of modernization. In the 1930s, when the fascist regime gained power in Japan, this very aestheticism was transformed into an ideology that equated everlasting nature with the imperial system in order to construct a new image of the homeland. During the war, Ayukawa saw surrealist and communist poets turn to writing nationalistic poems using traditional Japanese aesthetic images. I think that translators or scholars of modern Japanese literature have overlooked the historical background of Ayukawa's poetry, in which his sense of reality was shaped by this environment; living not only as a poet but also as a person, he was driven by an inconvertible need to create poems that rejected the concepts, images, and ideas conventionally thought of as "Japanese ways."

If translators overlook the creative force behind a poet's expression, the work loses its *raison d'être*. For example, *haiku*—which in the West must be the most popular form of Japanese poetry—seems to be defined as a short, three-line poem about a season. During the Edo period (1603–1867), *haikai* became popular because they rendered the larger world accessible through a mere seventeen syllables and used ordinary words. On the other hand, it is also true that this accessibility prevented *haikai* from progressing as a literary art. Before Bashō, the main source of *haikai* was the Danrin school (Danrin Haikai), which emphasized novelty and humor. From Bashō to Buson and Issa, most *haikai* were poems full of double entendres and the subjugation of ego. Outside of Japan, *haikai* seems to be lionized, but only works by Bashō, Buson, Issa, and a few of their contemporaries are good enough to be read now. In other words, only a few *haikai* poets elevated the form above mere wordplay. They did this by letting us see their inner conflicts. Bashō wanted to live a simple life, turning his back on the prosperity of the *Genroku* period. He examined the relationship between self and nature, and the lives of ordinary people. Buson lived in the mid-eighteenth century, when the merchant class controlled the economy, the *samurai* class was trying to regain its authority, and the farming class had fallen into poverty. He used a loose syllable-count to depict the lives of lower-class townspeople. Issa, who was one generation younger than Buson, wrote about nature from the perspective of someone who was forced to have a sense of humor (approaching self-scorn) in a time of perpetual riots and the downtrodden state of the villages in which he stayed on his travels.

Great writers are those who look inward while living in an environment shaped by the limitations of the age. I can't help thinking that if Bashō, Buson, and Issa were alive in this day and age, they would first view nature as being the inevitable victim of human economic pursuit.

If translators consider *haiku* to be a mere expression of *wabi-sabi* or *furyu* (elegance), they miss the radicalism and dynamism of the form. From this standpoint, translation fails in that it brings a superficial and temporal perspective to the work, overlooking the notion of a progressive history. As a result, the Japanese are seen alternatively as a nation of slaughterers who perpetrated genocide in Nanking, as victims of the atomic bomb, and as people who love their traditions.

The true traditional Japanese way to beauty has not been simply to adhere to conventional aestheticism. Whether the subject is nature or a social phenomenon, great works of literature have always been created by those who reject superficial words and create from an inner core of self-knowledge. There is no greater disservice to expression than to think that objectifying nature equals transcendence, or that writing about a current event or phenomenon truly represents the present reality. Only a consistent gaze inward can transform the disenfranchisement that surfaces in the gap between the self and the age into a necessary expression.

The impossibility translators face is in translating this expression born of the writer's disenfranchisement. The true mission of the translator is to translate works that embody this impossibility.

America

It was the fall of 1942.
"Farewell!
We will never meet again.
And if we livest or diest,
Our prospects are poor!"
So one by one we disappeared from the night town,
Laughing at the way we carried those rifles over our shoulders.
The old men with artificial flowers on their chests
Sent the highest words of praise to us,
Heading out for the battlefield to die.
The expectation bore the storm.
The storm contained the cold.
The cold was the drip of death—
The drip of death turned off each small light of life.
Dear M, according to our dark promise,
You erased your figure from this world,
Leaving behind your heavy army boots and the smell of medicine,
Leaving the trace of your anguished face upon us,
Who left dying behind.
Why were ash and flame your only ruin?

"We used to take long walks along the muddy river
Running through this city, didn't we?
Ships floated, contemplating,
Motionless on the water.
You remember, don't you?
We saw a black dog crouching down on the bridge,
Moved to tears, or sometimes not."
Yes, I remember well,
Even after your disappearance from this city, Dear M,
What you murmured wandering in its belly:
"What kind of science and philosophy do they have there?
What kind of rhythms and colors?
What kind of possibilities and impossibilities?"
And the wind never answered a thing.
Even now, when I stand on that bridge,

The cold of the drifting wind makes me shiver.
"The one whose star determines his life never looks back."
Dear M, holding out against the wind and fixing my gaze on the
     resistance,
I will travel on to the end of this desolate world—
Still, I glance back at the first alley.
"I am here. In order to get to the place where you are,
From the place where you are not,
The me that is here is not here."
When the tiny lights turn on, one by one along the circle of the sunset,
Did I stand without purpose, hoping you would appear from the mist,
Or did I not?
I will paint a scene from 1947 for the dead man.
Sitting on the other side of the barroom table,
I meet three wise friends almost nightly.
Like puppets, they start walking when I lift my hand,
And like puppets, they stop moving when I let my hand fall.
To make a vertical determination as to whether those men are stuffed,
Dear M, do we need to reach your height?
Sipping from a long-stemmed glass,
The student begins to speak in a low voice with a compassionate look.
"You all haven't forgotten, have you?
Second-class races, groups, citizens are only fodder
For more advanced nations, parties, personages.
That's what the young man in St. Petersburg told us.
Oh, to be in England now that Winston's out,
Now that there's room for doubt,
And the bank may be the nation's…
Oh, strip away your vanity!
Strip it away!
With your own dirty hands,
Pull down on your hanged mother's legs!
Yes, now is the time for the big river
And all great people to go calmly down
The crooked road!"

The poet who has sold his soul
Smiles fearlessly.
"I will leave from the closed room,

From backstage where the curtain has fallen.
I didn't overlook a thing.
The past begins right now,
And the future is already over.
Underneath the costumes and accessories,
Beneath faces covered in makeup,
In the people's smiles, dances and parties
Look, the slough of hatred and vanity—
Look, the euphoria and rapture of social graces, exposed.
You, who have turned in the keys to your memories,
I stole your keys and will not return them."
And the bachelor nods to himself,
"That's enough. Don't speak any more.
Turn your back to me.
Silent wall,
Yellow skin.
I know that in a flat back there is no backbone—
Okay, my solitude is enough for me.
But the twittering of birds appearing
From the sunset's bright colors at the fading horizon,
The trembling of trees as if calling to us,
The days past that brought people agony—
That they are hidden somewhere even now is difficult for me to believe.
I will leave these ghosts by saying goodbye to the past and the future.
Or, by drinking up the ghosts,
I will bless this cursed night.
Therefore, especially when I awaken,
Especially while you are sleeping,
Death will be just a much stronger liquor."

The bachelor shoots one last glance
At the student's long-stemmed glass,
The movement of his lips over his bad teeth
Turns beastlike when drawn
On the bottom of the student's small pupils.
The poet stands up, suppressing a yawn,
The old night smell emanating from his hat-covered head.
The adamant naysayer's sad face appears.
"See you again tomorrow. If there is a tomorrow,"

Someone says to someone.
The bachelor quickly leaves by the door,
Passing the streetlamp he'd spit under,
Proceeding to the bed of a dirty woman.
Then the poet and the student
Bid each other a long farewell at the station.

I am left behind, alone.
Tell me: Who was witness?
Now I gaze at my ego and remember a slight smile.
The shadow is changing into one world, one body.
The tiny light must not be turned out.
The picture must be in burning red.
The music must be the unending beat of madness.
"America—"
Suddenly I ignite.
Fired up, agitated,
My eyes glow and I babble like the waves,
But there is no one around.
The white rain dries in the empty frame.
The record on the phonograph spins silently.
"America—" answers the wall.
Like a gambler who reads his own fortune,
I frown and hide my hand.
My hand of four aces,
Kings with guardsmen and queens giving comfort
Jumbled together in my brain.
"America—"
Much more significantly, for the sake of all beings,
I wish I could speak in front of the people.
The Anti-Columbus did not discover America!
The Ur-Jefferson did not pen the Declaration of Independence!
Our America has not yet been found.

The waterfall of weariness and silence
Slowly shuts off existence.
Cruel Xenon!
The handkerchief I twisted in my hands
Flies from the edge of time,

Where dark existence will freeze into abstraction itself,
Onto the table, like a torn blue sky.
My body smells of salt.
The other side of the window
Broken open with a tie tack
From the room with no exit
Across the sea!
Light changes into an atom,
Into summer's hard sudden rain.

I, who am the mere shadow of miserable you,
Lean against the table in a perfectly fitting vest and jacket,
Dreaming of the new golden age,
And the unknown nation that will someday be born
In each of our eyes,
In our casual greetings,
And of the morning when the messenger—
Bearing transcendent words,
The symbol of a bright sun on his chest—
Jumps over the palace and government steps,
Pushes aside the excited crowd,
And knocks on the door of our house with that big fist!
Oh, from days long since gone,
Deeply have I been dreaming.

July 1947

Ayukawa Nobuo (1920–1986)

Translated by Shogo Oketani and Leza Lowitz

HIROAKI SATO

Forms Transformed:
Japanese Verse in English Translation

IN TRANSLATING POETRY, no one is *wrong,* except when the literal deciphering is. I remember, for example, a translator working on some poems of Hagiwara Sakutarō (1886–1942) misreading the Chinese character (*kanji,* in Japanese) for *sara* ("plate" or "dish") as the one for *chi* ("blood"). This was years ago, and I no longer remember his translations of the lines containing the misreading, although, checking my own translation, I see it must have occurred in places such as "I would like to steal and eat that love-plate of skylarks, which gleams in the sky," "I ate too much of the plate of *cabbage* this morning," and "I looked through the whitened plate." Sakutarō's imagery in these descriptions may be odd enough for this particular misreading not to matter much—at least to the reader ignorant of the original; still, it is an error.

But Hagiwara Sakutarō is mainly known for his *jiyū-shi* ("free verse"), which does not employ any discernible syllabic patterns. My focus in this essay is on two traditional forms: the 5-7-5-7-7-syllable *tanka* and, Japanese verse forms having developed genealogically, its grandchild, the 5-7-5-syllable *haiku.* Most translators routinely render these in five and three *lines,* obviously because the two forms consist of five and three syllabic units. The question is: does the 5- or 7-syllable unit constitute a "line," or are the two units so regarded by *tanka* and *haiku* writers? Also, in view of the recent emergence in the United States of translators who employ the same syllabic count in their translations of classical Japanese verse, you might ask what happens when they do so.

The first thing you find when you step out of the realm of traditional forms, where inherited notions may hold sway, is that, yes, the 5- and 7-syllable units can each be a "line." Miki Rofū (1889–1964), for example, wrote "Furusato no"—a poem that became famous because it was set to music—in lines that alternate 5 and 7 syllables. It begins:

Furusato no
  ono no kodachi ni
fue no ne no
  urumu tsukiyo ya.

In her village
  in a stand of trees by a field
a flute's sound
  blurs in the moonlit night.

(trans. Hiroaki Sato)

For that matter, the rendition by Ueda Bin (1874–1916) of Paul Verlaine's "Chanson d'automne," likely the most memorized French poem in Japanese translation, is done in a series of 5-syllable lines.

Yet, at the end of a prolonged period of verse experimentation—from the latter half of the Meiji era (1868–1912) and well into the Taishō era (1912–1926), when Western notions of poetry and poetics swamped the land in one wave after another—Hinatsu Kōnosuke (1890–1970), a scholar of English literature and a poet, concluded that neither the 5- nor the 7-syllable unit had "a general suitability in engendering poetic effect in Japanese." Indeed, among non-*tanka* and non-*haiku* poets, the usual practice was to compose poems with lines variously combining the two classical syllabic units. For example, the lines in the poem "Isago wa yakenu" (The sand is burnt), by Kambara Ariake (1876–1952), employed 7-5-7, 7-5-5, 5-5-7, or 5-7-5 syllables. In another famous translation of his, Ueda Bin gave 7-5-7-5, or a total of twenty-four, syllables to each line of Baudelaire's sonnet "L'albatros." Also, before free verse originating in France reached Japan and prevailed, poets worked out new syllabic patterns, such as 6, 8, and 9, and combinations thereof.

So, first, it may legitimately be asked: if the 5- and 7-syllable units in *tanka* and *haiku* are to be automatically regarded as "lines" because each forms a pattern, what to do with those "lines" Ariake composed? What to do with newly created syllabic patterns?

Second, free verse also affected the realms of *tanka* and *haiku*, prompting a substantial number of poets to stop using syllabic units and counts. I'll give one example from each genre.

Toki Aika (1885–1980)—who critically influenced the famous *tanka* trilineator Ishikawa Takuboku (1885–1912) and continued to experiment with *tanka* throughout his long life—has left some impressions of New

York, which he visited in 1927. Here's one of them:

Sotto yorisotte waki no shita ni mugon no pisutoru
o sashimukesō na otoko no aida o tōru

I pass between men who have the air of quietly
    sidling up to you and turning silent pistols
        up against your armpits

The original, written in one line, consists of forty-one syllables—ten more than the standard form—and cannot really be scanned.

As an example of the *haiku* genre, I cite Ozaki Hōsai (1885–1926):

Taikū no mashita bōshi kaburazu

Right under the big sky, I don't wear a hat

Also written in one line, the original consists of fifteen syllables, or two fewer than the standard seventeen, and, again, it is tough to scan, though the second half does form a 7-syllable unit. (I used this *haiku* as the title of a collection of my translations of Hōsai's work; as a reviewer noted, it is a rare book that has a complete poem for its title.)

Third, most *tanka* and *haiku* poets, along with their commentators, regard the *tanka* and *haiku* as one-line forms. At the same time, as you may discern from my use of the word "most," there are lineators in both genres. This fact has enabled the erudite popular writer Inoue Hisashi—not a poet as far as I know—to comment on Takuboku in this fashion:

> Had Takuboku followed the approach that no one had doubted
> till then and written *tanka* in one vertical line, or in two lines at
> most [the latter for reasons of space], he might have been able to
> make something like

Kishikishi to samusa ni fumeba ita kishimu kaeri rōka
    no fui no kuchizuke   [31 syllables]

Creakingly stepping in the cold the boards creak
    as I go back in the hall a sudden kiss

but he would not have been able to make

Aru hi, futo, yamai o wasure,   [12 syllables]
ushi no naku mane o shiteminu—   [12 syllables]
        tsumako no rusu ni.   [7 syllables]

One day, suddenly, I forgot my disease,
and mimicked a cow mooing just to see—
in wife and child's absence.

Inoue's point is that a deliberate use of space, here manifested as lineation, makes a big difference. Put another way: when poets string words together without spacing, they are aiming to create a certain effect—shall we call it agglutinative?—which they evidently feel they lose when they break the poem up into lines. And this is the sentiment of the majority. (As I show in the introduction to *Howling at the Moon* (Green Integer, 2002), Hagiwara Sakutarō, who took the *tanka* form very seriously, also tried to break up the 31-syllable form into lines, but in the end decided that doing so was unnatural. Something similar can be said about the *haiku* form.

Fourth, to go a few centuries back, a group of poets led by Kagami Shikō (1665–1731) tried to create a new poetic genre called *kana-shi*. The general idea worked out was that the units of 10 (5+5) and 14 (7+7) syllables would each form a "line," with the former corresponding to a 5-character line and the latter to a 7-character line in *kanshi* (verse composed in classical Chinese). This is significant because *kana-shi* rhymed in the manner of *kanshi* and, therefore, the concept of "line" was stronger.

Finally, to state the obvious, syllabic value differs from language to language. Japanese is a polysyllabic, vowel-laden tongue; English isn't. English can say, in my experience and on average, twenty to twenty-five percent more than Japanese can with the same number of syllables. You can guess what happens when the 5- and 7-syllable formations are applied in translating traditional *tanka* and *haiku*. Yes, the result usually says more than the original does.

Well, does all this matter? After all, Japanese and English are so different. With such differing languages, shouldn't the assumption be that forms, for instance, can't be transferred? Japanese poets may regard *tanka* and *haiku* as one-line poems, but it's highly doubtful that they have any notion of the "line" in the Western sense and, anyhow, one-line poems are nonpoems in English—even though, yes, come to think of it, there's something called the monostich in the English poetic tradition. But of the monostich, the *New Princeton Encyclopedia of Poetry and Poetics* says, "It is an interesting question whether a one-line poem is possible," doesn't it?

So, again, are Japanese views and practices, linguistic realities and such, of any import?

Not really. In large measure, the answer depends on what you are after. Some American poets have found my one-line approach intriguing because they'd never thought that the *tanka* and *haiku* are conceived as one-line poems, but they are an absolute minority. In this, as in many other things, American views and practices are the mirror images of those of the Japanese.

As I said at the outset, in poetry translation no one is *wrong*—or *right*. To show this, and to conclude, here are some translations of one poem from *tanka* and *haiku* each.

Murasaki Shikibu, author of *The Tale of Genji*, is represented in the canonical *Hyakunin isshu* (One hundred poems by one hundred poets) by the following *tanka*:

> *Meguriaite mishi ya sore tomo wakanu ma ni*
> *kumo gakurenishi yowa no tsuki kana*

The poem comes with a headnote: "Someone who was my childhood friend very early—I came across her years later, briefly, around the tenth of Seventh Month, but because she hurried away as if racing with the moon [I made the following poem]." (The original doesn't specify the gender of the friend.) In my translation the *tanka* reads:

> We met again but before I could tell I saw you,
> you hid in the clouds, midnight moon!

Steven D. Carter—who evidently enjoys immense admiration among his academic colleagues and who explains that in his translations he exploits such "natural resources" of English as "punctuation, capitalization, spacing, and a 'jogging' of lines"—has rendered the *tanka* this way:

> Quite by chance we met,
> and then before I was sure
>   who it really was,
> the moonlight had disappeared,
> hidden behind midnight clouds.

You will see that Carter has allocated exactly 5-7-5-7-7 syllables, although, as far as syllabic fidelity goes, he for some reason has ignored the fact that the opening phrase of the original is hypersyllabic, consisting of 6, rather than 5, syllables.

In contrast, consider this translation by F.V. Dickins:

> I ventured forth one moonlight night,
>   And then saw someone hastening past,
> Ere I could tell who 'twas aright,

With dark clouds was the moon o'ercast,
Whose pallid ray
    O'er th' middle night held tranquil sway.

Dickins, a physician attached to the Royal Navy, did, as far as I know, the first complete translation of an anthology of Japanese verse—the *Hyakunin isshu*. He worked on the translation in the 1860s, and it shows every sign of someone groping to find meaning in the opaque and obscure original, as he honestly admitted. Also to his credit, in his preface he didn't say the *tanka* was a five-line verse form, though that's probably because his Japanese informants didn't say that.

One hundred sixteen years later, another Englishman, Richard Bowring, gave this poem a try. With the headnote, his translation reads:

> I met someone I had known long ago as a child, but
> the moment was brief and I hardly recognized them.
> It was the tenth of the tenth month. They left
> hurriedly as if racing the moon.

> Brief encounter:
> Did we meet or did it hide
> Behind the clouds
> Before I recognized
> The face of the midnight moon?

In the headnote, Bowring, evidently in an attempt to avoid gender identification, uses "them" where its antecedent, in his translation, is "someone"; the same attempt, to some extent, is discernible in the poem as well. Such things may be a reflection of the time: by the mid-1970s, the use of "he" when the sex wasn't known or didn't matter was fast becoming a no-no.

What about translations of the other genre, the *haiku?*

In 1689, Matsuo Bashō carried out his famed journey to the interior of Japan and, in his celebrated account of it, included about fifty *haiku.* One of them, along with its preceding prose passage, may be translated:

> The glory of the three generations lasted only as
> long as a single nap. The place where the main gate
> stood was one *li* this side. Hidehira's site had turned
> into paddies, with only Kinkeizan retaining its
> shape. First, we went up to the Takadachi and saw
> the Kitagami was a large river flowing from Nambu.
> The Koromo River flows around Izumi Castle and

below the Takadachi pours into the large river. The
old site for Yasuhira and others was on the other side
of Koromo Barrier, with the Nambu side fortified
for defense, it seemed, against the Ezo. The most
loyal among his loyal vassals were selected and put
up in this castle, but their fame lasted only for a
moment and turned into clumps of grass. "The
country destroyed, the mountains and rivers remain.
In the castle it is now spring and the grass has
turned green." Sitting on our hats laid on the
ground, we shed tears for a while:

Natsukusa ya tsuwamono-domo ga yume no ato

Summer grass: where the warriors used to dream

Here, I will cite only translations by some of those who prepared the
complete translation of Bashō's account, *Oku no hosomichi:*

> The summer grasses:
> The high bravery of men-at-arms,
> The vestiges of dream.
>
> (trans. Earl Miner, 1969)

> A mound of summer grass:
> Are warriors' heroic deeds
> Only dreams that pass?
>
> (trans. Dorothy Britton, 1974)

> A dream of warriors,
> and after dreaming is done,
> the summer grasses.
>
> (trans. Helen Craig McCullough, 1990)

> Summer grasses:
> all that remains of great soldiers'
> imperial dreams
>
> (trans. Sam Hamill, 1991)

Of these four translators, Britton and McCullough use 5-7-5 syllables; Miner and Hamill don't, though Miner goes beyond the allotted seventeen syllables and Hamill arrives at exactly seventeen—accidentally perhaps. The effect of an inevitable amplification, which was only vaguely discernible in Carter's translation of Lady Murasaki's *tanka,* here becomes loud and clear, with the padding creating fancy results, such as "high bravery" (Miner), "heroic deeds" (Britton), "dream...dreaming" (McCullough), and "great...imperial" (Hamill).

But are they wrong? I don't think so.

At Midnight

The breathing next to me
suddenly cries out.
Pulled by an invisible hand,
he struggles, moans.
I get up,
kill my eyes,
turn into an ear.
He's already
stepped into
another world.
He's so close yet so distant.
If his voice stops
and he's dragged
to the other side,
that will be the end of one story.
For now
I don't want the story
to end,
so I call him back
to this world.
Then
holding each other
we sleep till morning.

Nagashima Minako (b. 1943)

Translated by Hiroaki Sato

Love

I thought of sleeping.
The man next to me, face turned this way,
is snoring comfortably.
Because he's asleep with his mouth open,
the smell comes.
Human innards smell rotten.
Fried chicken, salad, strawberries just eaten
change the moment they go down the throat.
Where and how do they change?
I'd like to stick my hand into his throat
and pull the single tube out of his body
for verification.
Where and how did we,
I and my man, change?
I'd like to pull in the core of our consciousness
for verification.

We go on rotting on the futon.
Both meat and fruit
are the most delicious when they begin to rot.
We're in the best moment to be eaten.

Do I love this man who comes with innards?
I ask myself.
At least the core of love
doesn't exist in the innards.
I turn his face away gently
lest I wake him.

Nagashima Minako (b. 1943)

Translated by Hiroaki Sato

The Messenger

"Maaaiiiil"
"Special Deliveryyyy"
The front door reflecting the morning sun is knocked on.
The buzzer cold with morning dew is pushed.
It is a dazzling messenger constantly dispatched
from the end of the world to the present.
The future, that is the end, is immovable.
What constantly moves and is shapeless is the present.
Myself, that is the present, is always short of sleep.
The door, that is myself, is repeatedly knocked on,
and the doorbell is repeatedly pushed.
"Telegram from tomorrooow"
"From five minutes from nooow"
This morning, too, draped in radiating light,
the bicycle arrives backward, noiselessly.
The end must be so bright
as to smash your eyes.

Takahashi Mutsuo (b. 1937)

Translated by Hiroaki Sato

Convalescence

Spread in the light of the backyard is the drying tree.
On its radiate three-stage branches is the laundry.
The white cutouts[†] of shirt-shapes and brief-shapes
of the one who'd worn them until a few minutes ago.
The one with a summer cold who'd just changed clothes,
sunk inert in his chair, is looking at them.
Now with the cutouts on the branches having shapes,
he has lost his own shape.
The cutouts have taken on shapes
continue to flap in the bright wind and dry.
This is time, this is healing,
the one with a fever thinks vaguely.

Takahashi Mutsuo (b. 1937)

Translated by Hiroaki Sato

[†] *Katashiro,* here given as "cutouts," are the shapes of people and objects
made to be buried with a dead person or to be used in a purification rite.
Its literal meaning is "shape substitute."

Spring Cold

So it may light your way
when you visit me again tonight,
as I'm sure you will,
I leave the light by my pillow on and close my eyes.
The backs of my eyelids
are like lanterns with lit candles.

In that light
peach blossoms fall, fluttering, fluttering.
It must be because you are coming,
I won't call it crude behavior,
slightly tipsy,
hitting, hitting flowering branches.
Yet you are like a silhouette on the paper sliding door
no matter how much time passes,
only peach petals remaining pink.

Fluttering, fluttering,
have I cried a little?
The lanterns waver,
your silhouette smudges and fades,
and tonight's dream
has turned into nothing but chilly, cold petals.

Kazue Shinkawa (b. 1929)

Translated by Hiroaki Sato

The Remaining Summer

To see him off, I stand at the gate after the rain.
The ivory roof of his car
has scarlet smudges of crepe myrtle
that the hard rainfall awhile back struck down.
—Shall I wipe them off?
—No, not necessary. It would wet your hands.
By the time he returns on the superhighway to his office downtown,
the roof will be dry, and so will the flowers sticking to it,
leaving no trace, blown away by the wind,
that's what he's figured out in his head.
The brief conversation like a bird's bath,
the faint scent transferred,
will fade, will be forgotten,
by the time he pushes the elevator button,
the transience of it all like an exclamation.
He's someone who promises to come
but often doesn't,
so when he hurries away without even saying "See you again,"
how can I, in the future, wait to see him again?
Telling myself not to wait anymore
I end up waiting again, morning and evening, which terrifies me.
Allowing the scattered red flowers, the last of this summer,
to smudge both heart and eyes, I remain standing,
thinking of the sadness of flowers
that peel off the roof of a speeding car
and are lost one after another.

Kazue Shinkawa (b. 1929)

Translated by Hiroaki Sato

ANDREW SCHELLING

Manuscript Fragments and Eco-Guardians: The Estate of Sanskrit Poetry

Nature Literacy

WITHIN SANSKRIT POETRY and the related vernacular lyrics that constitute northern India's classical tradition, a quality I find more and more compelling is the deep, studied regard shown the natural world. In our turn-of-the-millennium period an intense debate is in progress over the status of wilderness areas and the importance of nonhuman species. The urgency of concerns about wildlands and the disappearance of species across the planet—along with a stubborn archaic belief that one of the poet's jobs is to articulate the unique presence of birds and mammals, insects or river systems—has put contemporary poets on the alert for insights into nature or wilderness that distant artistic traditions might offer. I am convinced the best Sanskrit poems contain the tracks of something instructive. Rooted in Paleolithic habits of observation, they balance a finely tuned eco-literacy with a cosmopolitan delight in language, social patterns, and erotic behavior. Wild creatures were daily familiars to the Sanskrit poets, who studied them with a close unsentimental eye, observed how closely implicated they were in human behavior, and noted how parallel passions and enthusiasms animated them.

A poem attributed to Apanāgara, found in King Hāla's second-century anthology *Gāhākosa*, written in a vernacular of Maharashtra State:

> Stag and doe
> hard short lives
> ranging the forest for
> water and grass
> they don't
> betray each other they're
> loyal
> till death

For a North American poet working to become nature-literate on home territory, it is of enormous interest to see with what ease creatures of the natural world can become citizens of standing in a poem. The Sanskrit vocabulary for flowers and trees in particular is abundant and botanically accurate. Happening on this tradition at the remove of a thousand years, one might at first glance miss the precision of detail, but nonhuman elements of the landscape were carefully regulated inside the Sanskrit lyric. Poets worked specific flowers or blooming trees, particular birds, animals, or phases of weather, into compressed cultural ciphers. I don't mean they were employed symbolically. Rather, they provided a customary setting for the poem, instantly recognizable to a reasonably well traveled resident of India. The mere hint of fragrance off a nearby forested hill told not only in what calendar moment of what season the poem was located, but its bioregional particulars as well. A single detail could evoke a constellation of human relationships (also calibrated to the season), a precise mood, and of course vivid moments echoed from earlier poems.

There's good evidence this use of native creatures came into classical Sanskrit from the somewhat earlier Tamil tradition of the south. Classical Tamil poets (circa 100 B.C.E.–250 C.E.), writing in a Dravidian tongue, devised for their intricately erotic short poems an alphabet of natural elements, which they calibrated to distinct landscapes—what we now call bioregions. By invoking the name of a single plant or animal native to a known habitat, they would summon an image at once natural, cultural, regionally precise, and resonant with a particular emotion. The Tamil poets identified five wilderness regions; current natural history would classify them as montane, riparian meadow, forest, littoral shoreline, and arid scrubland. Each landscape set the scene for a particular erotic mood. Plant companions are so abundantly featured that A.K. Ramanujan's good book of translations, *Poems of Love and War,* includes a botanical index, which reads like the "List of Plants" that stands as an appendix to Henry David Thoreau's *The Maine Woods.*

In a looser way the Sanskrit poets, from the founding of the Gupta Empire in 320 C.E., used this type of alphabet for their own lyrics, introducing the kind of attention to seasonal changes in various bioregions that has been the stuff of natural history, and superimposing on the natural orders a sophisticated psychology of human life. Regional plants, weather patterns, bird migration, animal instincts, seasonal cycles: all were used emblematically. Though the intention was to provoke distinct emotional tones, their use lends sound testimony to Ezra Pound's counsel: "the natural object is always the adequate symbol."

Aside from one hundred rather fierce lyrics by Bhartṛhari (circa seventh century)—who was very likely a celebrated linguist and a bark-clad yogin at different times in his life—little Sanskrit poetry was written by hermits. The poets formed a professional guild—some doing double time as philosophers or scholars—and rarely chose to live outside human settlements or to develop yogic powers among the wild, nonhuman orders. The fact that poems minutely familiar with nature were not written by recluses gives Sanskrit short poems a different flavor from those of the adjacent Chinese tradition: the settings or landscapes seem closer to home; there are few brooding mountain escarpments, few unvisited gorges along thundering rivers.

In Sanskrit lyric, the human and nonhuman orders seem linked in unsensational daily intimacy. Local villages flocked with birds in flowering trees. The whiff of odors from a nearby forest grove. Farmland crops or native grasses in fertile alluvial soil. Sweet-smelling blossoms along a village path. To put it another way: what flowering creeper shares the details of your life because you walk past it every day to fetch water? What pliant reed did you collect one moonlit spring night in order to weave a couch for your lover?

Transcendentalist Tracks

The tricky, many-forked paths a poet takes into other centuries and other literatures are hard to trace. Sanskrit poetry—indeed, the thorny old language itself—seems a curious place to end up, and it's hard to be sure how I got there. There's a good poem by Dharmakīrti—it has a postmodern taste—that might serve as an entry point. Dharmakīrti was a Buddhist scholar from southern India who, late in the seventh century, wrote seven razor-witted treatises on Buddhist logic, several sūtra commentaries, and an unknown number of lyric poems, of which a handful survive. One of them reads:

> No one visible up ahead,
> no one approaches
> from behind.
> Not a footprint on the road.
> Am I alone?
> This much is clear—
> the path the ancient
> poets opened
> is choked with brush,
> and I've long since left
> the public thoroughfare.

I grew up in Transcendentalist country: the pre-Revolutionary townships that spread west of Boston. This meant that as a child I became familiar in a native way with the forests and meadows Henry David Thoreau surveyed. I dodged watchful rangers to swim the ponds he washed in or wrote about, and I lived on close terms with the little holy places of Emerson, Margaret Fuller, and the Alcott girls and their eccentric philosophic father.

An airy mixture of Asiatic books and thoughtful Romantic philosophies (which read like poetry) hung over the region. Thanks to early curators Ananda Coomaraswamy and Ernest Fenollosa, local museums offered world-class collections of Indian sculpture and Chinese landscape painting. These exposed viewers to archetypes of consciousness hewn in Indian sandstone, or forested crags rendered in Chinese ink. To stand in the presence of these was to catch a cool glimpse of the way one's own mind was fashioned.

Thoreau had been exposed to something similar, though in a rougher, more solitary way. In *Walden* he tells of waking at dawn and walking to the pond's edge to collect water. When he gets to the shore, time and space collapse for a moment and he catches sight of a Hindu arriving just at that moment at the bank of the Ganges, filling his own little water pot. This leap—what could it mean? That the *Bhagavad-gītā,* the *Upaniṣads,* some Buddhist sūtras, the Hindu *Purāṇas* were, by the middle of the nineteenth century, cross-fertilizing among New England hemlock, maple, and oak? That even the geographic error solidified in our use of the word "Indian" for this continent's native peoples expresses some unarticulated karmic link between North American landscapes and South Asian texts? Emerson and old man Alcott thought so.

It was the holy books of Sanskrit that I encountered first. Full of thunder and wind, craggy metaphysics, humorous folklore, shivery insight, they felt like poetry. No matter the available translations were largely in a not-very-lively prose. When I settled down to get what I could of Sanskrit into my head, it was because the familiar translations, many from the nineteenth century, no longer felt close enough. What had those British and German philologists left out? Looking into their translations, I glimpsed something tawny, a muscular flex back of the language: like snapping your glance around in the forest—an instant too late to identify the creature that's gone into the trees. At the time, I did not know there was also a classical tradition of poetry—secular, tenderly amorous, refined, and instructively nature-literate—lying in wait. This would have been hard for an American to know.

There have been few good translations of Sanskrit lyric poetry. Mostly there's been indifference, occasionally disdain, shown toward Sanskrit verse. Because there are no good translations? Or is it the other way around, that a colonialist *hauteur* has produced third-rate translation? Introducing his Chinese anthology, *The Jade Mountain: The 300 Poems of the T'ang Dynasty,* Witter Bynner states, "I doubt I could ever feel any affection for the ornate, entranced poetry of India." This was seventeen years after the first Imagist manifestos: two decades of Ezra Pound, H.D., Williams, Marianne Moore, and a handful of other writers working out that lean American hunger for poems shorn of adornment. Few adjectives could have been more damning than "ornate" and "entranced."

The English translations Bynner would have seen by 1929 could only have backed up his estimate. They're mostly worthless. British and American scholars put Sanskrit poems—surprisingly compressed, fleet-footed, and alert in the originals—into Tennysonian iambics. Furthermore, for complex reasons most translators seemed to require three or four times as many English words as Sanskrit. Given the distance between the two languages—one heavily declined, the other quite analytic—I realize it would be nearly impossible to define what constitutes a "word." Nonetheless, a survey of bilingual books on my shelf reveals that translations of Chinese poetry use only one and a half to two English words for each Chinese ideogram—though the originals show no verb tenses or pronouns and not much in the way of prepositions, all of which translators into English supply. Why such wordiness in Sanskrit translations?

A long-winded translation of a sprightly poem—Chinese, Indian, or any other—misses the one thing that counts: the poetry. John Dryden said it for all of us: "I cannot, without some indignation, look on an ill copy of an excellent original... A good poet is no more like himself in a dull translation, than his carcass would be to a living body." When in my studies I encountered *kāvya* (Sanskrit's short lyric poetry), I was unprepared to like it, and so was surprised to see how much vigor it had. Only two modern scholars have recognized this vigor, gone to the poetry on its own turf, and done good work: Daniel H.H. Ingalls, who has devoted himself to it and has written the best overview of Sanskrit poetry; and Barbara Stoller Miller, who throughout her life produced clean, modern translations based on good scholarship. Without their efforts, the trail might still be lost.

It is instructive to consider the effect China and Japan have had on American poetry. By contrast, India seems nearly invisible. There are two, possibly three Sanskrit words in Pound's *Cantos. The Waste Land* has three, all drawn from a single episode in the *Upaniṣads* (Eliot, interested in

Buddhism, studied Sanskrit as an undergraduate at Harvard). Only with Kenneth Rexroth's post–World War II poetry does Indian mythopoetics enter Anglo-American poetry in a compelling way.

Few Sanskrit scholars appear to like the poetry. The standard reference books—compiled by British scholars during colonial times—treat it with dismay or outright contempt. Closer to our own day, D.D. Kosambi, an influential literary Marxist and co-editor of the important twelfth-century anthology *Subhāṣita-ratna-koṣa,* dismisses it for other reasons. Following Plekhanov's theory of literary production, Kosambi maintains that good poetry can only be written by newly emergent classes that are advancing the means of production. The Sanskrit poets were courtiers or courtesans, scholars or schoolteachers—not labor revolutionaries. Their poetry, according to Kosambi's analysis, "necessarily carries with the rank beauty of an orchid the corresponding atmosphere of luxury, parasitism, decay."

If the professionals don't like it, readers will be indifferent. Predictably, the original texts remain hard to find. Only half a dozen libraries in our country have a workable collection. Where I live, along the front range of Colorado's Rocky Mountains, we're a thousand miles—the width of India—from the nearest Sanskrit collection of note. Luckily, a few dealers in Calcutta and Delhi have helped turn up useful books, but many volumes are hopelessly scarce: they went out of print in Bombay or Poona one hundred years ago.

Ragged Manuscripts

Classical Sanskrit poetry was written over the course of about eight hundred years, beginning around 320 C.E. with the founding of the Gupta empire. During those centuries, Indian civilization reached its height. The culture was abundant and cosmopolitan, drawing Chinese pilgrims, Arab merchants, and Greek philosophers to its courts. Most of India's exquisite classical sculpture, architecture, and mural painting, the manuals of science, erotics, theater, linguistics, and philosophy were also produced during this period. All these arts came to a violent end during the eleventh and twelfth centuries, when Muslim warriors of solid military capability rode on horseback through the Khyber Pass and down into the Indo-Gangetic plains, taking control of the cities and highways. They drove out the Buddhists, who had compiled extensive libraries in their *vihāras* (universities). Some manuscripts managed to survive, hidden away, especially in the South. But throughout the North the *vihāras* were sacked or burnt, and the libraries vanished.

Buddhist monks lucky enough to escape fled to Tibet, carrying what manuscripts they could: sūtra literature and Buddhist exegesis, accounts of Buddhist kings and yogins, but also volumes of secular writings. One of the notable examples is the *Subhāṣita-ratna-koṣa,* compiled between 1100 and 1130 by a likable scholar, Vidyākara, who served as abbot of Jagaddala *vihāra* in Bengal. A Buddhist monk with a keen ear for poetry, he saw no contradiction between his religious training and the teeming, playful, erotic poems he collected. His anthology—translated in full by Daniel H.H. Ingalls as *An Anthology of Sanskrit Court Poetry*—is open-minded and tolerant. Its 1,738 poems contain hundreds of erotic epigrams, cameos of tender moments, and portraits of lovers, children, poor people, rich people, animals, and accounts of the seasons. There's wit, despair, humor, irony, bitterness, affection; many of the poems are love poems, as good as those written in any language.

Vidyākara's anthology was entirely lost until the twentieth century, when two explorers a few years apart happened upon a readable twelfth-century palm-leaf manuscript, probably Vidyākara's personal copy, at the Ngor monastery in Tibet, about a one-day journey by foot from Shigatse. First, in 1934, Rahula Sankrityayana—an Indian *pandit,* a good scholar and good Sanskritist, possibly up in Tibet as a British spy—found the manuscript in a barn attached to the monastery. A few years later Giuseppe Tucci, the noted Italian art collector and scholar of Buddhism, also came across it. Each managed to produce, under challenging conditions, photographic plates of very poor quality ("execrable," says one account) and to transport them out of Tibet.

Working from these plates, which they compared against photos, manuscript fragments, and more recent anthologies—housed in libraries in Nepal and India—that held some of the same poems, Kosambi and fellow Indian scholar V.V. Gokhale managed to edit a clean edition for Harvard University Press's Oriental Series. Here, from Kosambi's 1957 introduction to the volume, is a representative estimate of the estate of the old poems:

> A chance still remains of getting better materials
> from Tibet, including the original manuscript or
> good new photographs... This was in fact promised
> me at Peking in 1952 by the authorities of the
> People's Republic of China... [However,] Tibet
> being completely autonomous in such purely inter-
> nal matters, the new evidence will not be forthcom-
> ing as long as the manuscripts remain sacred posses-
> sions of the monasteries, to be worshipped unread,

or sold in fragments for pilgrims to use as charms.
There is no doubt that the Tibetans themselves will
soon develop a modern scientific attitude towards
their priceless treasures, which are India's treasures
too. This implies the development of systematic
archaeology, which will open up images and stupas in
which many manuscripts may have been immured.

Two things strike me in this little account. First, though many went
unread, the old Sanskrit manuscripts were considered sacred items. That
Tibetans regarded them as holy is both why they were preserved and why
outsiders rarely got wind of them. The other notable thing is that decades
before global tourism entered the Himalayas—trekkers in Gore-Tex,
college students with granola bars, high-tech trophy mountaineers, interna-
tional dealers in cheaply bought antiquities, and all sorts of other travelers
willing to trade hard cash for old goods in the little mountain villages—
manuscripts were already being broken apart by monks and sold off to
visitors or, more interestingly, being ritually inserted into religious icons.
Might entire pages of high-quality Sanskrit poetry, tied into bricklike
amulets, be lying unread inside gilded icons or little prayer boxes?

I have instant sympathy with Buddhist mountain pilgrims, polyan-
drous Tibetan mothers, Tantric yogins, and energetic yak-herding yoginis
who worship texts without needing to read them. They have preserved oral
teachings that may prove more valuable than written texts. They've main-
tained techniques of personal insight, religious magic, and social ceremony
our planet dearly needs. They've saved fragile manuscripts. Still, I like to
imagine that one day in the twenty-first century a sheaf of unknown
poems by Lady Śīlābhaṭṭārikā, grown ragged over the centuries, will be
recovered from the base of a bare-breasted bronze Tārā and ably translated.

We know the sad history though. Two years after Professor Kosambi
wrote his account, Chinese soldiers moved artillery into Lhasa, the Dalai
Lama fled, and the People's Army set out on a savage wrecking spree which
may not yet be over. Statues were destroyed or melted down for bullion;
others were hustled away at great personal risk by Tibetans and secured in
remote caves. Tibet's "modern archaeology" seems no closer than it did in
1957. When it does come, if it does, archaeologists and scientists will need
to work alongside knowledgeable lamas who can preside over any excava-
tions, recording of lost texts, and subsequent resealing of holy images and
stupas.

Lady Śīlābhaṭṭārikā's Poem

Six short poems, distributed through several anthologies, bear the name of
Śīlābhaṭṭārikā, who most likely lived in the ninth century. Whatever else
she wrote has been lost. Her best-known poem is of a quick, almost unen-
durable beauty. If one believes Śīlā to have written it from direct personal
experience, she would have lived as a young woman in one of the villages
or towns along the Narmada River, close to the Vindhya mountain range
in western India. Her poem occurs in at least two versions; this is the one
from a fourteenth-century anthology, the *Paddhati* of Śārngadhara:

> Nights of jasmine and thunder,
> torn petals,
> wind in the tangled *kadamba* trees—
> nothing has changed.
> Spring comes again and we've
> simply grown older.
> In the cane groves of Narmada River
> he deflowered my
> girlhood before we were
> married.
> And I grieve for those faraway nights
> we played at love
> by the water.

According to ancient and modern critics, this version has a flaw.
Poetic convention does not permit the *mālāti,* a jasmine, to bloom in
Caitra, the lunar month of March-April, or spring. If Śīlābhaṭṭārikā got
the botany wrong, the critics' complaints would be a sound eco-critique of
her best poem.

Did Śīlābhaṭṭārikā herself make this mistake? Or could her poem,
going into the *Paddhati* five hundred years after she wrote it, have been
rewritten by someone unfamiliar with poetic convention or botanical
detail? Śīlā certainly recalls the *mālāti* blooming—blooming that season she
made love all night on the riverbank as a girl. But having aged, has she
confused the lunar month of Caitra with another? Mislocated the event?

Sanskrit's enormous vocabulary is full of words with complex over-
tones or several related but distinct meanings woven into one another.
Because the meanings are sometimes linked by something as subtle as a
fragrance, no word-by-word translation can hope to catch the *rasa,* the
mood or flavor, of a good verse. I find several early lexicographers give

mālati the additional meaning of "virgin." The scent of jasmine, the newly opened flower releasing its fragrance. Without denying the botanical fact, the image could stand for the poet herself in those faraway nights of Caitra.

The other version is from Vidyākara's anthology:

> The one who deflowered me
> is still my lover
> the moondrenched nights haven't changed.
> Scent from the newly
> bloomed *mālati*
> blows in from the Vindhya hills
> and the girl is still me.
> But her heart?
> It grieves for those nights
> we stole off and made love forever
> in the riverside cane.

Having gone deep into the jasmine-scented darkness, deep into the dictionary, deep into the poet's rhythm (set in a meter provocatively called *śārdūla-vikrīḍitā*, "tiger's play"), both poems grip me. Which would you give up: the moondrenched nights (*candra-garba-niśa*) or the breeze scented with torn *kadamba* blossoms (*kadamba-anilaḥ*)? If you could have only one, which would it be: the Vindhya Mountains or the Narmada River?

The Sanskrit short poem is a compressed moment of bedrock human emotion set into a briefly and accurately sketched landscape. Sīlā's temperament and training would have required a strict economy of language to reach that conjunction. Perhaps to write both mountains and river into a single poem was not in the Sanskrit grain. But the wild fragrant nights, wind off the hills, flowering branches, and moonlight; the abandon with which a girl takes her first lover; the bittersweet recollections of a middle-aged woman looking back on it all—it seems hardly extravagant to make two separate poems. What does it matter the critics consider one a bit ragged?

Nature Sentinels

From *Kavikaṇṭhābharaṇam*, a twelfth-century verse treatise on poetic training by Ksemendra, comes this good counsel:

> With his own
> eyes a poet
> observes the shape of a leaf.

He knows how to make
people laugh
and studies the nature of each living thing.
The features of ocean and mountain,
the motion of sun, moon and stars.
His thoughts turn with the seasons.
He goes among
different peoples
learning their landscapes,
learning their languages.

There's no explicit scholarship to cite, but it is my own belief that the way the Sanskrit poets continually and accurately named their trees, creepers, rivers, mountain ranges, and weather patterns reveals an archaic, "preliterate" habit of language. Recurring in endless variants, phrases like "newly opened jasmine," "black clouds mount the horizon," or "wind from the Vindhya mountains" did not originate as descriptions of nature, but were active spells set loose to summon the particular spirit controlling the event. The poetic handbooks of India, which were carefully consulted— their exacting rules cover not only grammar and metrics but also natural history—have similar roots in the customs of people who hunt and garden. They keep watch over the local calendar: animal migration and fertility, plant growth, weather cycles, river floodings.

The composers of the Vedic hymns (c. 1700 B.C.E.) bequeathed to India a treasury of ritual verse that summons the forces of a dramatic wilderness: thunder, wind, boiling clouds, sky-rending bolts of lightning, a mysterious female forest spirit, even frogs. We know those early *Ṛṣis,* or poet-priests, were specialists who compelled local spirits by ritual use of plants, animal products, and fire. After a lapse of two thousand years, the poets of classical Sanskrit took up the old energies and redirected them, bringing the poem to focus specifically on human affairs and old erotic imperatives. The archaic grain was not lost: the innovation was simply to lay patterns of human life across the earlier mythic orders.

From this perspective, most collections of classical Sanskrit poetry can be seen as ritual accounts of the Indian year. The short poems come down to us in anthologies ranging from collections of one hundred lyrics to over four thousand. A quick glance shows how often the anthologists ordered their books into seasonal and diurnal cycles, and patterned both alongside or on top of the rounds of human life: erotic, social, or simply biological. One can therefore read the anthologies as almanacs. The habits of animals, the tree groves, the seasonally flooding rivers, clouds bulking over the mountains, the fragrant blossoms—as in so much old poetry, these are the good companions, spirit guides on the human journey.

And the task of the poem? One of the oldest. To bring humans into right relation with denizens of the plant, animal, or geologic kingdoms. Some of these creatures took up lodging in the Sanskrit poem, others went into sculpture, architecture, painting, folklore, and the varied range of Hindu and Buddhist texts. A popular term applied to them was *lokāpala,* "place guardian," protective figures that formally watch over the eight directions or the neighborhood holy places: a temple door, a clear little runnel dropping out of the forest, a hillside grotto, the meadow at a bend in the river. Local and cosmological, they are "world guardians," sentinels of place.

What the Sanskrit poets accomplished was to secularize these sentinels and then to regard them with the naturalist's careful eye. It gives their writings a precise sense of ecology that seems nearly contemporary. Perhaps Ksemendra, Śīlābhaṭṭārikā, and their comrades—their writings scattered through fragmentary old manuscripts—can offer a few useful models as North Americans develop a poetry both cosmopolitan and minutely adapted to our own terrain. A poetry of romance, stout friendship, the sharp unforgettable image, the easy native wit. But also bristling with residents of our own ecosystems: cacti and piñon trees, granite outcroppings, migratory songbirds, the hardy native flowers of our upland meadows.

Won't the poets of old India clap their hands when they hear of it.

"Black swollen clouds"

Black swollen clouds
drench the far
forests with rain.
Scarlet *kadamba* petals toss on the storm.
In the foothills peacocks cry out
and make love and none of it
touches me.
It's when the lightning
flings her bright
veils like a rival woman—
a flood of
grief surges through.

Vidyā (c. seventh to eighth century)

Translated by Andrew Schelling

"The red fleshlike filament"

The red fleshlike filament
concealed in the
half-budded *kimśuka* flower—
faint crescent moon—
reminds me of
the love god's bow,
before he lifts it from its
      polished lacquer case.

                Vidyā (c. seventh to eighth century)

                Translated by Andrew Schelling

"A difficult journey"

A difficult journey
but he's returned.
Tears, unsteady eyes—
she steps from the house to gaze at his face.
Then lifts a mouthful of palm leaf and thorn
to his camel,
with her skirt
wipes the desert dust
from its mane.

Keśata, collected second century

Translated by Andrew Schelling

"Impenetrable clouds in the night"

Impenetrable clouds in the night,
deep constant rains
of the monsoon.
Pumpkin vines twisting
over the little hut's firmly thatched roof.
Who could be luckier?
Half asleep in the darkness
murmur of thunder and rain in his ears,
and a woman
tangled up in his arms
warm breasts against him.

Anonymous, collected early twelfth century

Translated by Andrew Schelling

"Hard rain"

Hard rain
then soft wind,
a sky smoking with clouds.
Flashes of lightning
stroke a horizon
that's there and then not there.
Moon and stars vanished,
fragrant wet flowers,
darkness creaking with frogs.
And a solitary traveler?
Can he get
through the night?

Yogeśvara (c. 850–900)

Translated by Andrew Schelling

"Calamity came to our region"

Calamity came to our region
with the cruel district
overlord.
Villages emptied.
A few ruined families
cling to degenerate homesteads.
Not a live blade of grass.
Not an uncrumbled wall.
But a mongoose pokes through the rubble.
And back in the trees
white pigeons are chattering.
They manage
to live without sorrow.

Anonymous, collected early twelfth century

Translated by Andrew Schelling

J.P. SEATON

Once More, on the Empty Mountain

AS YOU MAY BE ABLE TO GUESS from the title of this essay, I'm going to spend some time talking about Wang Wei's famous poem, perhaps his most famous: "Deer Park," known familiarly among its thousands of English-speaking admirers as "the empty mountain poem." You can, by my count, find twenty-one versions of the poem, including authoritative treatments by Burton Watson and Gary Snyder in Eliot Weinberger's *Nineteen Ways of Looking at Wang Wei,* plus an essay on Wang Wei by Octavio Paz. Since Weinberger's book first appeared, Arthur Sze and Willis and Tony Barnstone, with Xu Haixin, have also published notable versions.

In the face of this seeming surfeit of translations (several of which are excellent), I am going to dare to offer a new reading of the poem, one that attempts to take into account kinds of polysemy that only the Chinese written character can offer the poet—and his readers. Simply put, I'll try to show how Wang Wei uses the nature of his writing system to reinforce and deepen the experience offered in the poem. In order to do that, I have to talk briefly about the characters themselves.

Most English-speaking readers may not know Chinese, or much about it, but even many contemporary Chinese readers may find the approach I'm going to take a new one. Ezra Pound struggled to find something like it in his *The Chinese Written Character as a Medium for Poetry,* but failed because he knew, through the notes of Ernest Fenollosa, too little (a little knowledge—a dangerous thing, indeed). The French semioticist François Cheng certainly understands this approach, but beyond four short examples in his *Chinese Poetic Writing*—including the brilliant explication of a line from another quatrain by Wang Wei—he was sparing in his use of it. I'll give it full play here, attempting to point out in this well-known poem the places where the special attributes of the Chinese writing system contribute to the possibility of multiple and intertwining meanings for characters, lines, and the poem as a whole. The ease with which the characters now can be introduced into text, using the several excellent and relatively new Chinese word-processing systems, will make this sort of analysis more common in the future. Until very recently, none but the wealthiest of university presses could absorb the cost in money and time (for shipping to and from Hong Kong or Taiwan) of bilingual printing.

Before I begin my analysis, here is an extremely brief introduction for readers who don't know anything about the Chinese written character as a medium for poetry.

Three types of Chinese characters constitute more than ninety-nine percent of the writing system. The first type is the pictograph. The characters listed below are in a printed form that mimics the handwritten script that was stylized and standardized about twenty-two hundred years ago. From left to right, the characters below are "sun," "moon," "tree," "human being," "female," "child" (or—fine joke—"philosopher"), "ear," "eye," "mountain," and "gate."

日 月 木 人 女 子 耳 目 山 門

I suspect that for many readers, most if not all of these characters are, even in modern printed form, visually suggestive of the things that they are the words for. If, given the squared-off shapes of modern print, that seems a shaky position, you might note that all educated Chinese in Wang Wei's time, and most today, are also familiar with the less stylized, more clearly representational, older versions of the characters that were preserved in the scripts used both in the *chop* (personal seal) and in ceremonial and decorative calligraphy. This understanding of the printed form was reinforced, when necessary, by knowledge of the older forms.

Several hundred pictographs are commonly used in the written language, and more than a few of them are quite beautiful, even in their printed forms; but I've had to keep the examples to a minimum here and therefore have chosen ones, as you'll soon see, for reasons having to do with Wang Wei's poem.

The second major type of character, the ideograph, has two subgroups: the simple and the complex. Below are five simple ideographs: the numbers one, two, and three; and two words that can be interpreted, by extension, from "up" and "down" to "on" and "under;" "up from" or "up to" and "down from" or "down to;" and "superior" and "inferior."

一 二 三 上 下

As you might imagine, there are relatively few simple ideographs: it is very hard to draw an elegant image to suggest an abstraction or the action inherent in a verb. Below are examples of the type called compound ideographs, whose invention extended the writing system beyond the pictographic. The compound ideograph attempts to communicate an idea by parataxis: pointing toward meaning by juxtaposing visual images. Parataxis, important to character construction, is also a major structural feature of Chinese lyric poetry.

林 森 明 旦 好 仁 聞 曰

Beginning from the left in the line above, a character made up of two trees together (in the same square space on the page allotted by the writing system to every character, no matter how complex or how simple) make a "grove," and three a "forest." Sun and moon together mean not a full day (as bright students often suggest), but "brightness." Sun above the line of the horizon means "dawn" rather than "dusk." Woman and child together make a wonderfully earthy and fundamental word for "good," while a human (restylized for the sake of combination) standing beside the number two makes a nice abstraction: Confucius's "compassion" or "benevolence." An ear and a gate mean "to hear." The last character looks a lot like that for "sun," but notice that the horizontals are longer and the verticals shorter. It is a juxtaposition of tongue and mouth and means "to speak"—the verb in all those famous "the master says" passages in the Chinese classics.

Pictographs and ideographs of both types together comprise fifteen percent of the nearly fifty thousand characters included in the largest Chinese dictionaries. The earliest types of characters invented, they name the most obvious and important nouns and verbs of human life, and thus they often occupy a much higher percentage of a given text than one would expect, particularly in poetry. The third type of character, the phonetic-signific compound, is also important, if not quite as important as its numerical preponderance would seem to predict, and in fact has something very interesting to offer the poet.

As the name implies, the phonetic-signific compound gives some indication of both pronunciation (something that pictographs and ideographs do only arbitrarily) and meaning. Its sound-carrying elements can appear independently, as characters with meanings of their own, but in compound characters they merely indicate approximate pronunciation. The signifying elements are generally weak or nonspecific. The three characters below illustrate some of the range of information offered in a standard phonetic-signific compound.

Po (柏) consists of a tree element and an element that means "white." If it meant "white birch," anyone who knew the meaning of the two elements would recognize it as a compound ideograph, but it means "cypress," and since cypress trees are not white, we can tell that the character is a phonetic-signific: a word for a tree whose name is pronounced "po."

K'u (枯) is among a large number of the type of character that indicates that the people who originally created them were thinking to provide as many mnemonics as possible for their creations. Its signific, "tree," is very general, but its phonetic, *gu* (古), meaning "ancient," combines with "tree" in the manner of an ideograph: "tree" and "ancient" nicely suggest the character's basic meaning, "withered." Thus we end up with a word that is pronounced "ku" and means "withered" and has a supporting mnemonic: a juxtaposition of "ancient" and "tree."

Obviously, the phonetic-significs offer a great number of suggestive images for the poet, but the student of Chinese must be warned that a phonetic-signific may be the equivalent of the false cognate of French or Spanish—a slippery character that can easily humiliate the unwary translator. Pound liked to claim that his Parisian artist friends could sight-read Chinese characters: we can only shudder to think of what Gaudier-Brzeska might have made of *li* (瀉). It consists of a yak, an evil spirit or bogey, and three dots that represent the character for "water," simplified to function as an element of a complex character. A wet yak? The evil bogey of the waters? Neither, since it's not an ideograph, but rather a phonetic-signific—a weak one—pronounced "li" and having to do with water in that it means "drip." Without a context that clearly calls for the interpretation of phonetic elements according to their meaning, such interpretation is likely to leave the translator looking drippy. But with a context—where every possible signing element is being put to use to create a truly organic work of art—that may be another matter.

And now, language lesson done, let's turn to something that I hope is not, in Monty Python's immortal words, "completely different."

Wang Wei's "Deer Park," written in rows and from left to right, reads:

空 山 不 見 人

但 聞 人 語 響

返 影 入 深 林

復 照 青 苔 上

You'll immediately notice that you already know several of the characters in the poem, and if you look closely you'll see that you can also recognize pictographic elements within several others (which must therefore be either ideographs or phonetic-signific compounds). A word-for-word translation goes as follows (a colon denotes the meaning of a given character, and a slash marks the caesura):

Empty: Mountain: / Not: See: Human
But (only): Hear / Human: Language (spoken word): Sound (Echo)
Return: Sun or shadow: / Enter: Deep: Grove
Again: Shine on or reflect on or from: / *ch'ing:* Moss or lichen:
    On or up

To get a working prose version of the poem, we have to begin with the understanding that it is a convention of most forms of Chinese lyric poetry that the poem is written by the poet in his own voice, not in a persona, and that for reasons of economy and humility, the first-person pronoun is most often left out. Thus, the first line is not "The empty mountain doesn't see anyone," but rather "I, *on* empty mountain, don't see humans" or "Empty mountain: (I) don't see humans." The construction is paratactical rather than grammatical: that is to say, the mountain, as a topic, is simply juxtaposed to not seeing humans; no grammatical connective is present, and the subject of the sentence is, by convention, left out. With line one properly read, line two is straightforward and easy to understand:

Empty mountain: I don't see humans,
but I hear human language echo.

The ambiguity of the beginning of line three ("Return: Sun or shadow") is actually productive only of a truism: when light returns, shadows do too. There may be here an allusion to T'ao Ch'ien or to a *locus classicus,* one or another of Chuang Tzu's several playings with form and shadow, but for our purpose, we can let that question lie. The rest of the line certainly seems very straightforward: the subject (light or shadow) enters deep into the grove. It seems worth noting that the central characters in the lines of the central couplet—"human" (人) in line two and "enter" (入) in line three—are mirror images of each other, particularly when you consider the role of reflection and echo in the poem and of reflected images in Buddhist poetry in general. Failing to find a way to reflect this flourish in the translation, I can only offer the following to bring us to the end of the third line:

Empty mountain: I don't see humans,
but I hear human language echo.
Returning sun enters, deep, the grove

    The final line of the poem appears straightforward too, at first. The subject derives, clearly, from the preceding line. The returning sun again shines on, or reflects back from, the moss or lichen, which is *ch'ing. Ch'ing* is a color term with multiple denotations. It can be any color in the blue-green range of the spectrum, and in poetry it is usually used in the description of mountain scenery and is associated with colors ranging from bright blues and greens to their most muted tones, including black and the "color" of clear water in motion. In other contexts, it may also refer to the brilliant green of spring foliage: a metaphor for youth—the *ch'ing nien* (green years). Thus, though we might look to the color term to help us decide whether the penultimate character in the last line denotes moss or lichen, we actually get no help. The outline of the picture is clear: the poet (and by now his reader) is in a deep grove when a shaft of sunlight reenters the grove (at dawn or, following the usual Buddhist interpretation, at dusk). In either case, when the sun appears briefly below the line of the canopy of the grove, it casts slanting rays around and between the trunks of trees onto the moss or lichen, which is the only thing that will grow in the deep shade. Maybe only those who have seen late light on a tuft of moss know how vibrantly alive a green can be: sunlit gray lichen or reindeer moss is more sun than green.
    And does the sun shine "in and on," or "on and up from"? Logically, it has to shine in before it shines on, and then, of course, it reflects up from, into your eyes, and thence where? Notice that we hear the voice in line two only as an echo. (I wonder if that's actually possible?) The poem, beginning in the perhaps tranquilizingly vague permanence of the mountain, has come, riding its shaft of light, to rest on a little patch of lichen or moss. But it hasn't gone straight there, nor has it stopped when it's arrived.
    Zen teaches by pointing. Broad and flat on top and sharply pointed in the last line, Wang Wei's "Deer Park" is the point of an arrow. Vague, even unknowable, the mountain of permanence is an abstraction. There is no humanity in the flat top of the triangular form of the poem. When the poem narrows, you can hear human speech there, if only as an echo of itself, recognizable as language, but saying nothing. When enlightenment finds the deep grove, it comes as the sun strikes the simplest concrete thing: a single spot of life.
    However many times and in however many different versions you've seen this poem before, I hope what I've done will give you some indication

of the audacity of its translators. That the best of them have largely suc-
ceeded in the impossible is attested to by the popularity of the piece in
English, and by the thoughtful readings that it has been given by those
who have only read it in English.

Furthermore, the poet has a few other tricks up his sleeve. The word
for "echo," at the end of line two, consists of two elements: underneath, a
musical tone (anciently, "a man singing," 音); and on top, "countryside"
(鄉), a word with extremely positive connotations in Chinese. The char-
acter is a phonetic-signific, with the countryside element providing the
pronunciation. Yet when we read the character as if it were an ideograph,
we gain a connotative level of meaning. The echo of language is not heard
well enough to carry even the illusion of meaning, but for Wang Wei it
was a positive element. With a little humility, humans may hear their own
tongues on the level of birdsong: as simple notes in the complex music of
the outdoors.

The first character in the last line, the adverb for a repetition, is also
the name of hexagram number twenty-four in the Confucian classic the *I
Ching*. The fact that the characters are independent of sound means that
they can maintain their meanings even as change takes place in the spoken
language. Wang Wei lived a thousand years or more after the text of the *I
Ching* had taken form, but though he certainly used the character we now
pronounce "fu" to mean "again," he was also unquestionably very familiar
with the *I Ching* interpretation. The meaning of hexagram twenty-four is a
central one in Taoism and in traditional Chinese culture as a whole, where
it is part of the term *fu gu,* often wrongly translated by Western historians
and interpreters of Chinese culture as "going back to the ways of the
Ancients." Actually, it means something like "starting over," "from the
beginning," or simply "beginning again." Zen mind: beginner's mind?

All of this might seem off the point of the poem, except for the fact
that hexagram twenty-four

復

consists of five *yin* lines (dark, wet like moss or, even better, like lichen deep in a grove) being revisited, in the sixth place (by convention, the bottom of the hexagram is where a new line enters, bringing about change), by the *yang* line, which the poet presents embodied as sunlight. The picture this line of the poem paints is of a shaft of light reentering a grove, and the sun (*yang*) coming again into the place of *yin*, to begin again in a flash that is enlightening but not blinding—the rebirth of the simplicity that builds toward the complexity of the world. Through the use of an allusion, the Zen of the poem is to be found in a Confucian classic.

And one last little flourish from the poet: the first word in line two of the poem (㥯) is not an ideograph, but a phonetic-signific, and a weak one at that. It means "but" or "only" and is pronounced "tan," like its phonetic element, the character for "dawn" I cited in the language lesson. But what do we see when we look as closely at the character as we have been directed by the poet to look at the lichen? We see a man standing beside a sun on the horizon—at dawn or at dusk, at the time when we are reminded of the cycles of nature, of ending and of beginning again, the time when the rays of the sun penetrate the grove to alight upon the moist plants on the ground. Then we look again and see a man speaking of the *yang* line, or of the One all mystics speak of. *Fu* and *tan* are, in Chinese, what are called "empty words"; they are the only purely grammatical words in the poem. Through the use of classical allusion and visual play, Wang Wei has managed to fill both of them.

Wang Wei was an aristocrat. He knew his classics by heart. In a waning age (high T'ang was about to take a terrible fall from which it would never recover), he was a patron of a new way of approaching the problem of suffering in the world of humankind. A follower of Zen, he speaks here not just to converts like himself, but also to confirmed Confucians, men of his own class. It is a new light that enters, he says, but it is an old grove into which it comes. His poem says something we may have already known: it is time to begin again, anew, at the beginning. Always.

That this poem's structure and imagery alone, without allusion and deep wordplay, are sufficient to carry its meaning to the modern world through the medium of sensitive and talented translators is only the *most* obvious of the miracles of Wang Wei's art.

Leaving It to You

Self evident, truth mistakes no thing.
But my heart's a long way from there
and no thing's clear to me.
Yellow gold is almost all burned up
by my desire: white hair grows beside the fire.
Bitter indecision, choose This, or maybe That:
even spirit speaks in riddles,
and makes it hard to harvest
the essence of a single day.
Catch the wind, while you tether the shadows.
Faith, or a man who'll stand by his word, is all
there is, there is no disputing.

Kuan Hsiu (832–912)

Translated by J.P. Seaton

Bad Government

Sleet and rain, as if the pot were boiling.
Winds whack like the crack of an ax.
An old man, an old old man,
toward sunset crept into my hut.
He sighed, sighed he, as if to himself,
"These rulers, so cruel: why, tell me
why they must steal till we starve,
and then slice off the skin from our bones?
For a song from some beauty
they'll go back on sworn words;
for a song from some tart,
they'll tear our huts down...
for a song, for a sweet song or two,
they'll slaughter ten thousand like me, or
like you. You can cry as you will, let
your hair turn pure white,
let your whole clan go hungry...
no good wind will blow
no gentle breeze
begin again.
Lord Locust Plague, and Baron Bandit Bug,
one East, one West, one North, one South,
We're surrounded."

Kuan Hsiu (832–912)

Translated by J.P. Seaton

Dog Days

Empty mountain dog day door shut dwelling
Gown's light gauze: I drip with sweat
Yet I bless this burning wind: it shrivels visitors
Long as there's sun, at least,
I'll get some writing done.

Yuan Mei (1716–1798)

Translated by J.P. Seaton

At "Be Careful Bank"

Dangerous bank
           hard to get over
Careful indeed
           we help each other up
Might we, on flat ground too
Go on as we do
           when we're here?

Yuan Mei (1716–1798)

Translated by J.P. Seaton

Night Thoughts

Midnight, sudden jerk
Awake.
Wordless, heart still, sighs
Tonight the frost's first fall
That's all, and I
Forgot to cover the houseplants.

Yuan Mei (1716–1798)

Translated by J.P. Seaton

"When the clouds come"

When the clouds come the mountain ontologically dismanifests
When they go, I guess, it exhibits phenomenological
Mountain-ness.
Do you suppose
The mountain knows?

Yuan Mei (1716–1798)

Translated by J.P. Seaton

ERIC SELLAND

And Then the Whole Was Flooded with Light: Hiroya Takagai Translated

Art seems...to be the silence of the world.
Maurice Blanchot

The pure work implies the disappearance of the
poet as speaker, yielding his initiative to words.
Stéphane Mallarmé

Word becomes thing, and thing becomes word.
This is the central characteristic of poetry today,
and it is the most basic function of language.
Hiroya Takagai

WE BEGIN WITH MALLARMÉ, with the originary silence behind language—the emptiness of the word; the abyss of meaning. Language, or writing, as an open wound. It is not possible to speak of translation outside the context of poetics. It must confront the poetics of the original, the text under examination (or exhumation). Even translation itself is a poetics.

There is a paradox at work that involves entering into a total intimacy with the poem, entering into its space, and yet encountering an otherness that brings meaning into question; this comes from the fact that the original word and its associations must be broken open, initially lost, and then recreated in a different form. Many meanings and associations present in languages that differ radically from each other simply cannot be brought across. They can be explained, but then the poetry is lost.

Being absorbed in the work is like being absorbed into a painting, or a piece of music. This comes out of the experience of poetry itself and its making, which is perhaps itself a form of translation. The poem is like a form of prayer or meditation, in which God is experienced as being at once totally other and yet more inward than inward.

> The sound out of silence of language speaking.
> The poem speaks to me out of this silence.

> Spearheads
>
> The buoyant particles of grass separate, and connect
>
> Packets of white flesh
>
> [Binding the hems, the flames of the <hidden interiors>
> join, trembling
>
> (They call)
>
> Binding, the hems are shaken and returned to the
> <exterior>]

Of course, one could make the decision to decontextualize the poem from its original root for one's own poetic purposes, but in doing so one must be completely conscious of what is happening in language and the poem. To produce a translation that may be accurate according to the dictionary, but bland and distant from the spirit of the poem because one has either ignored or misunderstood the author's poetics is not at all the same thing as performing a translation from the viewpoint of a radical poetics or creating a version. There is no correct or incorrect way of translating a poem. Translation is not a means of testing foreign-language skills. Translation is a total engagement with language and identity. It is an important and essential part of the production of literature.

Who speaks in the poem, in Hiroya Takagai's poem? Language speaks.

> *If only the poem dwells, it dwells in this suspension, almost in levitation in a space it does not create but that it nonetheless makes come, that it calls to come.*
>
> Marc Froment-Meurice,
> *That Is to Say: Heidegger's Poetics*

Tilting, there is a young branch,

And there are stems,

(The child which becomes a circle, and feeds
        on its own parent)

[Tree which becomes disentangled]

(A <collar> is dropped from the hem's tip)

Dark ring

Earth's ear breaks open

These poems from *Rush Mats* present a series of discrete signs that form a complex of archetypes—fundamental blocks representing bits and pieces of memory, sense experience, the actual and the dreamed—that themselves form a kind of body or "inner weave," as well as an invisible bridge between the personal and the communal.

The importance of the function of empty space should not be ignored here. Behind each of these sparse sections of text—and behind each line and each word—there is a gap where emptiness and silence lie still in their pure echo. This emptiness, this silence, is the sound of memory.

We must allow silence to speak, to incorporate silence into the translation. For this reason, spacing and usage of graphic markings and punctuation are very important. Is the silence a framing mechanism, or is it the text that frames silence?

The word *translation* means "transfer": to pass over or to be passed over. In usage up until the twelfth century or so, it referred primarily to a holy person being transported instantly to heaven without death, or to the body of a saint being disinterred and buried elsewhere. In "The Task of the Translator," Walter Benjamin speaks of the afterlife of a work.

Translation involves value judgments—a whole complex of cultural, personal, and poetic assumptions. It is not, and cannot be, a transparent process. There is too much at stake. If translation were so simple, it would not be generating so much discussion in contemporary intellectual circles.

Finally, translation is, essentially, an engagement with the poem. It is a reading. So we speak here more of how one person has read the poems of Hiroya Takagai—rather than of translation in general.

The walls of the house

The sliding partitions

([The going around] of things that do not
    move   things that move, a lost child)

Screen of a solid color

Behind a stone, cramped and twisted

Many of the poems in this collection, which should perhaps be retitled *The Inner Weave* (*Shiki-i*, the original title, refers to the underside or inner part of the *tatami*), present a problem for English because they form a kind of stasis. In the poem above, entitled "The Condition of Movement" in translation, hardly any movement occurs at all: most of the poem is made up of noun phrases. Some translators might try adding more verbs or explanatory phrases to evoke more of the associations inherent in the original. For myself, I would prefer to leave the English more "troubled," somewhat more floating and off-kilter, so that it carries the strangeness that is in the original, and allow the reader to create a picture in her own mind, without the need for extraneous explanation. Perhaps it might also help to retitle the translation "Movement and Quietude" or "Movement and Rest," to match more exactly the original, which, though its dictionary meaning is "conditions" or "the condition of things," is made up of two characters whose literal meaning is "movement-quiet."

This collection, made up of real and imagined childhood memories placed within a traditional Japanese architecture, presents a series of archetypal opposites, such as "interior" and "exterior," and an odd collection of ambiguous identities—a child that is both human and insect, an "adopted orphan" whose other reading is a "nest of boxes." In the translation of such a text, the pull of the other language interrupts our own identities, and in a sense liberates our true selves when the new language is liberated and emerges from the original text.

But why a foreign poet in speaking of Takagai? Because Takagai himself alludes to Mallarmé's "throw of the dice" in speaking of his own poetics, and it is the cultural paradox of the Japanese that it is often precisely those points at which they seem to us to have become "Westernized" that they are the most themselves, most Japanese. This paradox of identity runs straight through the process of translation and, indeed, the process of original poetic production itself.

> *Why does poetry raise the human to a higher spiritual plane? The key may be in the spirit of word and the spirit of thing. Never quite reaching the light, perhaps we move closer to the sky on distant steps whispering from within the word spirit— thing spirit and silence.*

—Hiroya Takagai

There is nothing but translation, "that is to say that saying means translating" (Froment-Meurice).

There is something in the very nature of language itself, and in the nature of poetry, that calls out for translation and retranslation—not simply on the level of communication between peoples of different nations for practical purposes. It is rather something in the said, where the nature of the human asks that it be told and retold again. Walter Benjamin felt that it was in the nature of certain works that they be translated: that within them, as a part of their inner structure, resided not only the possibility, but also the necessity of translation into a language with which, somehow, they were already in relation, and through which they could truly attain their own being and identity.

One finds this calling in many Japanese works, despite the linguistic and cultural distance from English. Perhaps it is the very absence of a historical or linguistic relationship that calls. It is often the more difficult works that call out to us, and challenge us to an engagement in translation (from within translation). This is because they insist that we enter that much more deeply into the very root of poetry, and of language itself, where we are required less to perform some mechanical act of transference than to return to the originary act of saying and to the process of the poem. The poem, whose existence from the very beginning was something somewhat ephemeral, must in this way be reborn. A simple, surface act—that of linguistic transference—is in a sense an impossibility. The poem, the writer-translator, and language must give themselves over to the experience of death and transfiguration, in which new life appears.

We must begin talking again. This speech out of lack.

Chicken Coop

Raising up fire

The case a shell within a shell, from both of its sleeves to the opposite side
Touch it

Sauntering along, swinging the fire

A dry wind

Scantlings at the wall shake,

(Reclining there is a thin desolate field of railroad ties)

The sun

[Brandishing a pole, the skin, looking at the fire outside]

Spearheads which gather

Book covers which couple

(The lost child moving along the road)

Twisting a rope in the sand

Gathering fire

Hiroya Takagai (b. 1961)

Translated by Eric Selland

Hidden Marsh

Carp in the branches

Sky

(Opening their mouths, they are trying to catch them from behind the leaves)

Left at the edge, still out to dry
The white, dried fish

Twisted, corpse of flower
Begins to unravel

Begins to rot fallen tree

[Water hollow]

Fished, transparent boat

Below the edge, scales fallen everywhere

Hiroya Takagai (b. 1961)

Translated by Eric Selland

Neck of the Bamboo Pole

At the mouth of the split,

the dried bamboo hangs suspended

[The interior's

Eaves

(From the mouth, rotten twigs spring up

As if to mend

A sapling

Ear of growth

In the garden a child of the fields chewing, silkworms scattered,

Mulberry and the youngest child)

Shaking the white pendulum the interior of the bamboo pole

A child is being shaken]

Hiroya Takagai (b. 1961)

Translated by Eric Selland

GARY SNYDER

Reflections on My Translations of the T'ang Poet Han-shan

A TRULY APT TRANSLATION OF A POEM may require an effort of imagination almost as great as the making of the original. The translator who wishes to enter the creative territory must make an intellectual and imaginative jump into the mind and world of the poet, and no dictionary will make this easier.

In working with the poems of Han-shan, I have several times had a powerful sense of apprehending auras of nonverbal meaning and experiencing the poet's own mind-of-composition. That this should happen is not altogether odd, for although Han-shan is intense, the range of his sensibility is not as strongly tied to Chinese cultural and historical phenomena as the sensibility of Po Chü-i, Tu Fu, or Tu Mu. Also, the purely physical side of the Han-shan world—the imagery of cold, height, isolation, mountains—is still available to our contemporary experience: I have spent much time in the mountains, and feel at home in the archetypal land of Han-shan. It would be well-nigh impossible to feel similarly at home with the concubines, summer palaces, or battlefields of much of Chinese poetry.

Part of my translation effort was an almost physical recall of the ponderosa and whitebark pine, granite cliffs, and frozen summer lakes of my own Sierra Nevada experience. The mountain imagery in my translation can be taken as an analog (a "translation") of the lower, wetter, greener mountains of southern China. My initial blocking-out was done in the fall of 1955 in a graduate seminar in T'ang poetics at the University of California, Berkeley. The instructor was Chen Shih-hsiang. As I wrote elsewhere, "Chen was a friend and a teacher. His knowledge and love of poetry and his taste for life were enormous. He quoted French poetry from memory and wrote virtually any Chinese poem of the T'ang or Sung canon from memory on the blackboard." I had just returned from a summer working as a trail-crew laborer in the northern Yosemite backcountry, which attuned me to working with a "mountain poet."

As the poem here makes adequately clear, though, Han-shan was not exactly a "nature poet." He was a person who left his old self behind to walk in the world of *jijimuge* ("fact-fact-no-obstruction"), which is, in the philosophy of Avatamsaka (Hua-yen) and in the practice of Zen, just this very world. The recurrent image of Cold Mountain and its roughness is the narrow gate through which Han-shan tried to force his perception of a *whole* world, and this helps to explain his poetry's calm intensity.

In some ways, our contemporary idea of Han-shan is the creation of the Zen tradition and the Chinese delight in eccentrics. His poems are much loved in Japan, and formal Zen lectures are given on his work. The mountains and caves that are associated with him are still there: people visit them regularly. According to traditional scholarship, Han-shan lived from A.D. 627 to 650. The scholar Hu Shih places him circa A.D. 700 to 750.

> In a tangle of cliffs I chose a place—
> Bird-paths, but no trails for men.
> What's beyond the yard?
> White clouds clinging to vague rocks.
> Now I've lived here—how many years—
> Again and again, spring and winter pass.
> Go tell families with silverware and cars
> "What's the use of all that noise and money?"

"Men ask the way to Cold Mountain"

Men ask the way to Cold Mountain
Cold Mountain: there's no through trail.
In summer, ice doesn't melt
The rising sun blurs in swirling fog.
How did I make it?
My heart's not the same as yours.
If your heart was like mine
You'd get it and be right here.

Han-shan (627–650 or 700–750)

Translated by Gary Snyder

"Cold Mountain is a house"

Cold Mountain is a house
Without beams or walls.
The six doors left and right are open
The hall is blue sky.
The rooms all vacant and vague
The east wall beats on the west wall
At the center nothing.

Borrowers don't bother me
In the cold I build a little fire
When I'm hungry I boil up some greens.
I've got no use for the kulak
With his big barn and pasture—
He just sets up a prison for himself.
Once in he can't get out.
Think it over—
You know it might happen to you.

Han-shan (627–650 or 700–750)

Translated by Gary Snyder

"Clambering up the Cold Mountain path"

Clambering up the Cold Mountain path,
The Cold Mountain trail goes on and on:
The long gorge choked with scree and boulders,
The wide creek, the mist-blurred grass.
The moss is slippery, though there's been no rain
The pine sings, but there's no wind.
Who can leap the world's ties
And sit with me among the white clouds?

Han-shan (627–650 or 700–750)

Translated by Gary Snyder

"I settled at Cold Mountain long ago"

I settled at Cold Mountain long ago,
Already it seems like years and years.
Freely drifting, I prowl the woods and streams
And linger watching things themselves.
Men don't get this far into the mountains,
White clouds gather and billow.
Thin grass does for a mattress,
The blue sky makes a good quilt.
Happy with a stone underhead
Let heaven and earth go about their changes.

Han-shan (627–650 or 700–750)

Translated by Gary Snyder

ARTHUR SZE

Introduction to *The Silk Dragon: Translations from the Chinese*

THE TRANSLATION OF CHINESE POEMS INTO ENGLISH has always been a source of inspiration for my own evolution as a poet. In 1971, as a student at the University of California, Berkeley, I majored in poetry. Also studying Chinese language and literature, I became interested in translating the great T'ang dynasty poets—Li Po, Tu Fu, Wang Wei, among others—because I felt I could learn from them. I felt that by struggling with many of the great poems in the Chinese literary tradition, I could best develop my voice as a poet. Years later, in 1983, after publishing *Dazzled,* my third book of poetry, I translated a new group of Chinese poems, again feeling that it would help me discern greater possibilities for my own writing. I was drawn to the clarity of T'ao Ch'ien's lines, to the subtlety of Ma Chih-yüan's lyrics, and to Wen I-to's sustained, emotional power. In 1996, after completing my book *Archipelago,* I felt the need to translate yet another group of Chinese poems: I was particularly drawn to the Ch'an-influenced work of Pa-ta-shan-jen and to the extremely condensed and challenging, transformational poems of Li Ho and Li Shang-yin.

I know translation is an "impossible" task, and I have never forgotten the Italian phrase *traduttori/traditori:* "translators/traitors." Which translation does not in some way betray its original? In considering the process of my own translations, I am aware of loss and transformation, of destruction and renewal. Since I first started to write poetry, I have only translated poems that have deeply engaged me; and it has sometimes taken me many years to feel ready to work on one. I remember that in 1972 I read Li Shang-yin's untitled poems and felt baffled by them; now, more than twenty-five years later, his verses—veiled, mysterious, and full of longing—strike me as some of the great love poems in classical Chinese.

To show how I create a translation in English, I am going to share stages and drafts of a translation from one of Li Shang-yin's untitled poems. I like to begin by writing the Chinese characters out on paper. I know that my own writing of Chinese is awkward and rudimentary, but by writing out the characters in their particular stroke order I can begin to sense the inner motion of the poem in a way that I cannot by just reading the characters on the page. Once I've written out the characters, I look up each in Robert H. Mathews's *Chinese-English Dictionary* and write down the sound and tone along with a word, phrase, or cluster of words that helps mark its field of energy and meaning. I go through the entire poem doing this groundwork. After I have created this initial cluster of words, I go back through and, because a Chinese character can mean so many different things depending on its context, I remove words or phrases that appear to be inappropriate and keep those that appear to be relevant. In the case of Li Shang-yin's untitled poem, I now have a draft that looks like the illustration on the following page:

In looking at this regulated eight-line poem, I know that each of its seven-character lines has two predetermined caesuras, so that the motion in Chinese is 1–2 / 3–4 / 5–6–7. I try to catch the tonal flow and to sense the silences. I know that the tones from Mathews's dictionary only give me the barest approximation. T'ang-dynasty poems are most alive when they are chanted. The sounds are very different from the Mandarin dialect that I speak. Yet I can, for instance, guess that the sound of *tuan*[4], the first character in line six, is sharp and emphatic. I also sense that characters three and four in line six—*hsiao*[1] and *hsi*[2]—have an onomatopoeic quality to suggest ebb and flow. In double-checking this phrase in the dictionary, I realize it has the primary meaning of "news and information"; there is no news, and the speaker is in a state of heightened isolation. In looking at the visual configuration of the characters, I am again struck by the first character in line six, *tuan*[4]. Here the character contains the image of scissors cutting silk, and I wonder if this can be extended to develop an insight into the poem.

I proceed by writing a rough draft in English: trying to write eight lines in English that are equivalent to the eight lines in Chinese. I realize immediately that the translation is too cramped. I look back at the Chinese and decide to use *two* lines in English for each line of Chinese. I also decide to emphasize the second caesura of each line in Chinese so that in English there's a line break after the meaning of the fourth character in each line of the Chinese original.

I write out another draft in which sixteen lines in English now stand for the eight lines in Chinese. All of the lines in English are flush left, but the blocklike form does not do justice to the obliquely cutting motion of the poem. To open it up and clarify the architecture, I decide to indent all of the even-numbered lines. I go through another series of drafts, which

鳳 male phoenix feng4	尾 tail/s wei3	香 fragrant hsiang1	羅 gauze, thin silk lo2	薄 thin, slight po2	幾 how many chi3	重 layers, folds ch'ung2
碧 green jade pi4	文 elegant, refined wen2	圓 round yüan2	頂 the top ting3	夜 night yeh4	深 deep shen1	逢 meet with feng2
扇 fan shan4	裁 to cut ts'ai2	月 moon yüeh4	魄 form, shape p'o4	羞 shame, blush hsiu1	難 difficult nan2	掩 conceal yen3
車 carriage ch'e1	走 departs tsou3	雷 thunder lei2	聲 sound/s sheng1	語 word/s yü3	未 not yet wei4	通 get through t'ung1
曾 once, already ts'eng2	是 is shih4	寂 silent chi4	寥 empty liao2	金 gold chin1	燼 ashes, embers chin4	暗 dark, cloudy an4
斷 cut off tuan4	無 no, without wu2	消 —ebb and flow— hsiao1	息 hsi2	石 —pomegranate— shih2	榴 liu2	紅 red hung2
班 mottled pan1	騅 piebald horse chui1	只 only, but chih3	繫 tie, bind hsi4	垂 hang down ch'ui2	楊 —willow— yang2	柳 liu3
何 what, which ho2	處 place ch'u4	西 —southwest— hsi1	南 nan2	任 allow, confide in jen4	好 good hao3	風 wind feng1

oftentimes incorporate English words that I've listed on the page with Chinese characters, though I don't feel compelled to use all of them. At this transitional stage, I have something that looks like the version below (without any of the crossed-out or underlined words):

phoenix tails, fragrant silk,

┌folds

how many thin ~~layers~~.

under the ~~elegant~~ green round canopy

┌opens to

she ~~encounters~~ the deep night.

the fan cuts the moon's shape

┌ but   *┌ blush*

~~and~~ can't conceal her ~~shame~~.

a carriage goes, thunder sounds,

┌ didn't

the words ~~can't~~ get through.

a while in the ~~desolate~~ quiet

gold embers in the dark.

nothing now but   *┌ the ebb and flow of*

↳ ~~cut off, no word, who could be pouring~~

~~a measure of~~ red pomegranate wine?

a piebald horse is yet tied

┌ dangling

to a ~~trailing~~ willow.

┌from

and where is the place ~~in~~ the southwest

where the fine breeze can blow?

At this point, if there are books of Chinese translations that I think might be helpful, I look at them to see if they have any commentaries that are relevant. In François Cheng's *Chinese Poetic Writing* I find that lines one and two "describe the bedcurtain of a bridal chamber," that "to pluck a willow branch" means to visit a courtesan, that red pomegranate wine might be served at a wedding feast and connotes explosive desire, and that the southwest breeze alludes to a phrase by Ts'ao Chih (192–232), "I would become that southwest wind / waft all the way to your bosom." I find these comments insightful but do not want to incorporate them overtly into my translation. Because Li Shang-yin's great strength is his oblique exactitude, I want my translation to hint at these elements.

I now look at my very rough translation and go back to the original Chinese. My experience of the poem is that a solitary woman is lamenting the absence of her lover and longs for him even as she worries that he is unfaithful. I go back through my translation, cross out certain phrases, and substitute new phrases wherever they seem better. With the second line, I decide that it is more appropriate to have the silk in folds than in layers. In line three, the phrase "elegant green round canopy" is cumbersome; I decide the word "elegant" is too stated and should be removed. It's so hard in a contemporary poem to use an adjective like "elegant" and not cause a boomerang effect. I read on and decide that "encounters" is too neutral. To make the longing more overt, I change it to "opens to the deep night." In line six, I change "and" to "but" and substitute "blush" for "shame." I'm happy with this last change: the "blush" will help foreshadow the "red pomegranate wine" and also suggests the red of desire. In line eight, I change "can't" to "didn't," though I'm not sure this is better. In line nine, I mark with an *x* and double-underline the word "desolate." This word is another loaded adjective, but nothing comes to mind as a good replacement, so I mark it with an *x* to tell myself to come back to it. I am totally dissatisfied with line eleven and strike it out. I go back to the page with characters and reincorporate "ebb and flow." With line fourteen, I am uneasy about "trailing" and insert "dangling." Line fifteen strikes me as too wordy, but again nothing comes to mind, so I mark it with an *x* and a double-underline.

At this point, I put the translation away for a few weeks. I brood on it and, if some changes come to mind, I jot them down on the side. But I usually wait until I'm ready to revise with intensity and clarity. When I finally sit down and rework the translation, I decide that "the deep quiet" opens up the emotional space in a way that "the desolate quiet" can't. I decide to foreground the gold embers and make them a more active presence; the verb "scintillate" leaps into my mind. To suggest that red pomegranate wine connotes explosive desire, and to make the configuration of sounds more alive, I replace the static "a measure of red pomegranate wine" with the active "pulsing red pomegranate wine." I also decide to break the symmetry of the indented lines by further indenting the very last line; I think this heightens the cutting effect of the ending. You can see these significant changes incorporated into the final version:

UNTITLED (II) *by Li Shang-yin*

Phoenix tails, fragrant silk,
    so many thin folds.

Under the round green canopy,
    she opens herself to the night.
A fan cuts the moon's shape
    but can't conceal her blush.
The carriage goes, thunder sounds;
    the words couldn't get through.
A while in the deep quiet,
    gold embers scintillate:
nothing now but the ebb and flow of
    pulsing red pomegranate wine.
A piebald horse is yet tied
    to a dangling willow.
And where out of the southwest
    can the fine breeze blow?

Drinking Wine (1)

A green pine is in the east garden,
but the many grasses obscure it.
A frost wipes out all the other species,
and then I see its magnificent tall branches.
In a forest men do not notice it, but
standing alone, it is a miracle.
I hang a jug of wine on a cold branch;
then stand back, and look again and again.
My life spins with dreams and illusions.
Why then be fastened to the world?

T'ao Ch'ien (365–427)

Translated by Arthur Sze

Return to Chiang Village

Shaggy red clouds in the west—
the sun's foot is down to level earth.
By the wicker gate, sparrows are chirping.
The traveler returns from over a thousand *li*.

Wife and children panic at my presence;
quieted, they still wipe tears.
In this age of turmoil, I floated and meandered.
A miracle of chance to return alive!

Neighbors crowd the fence tops
and also sigh and sob.
In the deep night, we are again holding candles,
facing each other as in a dream.

Tu Fu (712–770)

Translated by Arthur Sze

Miracle

I never wanted the red of fire, the black at midnight
of the Peach Blossom Pool, the mournful melody of the *p'ï-p'a,*

or the fragrance of roses. I never loved the stern
pride of the leopard, and no white dove ever had

the beauty I craved. I never wanted any of these things,
but their *crystallization*—a miracle ten thousand

times more rare than them all! But I am famished and harried.
I cannot go without nourishment: even if it is

dregs and chaff, I still have to beg for it. Heaven knows
I do not wish to be like this. I am by no means

so stubborn or stupid. I am simply tired of waiting,
tired of waiting for the miracle to arrive; and

I dare not starve. Ah, who doesn't know of how little worth
is a tree full of singing cicadas, a jug of turbid wine,

or smoky mountain peaks, bright ravines, stars
glittering in the empty sky? It is all so ordinary,

so inexorably dull, and it isn't worth our ecstatic joy,
our crying out the most moving names, or the

longing to cast gold letters and put them in a song.
I also affirm that to let tears come

at the song of an oriole is trivial, ridiculous,
and a waste of time. But who knows? I cannot be otherwise.

I am so famished and harried I take lamb's-quarters
and wild hyssop for fine grain—

                              but there's no harm
in speaking clearly as long as the miracle appears.

Then at once I will cast off the ordinary. I will never
again gaze at a frosted leaf and dream of a spring blossom's

dazzle. I will not waste my strength, peel open
stones, and demand the warmth of white jade.

Give me one miracle, and I will never again whip ugliness,
and compel it to give up the meaning of its

opposite. Actually, I am weary of all this,
and these strained implications are hard to explain.

All I want is one clear word flashing like a Buddhist relic
with fierce light. I want it whole, complete,

shining in full face. I am by no means so stubborn
or stupid; but I cannot see a round fan without

seeing behind it an immortal face. So,
I will wait for as many incarnations as it takes—

since I've made a vow. I don't know how many
incarnations have already passed; but I'll wait

and wait, quietly, for the miracle to arrive.
That day must come! Let lightning strike me,

volcanoes destroy me. Let all hell rise up and crush me!
Am I terrified? No, no wind will blow out

the light in me. I only wish my cast-off body
would turn into ashes. And so what? That, that minutest

fraction of time is a minutest fraction of—
ah, an extraordinary gust, a divine and stellar hush

(sun, moon, and spin of all stars stopped;
time stopped, too)—the most perfectly round peace.

I hear the sound of a door pivoting: and with it
the rustling of a skirt. That is a miracle.

And in the space of a half-open gold door,
you are crowned with a circle of light!

Wen I-to (1899–1946)

Translated by Arthur Sze

The Last Day

Water sobs and sobs in the bamboo pipe gutter.
Green tongues of banana leaves lick at the windowpanes.
The four surrounding whitewashed walls are receding,
and I alone cannot fill such a large room.

A fire in a bowl burns and burns in my heart.
Silent, I wait for the faraway guest to arrive.
I feed the fire cobwebs, rat droppings,
and also the scaly skins of spotted snakes.

Now the crowing of a cock hastens a heap of ashes.
A gust of dark wind gropes at my mouth.
Ah, the guest is right in front of me!
I close my eyelids then follow him out.

Wen I-to (1899–1946)

Translated by Arthur Sze

MICHELLE YEH

The Chinese Poem: The Visible and the Invisible in Chinese Poetry

IN HIS 1928 INTRODUCTION to Pound's *Selected Poems,* T.S. Eliot lauded Pound as the "inventor of Chinese poetry for our time," but continued: "This is as much as to say that Chinese poetry, as we know it today, is something invented by Ezra Pound. It is not to say that there is a Chinese poetry-in-itself, waiting for some ideal translator who shall be only translator." Eliot clearly recognized the creative transformation involved in translating poetry from one language to another; hence his distinction between Pound's translation and "Chinese poetry-in-itself."

Although it is well known that Pound's translation is a particularly free, often ingenious rendition of the Chinese—fully justified in view of his Imagist project—what neither he nor Eliot could have foreseen was how powerful and lasting this translation would be in shaping poets' and translators' perceptions of Chinese poetry. In recent decades translators of Chinese poetry have given us many wonderful translations that are far more faithful to the originals than Pound's; interestingly, however, the "Chinese poetry-in-itself" that they strive for remains informed by aesthetic and cultural assumptions that underscore the earlier modernist model. In "The Poem behind the Poem," Tony Barnstone expands on the work of a long line of poet-translators—from Pound to Kenneth Rexroth, Gary Snyder, and, most notably, Wai-lim Yip—in describing the Chinese poem as "imagistic," consisting of "largely pictographic characters," and presenting a moment of "empty, pure perception." If for Pound the metaphoric basis of Chinese characters was central to his translation of Chinese poetry, Snyder, Yip, and Barnstone tend to emphasize the nonfigurative quality of Chinese poetic imagery and further link it to a state of mind that resonates with a Daoist or Zen Buddhist sensibility.

Despite some modifications, Pound's formulation of Chinese poetry as "ideogrammic" underlies what Robert Kern calls "the standard conventions for the representation of Chinese poetry in English." Borrowing from

Eliot, may we not say that "the Chinese poem" in the English-speaking world is a Western invention?

By referring to the Chinese poem described above as an "invention," I am not denying that those qualities exist in Chinese poetry. I am suggesting, however, that the act of choosing certain poems for translation always presupposes what a Chinese poem is in the mind of the translator, which further influences the way the poems are translated. What does not get translated is at least as revealing as what does. It is therefore meaningful to look at the Anglo-American modernist paradigm of the Chinese poem in terms of what it accentuates as well as downplays, what it gives a value to and at the same time excludes.

The quintessential Chinese poem is, as suggested by many American poet-translators, imagistic. Pound points out in "How to Read, and Why" (1929) that visual image—*phanopoeia*—is the most translatable part of poetic language. It is natural, then, that visual imagery receives the most attention in translation. But the tendency to see the Chinese poem as a concatenation of concrete visual images with few discursive elements is inseparable from the conception that the Chinese language is "largely pictographic" or ideographic. Such a view, with a long history that goes back to Catholic missionaries in the sixteenth century, is based on the notion that Chinese written symbols are visual embodiments of particular things in nature rather than artificial signs of phonetic import. Despite efforts by sinologists—for example, Peter Boodberg, Yuen Ren Chao, and John DeFrancis—and others to dispel the myth, it remains strong to this date, and it is but a short step from seeing the Chinese language as pictographic to seeing Chinese poetry as an unmediated expression of the concrete world of experience.

While it is generally true that imagery is a major component of all poetry, the kind of imagery emphasized in the Chinese poem is typically nonfigurative, descriptive of nature, and juxtaposed in a nondiscursive way. Further, these traits are often attributed to an aesthetic informed by Daoist or Zen Buddhist philosophy, which supposedly espouses such a treatment of nature. If separately these characterizations are valid, it becomes problematic when they are seen as somehow intrinsically related to one another in Chinese poetry. In other words, implicit in the Anglo-American perception of the Chinese poem is a particular kind of correlation between stylistics and epistemology. It is this correlation that I find questionable.

The dense juxtaposition of imagery in a Chinese poem has much to do with the economy of space prescribed by certain—albeit not all—poetic forms and the dominant Chinese convention of parallelism in classical poetry. In itself, juxtaposition of imagery is unrelated either to the kind of imagery used in a poem or to its philosophical underpinnings. As to the other two qualities, again I find no correlation between nonfigurative imagery and Daoist or Buddhist aesthetics in Chinese poetry. It has been argued by some sinologists that the concept of metaphor is foreign to Chinese culture because it can only exist in a dualistic worldview predicated on what Pauline Yu calls a "fundamental disjunction…between two ontologically distinct realms, one concrete and the other abstract, one sensible and the other inaccessible to the senses." It is as if metaphor and other such figures of speech represented an intrusion of artifice, which destroys the primeval unity of humans and the universe. Metaphor seems to have no place in a culture that believes in harmony between man and nature and noninterference of the human ego. Without going into the counterarguments that have been advanced by critics, I will turn to the poems themselves to show that this concept is, by and large, yet another myth about Chinese poetry and culture.

Wang Wei is the favorite poet of contemporary American translators mainly because of his Zen-flavored nature poems. Indeed, Wang was deeply Buddhist in his old age, and his poetry is replete with nature imagery. But his nature images often do not depict nature as such but are metaphorical, allusive, or symbolic. For instance, the red peony in the poem of the same title is clearly a personification, and the seemingly happy appearance of the peony flower—a symbol of fame and fortune in Chinese culture—is contrasted with its hidden sorrow. A standard symbol in Buddhist scriptures, the moon in Wang's poetry often evokes Buddhist enlightenment, while the water image in his famous "Villa in Mount Zhongnan" intimates the Daoist notion of constant cyclical change. Neither Daoism nor Buddhism shuns metaphors or symbols.

In other words, what appear to be literal images in Chinese poetry may have deeper significance within the cultural context. The willow tree, to give another example, often appears in farewell poems—an important genre in Chinese poetry—because *liu* ("willow") is a near homonym of the verb meaning "to [ask someone to] stay." Breaking off a willow twig when seeing someone off and waving it became a way to express the sadness of having to part with one's friend or loved one.

Nature in Chinese poetry is imbued with symbolic meaning, but Chinese nature poetry often includes such man-made things as the zither or the bell. The zither, which appears frequently in Wang Wei and Meng Haoran, two T'ang poets famous for their nature poetry, evokes the ancient story of Zhong Ziqi in which the musical instrument is equated with the heart and spirit of the musician. The bell is commonly associated with a Buddhist monastery; it neither sings, nor growls, nor tinkles, but its deep, slow, reverberating sound evokes, paradoxically, quiet and serenity.

Cultural symbols play an equally important role in Liu Zongyuan's "River Snow," a poem that seems to contain only literal images. Let me quote Barnstone and Chou's beautiful translation:

> A thousand mountains. Flying birds vanish.
> Ten thousand paths. Human traces erased.
> One boat, bamboo hat, bark cape—an old man.
> Alone with his hook. Cold river. Snow.

Even with this fine interpretation, I doubt that reading the poem only imagistically would suffice to convince a student who truly understands the poem to describe, say, the hardship of an old fisherman having to make a living in bitter winter.

The fact is that the fisherman in Chinese culture is an emblem, an archetype. It can be traced back to the autobiographical poem by Qu Yuan (c. 343–278 B.C.), the first fully identifiable poet in Chinese literature. In "The Fisherman," the loyal poet-minister, who has been wrongfully rejected and exiled by his prince, encounters a fisherman. Their brief exchange presents two contrasting approaches to the vicissitudes in life: the poet would rather die than compromise his "spotless purity" by associating himself with the dark, "muddy" world; the fisherman advises detachment from external circumstances so as to keep one's equanimity intact. When the poet fails to heed his words, the fisherman rows off in a boat while singing this song:

> When the Canglang's waters are clear,
> I can wash my hat-strings in them;
> When the Canglang's waters are muddy,
> I can wash my feet in them.

> (trans. David Hawkes)

If the poet-minister is an exemplar of Confucian loyalty and self-sacrifice (Qu threw himself into the Milo River and drowned), then the fisherman represents the Daoist master, who is *in* but not *of* this world. The title of the first chapter of *Zhuangzi* sums it up: the Daoist fisherman is unperturbed as he engages in "free and easy wandering" through the human world.

Perfect equilibrium between the fisherman and the world is achieved in "River Snow" at multiple levels. Formal parallelism exists, first of all, between the beginning of the first two lines: "a thousand" and "ten thousand" together form a compound word in Chinese—*qianwan*—which refers to all things in the world. There is also a parallel between the third and fourth lines: the first words, "one" and "alone," are synonyms and also constitute a compound word (*gudu*) with the same meaning. Contrasts are found between the first and second couplets: between the concepts of all and one, between the multiplicity of heaven and earth and the singularity of the old fisherman, between absence (of many) and presence (of one).

The verb in the last line of the original—*diao,* which is rendered as a noun, "hook," in Barnstone and Chou's translation—reads more like a transitive verb than an intransitive one. Literally, the line reads: "alone, [the old fisherman] angles [for] the cold-river snow." The river and the snow have merged into one, just as snow falling on the surface of the water slowly melts into, and can no longer be distinguished from, the river. Paradoxically, the diminutive fisherman is the center of the snow-covered universe.

Whether structurally, syntactically, or imagistically, "River Snow" achieves a perfect equilibrium that endows the solitary human figure with the same significance, the same weight, as the immensity of earth and sky. The nonintrusive yet dignified, self-sufficient presence of the fisherman illustrates well Zhuangzi's maxim in "Discussion on Making All Things Equal" (as translated by Burton Watson): "Heaven and earth were born at the same time I was, and the ten thousand things are one with me."

I fully agree that some Chinese poems are more translatable than others, and that culture-specific symbols and allusions don't always come across effectively without footnotes, which should be used minimally, if at all. What I have tried to demonstrate is that the modernist paradigm of the Chinese poem as a minimalist gem of imagery—nature imagery at that—tends to favor certain works of a poet over other works or to favor certain writers over others. Such favoritism hardly does justice to Wang Wei, who is more than a Zen Buddhist nature poet, and even less to Li Bo and Du Fu, generally considered by the Chinese to be the greatest poets of all time. However creative and powerful it may be, "the Chinese poem" in much contemporary English translation is a select representative of an essentialized view of Chinese language and culture. Once we decouple Chinese pictographs from poetic image, and nonfigurative nature imagery from Daoist or Buddhist aesthetics, we are better able to appreciate a broad range of Chinese poetry.

The other limitation of "the Chinese poem," as I see it, is that it is based on classical Chinese poetry and hardly applies to modern Chinese poetry, which emerged after 1910. Modern Chinese poetry seems like an alien species compared to classical Chinese poetry because of profound differences in language (the modern vernacular versus classical Chinese) and form (complete formal freedom versus prescribed traditional forms). It is no wonder, then, that when the classical poem is held up as the paragon of Chinese poetry, modern poetry appears wanting.

It is ironic, the claim that classical Chinese poetry is superior to its modern counterpart *because* the former has exerted such influence on modern American poetry. Such an argument is curiously circular. Rather than recognizing the modernist-postmodern American model of the Chinese poem as a highly select and creative appropriation of classical Chinese poetry, the critics accept it as definitive and measure modern Chinese poetry against it. The inevitable result is that modern Chinese poetry is described in terms of loss, lack, or deficiency.

In contrast to "the Chinese poem," modern Chinese poetry often seems expansive, discursive, even prosaic. The modern vernacular allows infinitely more syntactical variations, which in turn engender new semantic and stylistic nuances; and the freedom from traditional forms allows poets to set aside the parallelism central to classical Chinese poetry. A modern poem may be elliptical and compact, or it may be discursive and long-winded.

For the purpose of contrast, I'd like to look at a modern prose poem written by Shang Qin. Prose poetry is a notable accomplishment in twentieth-century Chinese poetry. Lu Xun, better known for his fiction from the 1910s and 1920s, wrote the first volume of prose poetry in Chinese: *Wild Grass,* published in 1926. He was an early influence on Shang Qin, a native of Sichuan who was coerced into the nationalist army at the age of fourteen and moved to Taiwan in 1949. Qin has been writing poetry since the 1950s and is best known for his prose poetry. Here is my translation of "The Cat That Passes Through the Wall," which he wrote in 1987:

> Ever since she left, this cat has been coming in and out of my place as she pleases; doors, windows, even walls can't stop her.
>
> When she was with me, our life made the sparrows outside the iron gate and iron-barred windows envious. She took care of me in every way, including bringing me the crescent moon with her hands on

nights when there was a power outage, and emitting
cool air by standing next to me on humid summer
nights.

I made the mistake of discussing happiness with her.
That day, contrary to my usual reticence, I said:
"Happiness is the half that people don't have." The
next morning, she left without saying goodbye.

She's not the kind of woman who would write a
note with lipstick on the vanity mirror. She didn't
use a pen either. All she did was inscribe these words
on the wallpaper with her long sharp fingernails:
"From now on, I will be your happiness, and you
mine."

Ever since this cat started coming in and out of my
place as she pleases, I have never really seen her, for
she always comes at midnight, leaves at daybreak.

The contrast between this prose poem and the Anglo-American
model of the Chinese poem cannot be sharper. Contrary to the minimalist
lyric, this poem is a first-person narrative, a running monologue. Contrary
to a concatenation of clean, sharp images, this poem has prepositions, arti-
cles, participles, adverbs, and adverbial phrases, which lengthen the sen-
tences considerably. Contrary to a quiet meditation on nature, this poem
depicts a human drama in an urban setting separated from nature by an
iron gate and iron-barred windows, common sights in crime-infested big
cities.

In translating the poem, it is important to duplicate the author's
prosaism and wordiness because these are central to its theme and effect.
As is typical in Shang Qin, the narrator is an ordinary man, one who is
not very smart or articulate and is somewhat naive. He narrates a personal
experience in a straightforward manner, never bothering to figure out what
it means. Through this character, the poet creates a discrepancy between
the matter-of-fact tone of the reminiscence and the surrealistic details,
between the literal surface narrative and the depths beneath.

In a low-key, chatty way, the narrator tells us of the supernatural
feats of which the woman is capable: she can fetch the moon and emit
cool air from her body. Her emotions, however, are all too human, as indi-
cated by her abrupt departure after hearing the narrator's innocent remark

about happiness. With the same matter-of-factness, the narrator describes the mysterious cat, which seems to take the place of the absent woman.

The identification between the woman and the cat is intimated throughout the poem, first by the blurring of the references to "she" in the first and second stanzas. The woman and the cat also share such attributes as individuality, aloofness, sultriness, and long, sharp nails or claws. At the end, both the cat and the woman are invisible to the narrator. Although the cat replaces the woman chronologically as well as psychologically, the narrator never actually sees the cat, which only visits him during the night, supposedly when he is asleep. Like the absent woman, the cat exists only in his dreams: she is real and unreal at the same time.

The poem is highly suggestive, yet it is difficult to pin down what it is about. It makes a humorous comment on human nature: we always desire that which we don't have and are never fully content with what we do have. It also suggests that happiness is intangible, elusive, beyond human comprehension. Finally, the coexistence of the naive, prosaic narrator with the mysterious woman/cat points to the hidden mystery and marvel of everyday life.

In both form and content, "The Cat That Passes Through the Wall" cannot be more different from "the Chinese poem." Although image still plays an important role, the construction of tone and texture, in my view, accounts more for the power of Qin's poem. Still, in the metamorphosis of the woman/cat we can find a distant echo of Zhuangzi's "butterfly dream." Just as the Daoist philosopher, on waking, couldn't tell whether it was he who had dreamed of being a butterfly or the butterfly who had dreamed of being him, so the narrator in Shang Qin's poem suspends judgment about the identity of the woman/cat. There is an affinity between the ancient philosopher and the modern poet in their embracing of the mystery—both the visible and the invisible—of life.

If poetry renders the invisible visible, then translation must do the same. Despite great challenges at the linguistic and cultural levels, Chinese poetry deserves to be represented with more poets, periods, and places of origin. Returning to Eliot, whom I quoted at the beginning of this essay, the answer to whether or not we can ever create "Chinese poetry-in-itself" is both yes and no. For a bilingual reader, the answer is probably no: a Chinese poem and its English rendition can never have exactly the same effect, whether we are speaking of the music, ambience, or associations of a poem. But it is possible, as Tony Barnstone has demonstrated, to create beautiful English equivalents. I have tried to point out that Chinese poetry-in-itself is far more varied and interesting than "the Chinese poem," which is a modernist and postmodern American construction. It is only

when we go beyond the received tradition of "the Chinese poem" that we
see behind the veil into Chinese poetry-in-itself.

Purple Hare

On the snow-covered prairie
Where a purple hare leaps
In the blink of an eye
Clovers grow everywhere

This winter
We scissor the cloth of the Milky Way
Garner the brightest star of Sirius
For a burial button
A hundred years from now

Ah purple hare purple hare
There goes a clever hare
Without a shred on

Xu Huizhi (b. 1966)

Translated by Michelle Yeh

The Simple Future Tense

When I'm a hundred years old,
I will squat in a corner in the dingy room
and write a weak, sentimental letter:
"I'm so destitute
and I keep gaining weight—
an eternal
pure contradiction!"

When I'm a hundred years old,
I will let the world climb into my lap
to do a perfect handstand,
even though we won't achieve better understanding
because of this.

I will still remember my funeral,
which will take place when I'm a hundred and one.
The world will be at the beginning of a new civilization
and tend to be conservative, untrusting.
I will hear someone say:
"She looks more honest now."
Dream is the shortest distance between two points,
dream is the truly smart one.
An aging surrealist,
I will fall asleep smiling.

But according to them, that is death.
My burial clothes will be too big, my casket too small,
the plot they give me will have too many ants…

All those men will come
whom I once loved,
some holding umbrellas,
others shedding tears.

Xia Yu (b. 1956)

Translated by Michelle Yeh

Rooster

Sunday, I sit on an iron bench with a missing leg in a quiet corner of the park to enjoy the lunch I bought at a fast-food place. As I chew, all of a sudden it occurs to me that I have not heard a rooster crow in a few decades.

With the bones I try to put together a bird that can summon the sun. I can't find the vocal cords, because they no longer need to crow. Their work is incessant eating and they produce themselves.

> Under the artificial sunlight
> there is neither dream
> nor dawn.

Shang Qin (b. 1930)

Translated by Michelle Yeh

A Tale—to the Tune "Metamorphosis Two" by Philip Glass

If the tide, at the speed of memory, unceasingly
if I, with the same heart, if the tide, just once
during all the nights and days when we are apart
told the story from beginning to end—
a circular tune, a meandering
discourse, about life and death, highs and lows
an answer to a call coming from afar

On the surface of the steadily cooling sea
like the frail breaths of white birds who, deep into the season
fly over the faint wakes of passing ships
if the tide once did
if I, with the same heart

Yang Mu (b. 1940)

Translated by Michelle Yeh

The Colonel

That was simply another kind of rose
Born of flames
In the buckwheat field they fought the biggest battle of the campaign
And his leg bade farewell in 1943

He has heard history and laughter

But what is immortality?
Cough syrup, razor blade, last month's rent, so on and so forth
While his wife's sewing maching engages in skirmishes
The only thing that can take him captive, he feels
Is the sun

Ya Xian (b. 1932)

Translated by Michelle Yeh

ABOUT THE CONTRIBUTING
TRANSLATORS

JOHN BALABAN is the author of twelve books of poetry, fiction, and non-fiction, which have been recognized with such awards as the Lamont Prize from the Academy of American Poets and the William Carlos Williams Award from the Poetry Society of America. His publications as a translator of Vietnamese poetry include *Ca Dao Việt Nam: Vietnamese Folk Poetry; Vietnam: The Land We Never Knew,* and *Spring Essence: The Poetry of Hồ Xuân Hương.*

TONY BARNSTONE teaches Asian studies and creative writing at Whittier College. His books of translation include *Out of the Howling Storm: The New Chinese Poetry; Laughing Lost in the Mountains: Selected Poems of Wang Wei; The Art of Writing: Teachings of the Chinese Masters;* and (with Willis Barnstone) *Literatures of Asia, Africa, and Latin America.* Books of his own poetry include *Impure.*

WILLIS BARNSTONE is the author of more than fifty books of criticism, translation, essays, memoir, and poetry. He is a distinguished professor of comparative literature, East Asian languages and literatures, Spanish, and a member of the Institute for Biblical and Literary Studies at Indiana University. His books include *Six Masters of the Spanish Sonnet; The Politics of Translation; With Borges on an Ordinary Evening in Buenos Aires; Modern European Poetry; The Other Bible; To Touch the Sky; The New Covenant: The Four Gospels and Apocalypse;* and (with Tony Barnstone) *Literatures of Asia, Africa, and Latin America.*

MARK BENDER has lived for many years among the minority peoples of southwest China, such as the Yi in Yunnan and the Miao in Guizhou, studying their folk-song and epic traditions. His books include *Seventh Sister and the Serpent: A Narrative Poem of the Yi People; Elephant Trunk Hill; Daur Folktales; The Bride's Boat: Marriage Customs of China's Fifty-five Ethnic Minorities;* and *Plum and Bamboo: China's Suzhou Chantefable Tradition.* He teaches at Ohio University in Columbus.

WILLIAM I. ELLIOTT is the director of the Kantō Poetry Center in Yokohama, Japan. He has translated numerous books by the poet Shuntarō Tanikawa, including *Selected Poems of Shuntarō Tanikawa,* which won the translation prize of the Society of Authors/ *TLS* in London. His other translations of Tanikawa (with Kawamura Kazuo) include *With Silence My Companion; At Midnight in the Kitchen I Just Wanted to Talk to You; Coca-Cola Lessons; Floating the River in Melancholy; Naked;* and *Two Billion Light-Years of Solitude.*

OK-KOO KANG GROSJEAN is the author of two books of her own poetry, *Horizon* and *A Hummingbird's Dance,* and a collection of essays, *Path with No Mind.* She translated into Korean the Dalai Lama's *Policy of Kindness and Ocean of Wisdom;* Thich Nhat Hanh's *Being Peace* and *The Heart of Understanding;* Krishnamurti's *Flame of Attention* and *Education and the Significance of Life;* and Gary Snyder's *No Nature.* She also translated into Korean the work of many American poets. She translated from Korean into English the poetry of Park Nam Soo and assisted in the translation of Oh Sae Young and Ko Ŭn. She died in 2001.

SAM HAMILL is the author of a dozen volumes of original poetry, including *Dumb Luck; Gratitude,* and *Destination Zero: Poems 1970–1995.* He has also published twenty volumes of poetry translated from ancient Chinese, Japanese, Greek, Latin, and Estonian, including (with J.P. Seaton) *The Essential Chuang Tzu; Narrow Road to the Interior and Other Writings of Bashō; The Spring of My Life;* and *Selected Haiku of Issa;* (with Keiko Matsui Gibson) *River of Stars: Selected Poems of Yosana Akiko;* and *Crossing the Yellow River: Three Hundred Poems from the Chinese.* He has received fellowships from the National Endowment for the Arts, the John Simon Guggenheim Memorial Foundation, the Lila Wallace–Readers Digest Fund, The Japan–U.S. Friendship Commission, and two Washington Governor's Arts Awards.

JANE HIRSHFIELD is the author of five collections of her own poetry, including *Given Sugar, Given Salt* and *The Lives of the Heart,* and a book of essays on poetry, *Nine Gates.* She also edited and cotranslated (with Mariko Aratani) two poetry anthologies: *The Ink Dark Moon: Love Poems by Ono no Komachi and Izumi Shikibu, Women of the Ancient Court of Japan* and *Women in Praise of the Sacred: 43 Centuries of Spiritual Poetry by Women.* Her honors include The Poetry Center Book Award, fellowships from the Guggenheim and Rockefeller Foundations, Columbia University's Translation Center Award, and the Commonwealth Club of California's Poetry Medal.

SUSIE JIE YOUNG KIM has published translations of poetry by Kim Chiha and Kim Nam-ju, as well as fiction by Kim Hyong Kyong, Shin Kyong-suk, and Yun Chong-mo. She teaches in the East Asian Studies Program at Yale University.

LEZA LOWITZ has published six books of translations, including the award-winning anthologies of contemporary Japanese women's poetry, *A Long Rainy Season* and *Other Side River*. She is the recipient of a PEN Syndicated Fiction Award, an NEH fellowship, and a Tokyo Journal Fiction Translation Prize. She has taught writing at San Francisco State University and Tokyo University.

DAVID R. MCCANN is Korea Foundation Professor of Korean Literature in the Department of East Asian Languages and Civilizations at Harvard University. His many published volumes of translation and scholarship include *Early Korean Literature: Selections and Introduction; Selected Poems of Sŏ Chŏngju;* and *Form and Freedom in Korean Poetry.*

KEN MCCULLOUGH teaches at Winona State University in Minnesota. Books of his own poetry include *Obsidian Point: A Triptych, Travelling Light,* and *Sycamore Oriole.* He has received numerous awards for his work, including the Academy of American Poets Award and a National Endowment for the Arts fellowship. In addition to translating *Sacred Vows,* the poetry of U Sam Oeur, he worked with U on his autobiography, *Crossing Three Wildernesses.*

W.S. MERWIN's many awards include the Pulitzer Prize for Poetry, the Bollingen Prize in Poetry, and the Tanning Prize. In addition to books of poetry and prose, he has published eighteen volumes of translation, including *East Window: The Asian Translations; Sun at Midnight: Poems by Musō Soseki* (with Sōiku Shigematsu); and *Asian Figures.*

SHOGO OKETANI worked as a journalist in Tokyo then as a professor of translation at the Monterey Institute of International Studies in California. A collection of his own poems, *Cold River,* was published in Kobe. With Leza Lowitz, he received a grant from the NEA to translate Ayukawa Nobuo. He is also in the process of translating the postwar Decadent novelist Sakaguchi Ango.

HIROAKI SATO translator, essayist, and columnist, lives in New York. Among his recent books is *My Friend Hitler and Other Plays of Yukio Mishima*. Among his forthcoming books is an anthology of Japanese women poets from ancient to modern times. He writes a column for *The Japan Times*, "The View from New York."

ANDREW SCHELLING teaches poetry, Sanskrit, and bioregional writing at the Naropa Institute. His recent books include *Wild Form Savage Grammar: Poetry, Ecology, Asia; Tea Shack Interior: New and Selected Poems; The Road to Ocosingo;* and *The Cane Groves of Narmada River: Erotic Poems from Old India*. His book *Dropping the Bow: Poems from Ancient India* received the Academy of American Poets prize for translation.

J.P. SEATON teaches Chinese at the University of North Carolina, Chapel Hill. His nine books of translation include *The Wine of Endless Life: Taoist Drinking Songs from the Yuan Dynasty, I Don't Bow to Buddhas: Selected Poems of Yuan Mei* and (with Sam Hamill) *The Essential Chuang Tzu.*

ERIC SELLAND's translations of Japanese experimental poets have appeared in a variety of journals and anthologies as well as on the Internet. His books of translation include Yoshioka Minoru's *Kusudama* and Hiroya Takagai's *Rush Mats*. A book of his own poems, *The Condition of Music*, was released in 2000.

GARY SNYDER has published more than fifteen books of poetry and prose, including *The Gary Snyder Reader, Mountains and Rivers Without End; No Nature: New and Selected Poems; The Practice of the Wild; Left Out in the Rain, New Poems 1947–1985; Axe Handles,* for which he received an American Book Award; and *Turtle Island,* which won the Pulitzer Prize for Poetry. Among other honors, he has received an American Academy of Arts and Letters Award, the Bollingen Prize, a Guggenheim Foundation fellowship, the Robert Kirsch Lifetime Achievement Award from the Los Angeles *Times*, and the Shelley Memorial Award.

ARTHUR SZE is the author of seven books of poetry and translation, including *The Redshifting Web: Poems 1970–1998,* and *The Silk Dragon: Translations from the Chinese*. His awards include fellowships from the John Simon Guggenheim Memorial Foundation, Lannan Foundation, the Lila Wallace–Reader's Digest Foundation, the Witter Bynner Foundation for Poetry, and the National Endowment for the Arts. He teaches at the

Poetry, and the National Endowment for the Arts. He teaches at the Institute of American Indian Arts.

MICHELLE YEH is professor of Chinese and Japanese at the University of California, Davis. Her books of translation include *Frontier Taiwan: An Anthology of Modern Chinese Poetry* (with N.G.D. Malmqvist), and *No Trace of the Gardener: Poems of Yang Mu* (with Lawrence R. Smith).

ABOUT THE EDITOR

FRANK STEWART settled in Hawai'i in 1966. His most recent book of poetry is *By All Means* (2003). Others include *Reunion, Flying the Red Eye,* and *The Open Water,* for which he received a Whiting Writers Award in 1986. In 1995 he published a book of prose, *A Natural History of Nature Writing.* He has edited over two dozen anthologies concerned with contemporary translations of literature from China, Tibet, Korea, Japan, Indonesia, Việt Nam, and elsewhere in Asia and the Pacific. Since 1989 he has been the editor of *Mānoa: A Pacific Journal of International Writing.* He lives in Honolulu, on the island of O'ahu, and near Kalopā, on the island of Hawai'i.

ASIAN TRANSLATIONS FROM
COPPER CANYON PRESS

BENGALI

Rabindranath Tagore, *The Lover of God**, translated by Tony K. Stewart
and Chase Twichell

CHINESE

Han-shan (Cold Mountain), *The Collected Songs of Cold Mountain**,
translated by Red Pine

Su Tung-p'o, *Selected Poems of Su Tung-p'o*, translated by Burton Watson

T'ao Ch'ien, *Selected Poems of T'ao Ch'ien*, translated by David Hinton

Yuan Mei, *I Don't Bow to Buddhas: Selected Poems*, translated by
J.P. Seaton

*Poems of the Masters: China's Classic Anthology of T'ang and Sung Dynasty
Verse**, translated by Red Pine

The Silk Dragon: Translations from the Chinese, translated by Arthur Sze

JAPANESE

Ikkyū, *Ikkyū: Crow with No Mouth*, translated by Stephen Berg

Like Underground Water: The Poetry of Mid-Twentieth Century Japan,
translated by Edward Lueders and Naoshi Koriyama

KOREAN

The Moonlit Pond: Korean Classical Poems in Chinese, translated by
Sung-Il Lee

VIETNAMESE

Hồ Xuân Hương, *Spring Essence: The Poetry of Hồ Xuân Hương**,
translated by John Balaban
Ca Dao Việt Nam: Vietnamese Folk Poetry*, translated by John Balaban

VARIOUS

East Window: The Asian Translations, translated by W.S. Merwin

* bilingual presentation

The Chinese character for poetry is made up of two parts: "word" and "temple." It also serves as pressmark for Copper Canyon Press.

Founded in 1972, Copper Canyon Press remains dedicated to publishing poetry exclusively, from Nobel laureates to new and emerging authors. The Press thrives with the generous patronage of readers, writers, booksellers, librarians, teachers, students, and funders—everyone who shares the conviction that poetry invigorates the language and sharpens our appreciation of the world.

The Allen Foundation for The Arts
Lannan Foundation
National Endowment for the Arts
Washington State Arts Commission

THE ALLEN FOUNDATION *for* THE ARTS

NATIONAL
ENDOWMENT
FOR THE ARTS

Lannan

For information and catalogs:
COPPER CANYON PRESS
Post Office Box 271
Port Townsend, Washington 98368
360/385-4925
www.coppercanyonpress.org